Supervisors & Teachers: A Private Cold War

SECOND EDITION

ARTHUR BLUMBERG

Syracuse University

McCutchan Publishing Corporation
2526 Grove Street
Berkeley, California 94704

ISBN: 0-8211-0133-1
Library of Congress Catalog Card Number: 79-89771

Once More,
to Phyllis

Preface

The first edition of *Supervisors and Teachers: A Private Cold War*, published in 1974, represented the gathering together in one place of papers that I had written and ideas that I had developed over a period of ten years or so. This second edition of the book, being finished five years after initial publication, represents increments in my thinking, such increments all being focused around the continuing theme of the human side of the supervisory enterprise. Though much of the book has remained as originally written, four new chapters have been added, and one of the original ones has been completely rewritten. Essentially, then, about one-third of the book is new, although some of the new chapters have appeared in print elsewhere.

I hold pretty strongly to the idea that we discover what a person's goals are, not by what he says he wants to do, but by our analysis of what he, indeed, does. Thus, it did not occur to me until after publication of the first edition—on talking with, and listening to the reactions of, students and colleagues who read it—that what I really wanted to do in it, which I apparently succeeded in doing to some extent, was to speak directly to the experience of both supervisors and teachers. It is my hope that this edition continues, and perhaps even goes beyond, this pattern in suggesting some images of what the future experience of supervisors and teachers might be in a different educational world.

It has also occurred to me as I went about the task of revision, and of reflecting back on the innumerable conversations I have had with supervisors, teachers, and colleagues since the book was first published, that I must offer it to the reader with a good bit of humility. That is, it seems to me that the people toward whom my ideas are aimed—supervisors and teachers—confront and deal with problems on a daily basis that are infinitely more taxing, physically and emotionally, than the ones I confront in my work. But they do it, and I do not. For me to pretend that, from the calm of my university office, I am able to prescribe answers to their problems would be arrogant beyond belief. But perhaps I have been able to suggest some ways to describe and analyze the supervisor-teacher relationship in a manner that will prove helpful both to them and to people in colleges and universities who are attempting to understand that relationship. That, at least, is my intent.

Other people have, of course, helped me. In particular I wish to thank my colleague, Professor William Greenfield, for his contribution on the socialization of supervisors. My deep thanks also go to Mrs. Marilyn Stauffer for her help with manuscript preparation and for her unfailing good humor.

Finally, I repeat a note on usage that appeared in the preface of the first edition: "Throughout the book I have used the pronoun 'he' when referring to a supervisor or a teacher. I have been following convention, which I find less clumsy than the possible alternatives, 'he/she' or, worse 's/he' and intend no slight."

Preface to First Edition

It seems, frequently, that much of what develops in life is the result of the fortuitous meeting of people and events. In any event, as will shortly be clear, that is the case with this book.

When Dr. Ted Amidon and I conducted our initial study of interaction between supervisors and teachers about nine years ago, the idea of writing a book on supervision was far from my mind. What we were doing, it seemed to me, represented a transient interest. We uncovered some interesting findings about supervisors and teachers; we published our results; but, mostly, we had fun.

All this changed when I moved from a department of educational psychology at Temple University to a department of educational administration at Syracuse University. Suddenly I was confronted with a new situation: I was to teach a course in supervision. What had been a passing interest became a major concern. I had to confront forty or so students each semester and—do something! I wasn't completely lacking in qualifications. In addition to my research on the behavior of supervisors and teachers, I had conducted a workshop for supervisors, and had trained some supervisors in industry. But I had never been a supervisor; I had never taken a course in supervision; and my reading in the field had been minimal. What all this meant was that the course I developed was experimental in the sense that it was an opportunity to test the ideas in which I previously had but a passing interest.

It has been an exciting experience, mostly, I think, for two reasons. First, the ideas I had about the dynamics of supervisor-teacher interaction and the concept of the supervisor's role as that of a helping agent seemed to strike a responsive chord among students. What we dealt with was behavior—theirs, supervisors', and teachers'—and it was relevant to their experience. Second, the teaching experience forced me to bring my ideas together so that they would fit, so that my concerns were not merely random but organically related to one another.

Still, there was no book forthcoming. What provided the impetus was the urging of my longtime colleague and friend, Dr. Robert Golembiewski of the University of Georgia. I owe him a great debt for sparking me to put it all together.

When I finish writing a manuscript, I usually experience a mixed sense of relief and tension: relief that the job is done and now I can go on to other things; tension because I don't know how what I have written will be received by a reader—even though I think it's good. So it was with a bit of trepidation that I asked my treasured friend and valued critic, Dr. Burton Blatt, Director of the Division of Special Education at Syracuse University, to read this manuscript. For his evaluation and encouragement, I am truly grateful.

Most importantly, however, I owe thanks to the several hundred students with whom I have worked over the last few years. They made me think. They accepted little on my undocumented assertion. They helped me grow. It is clear to me that, without them, there would be no book. My thanks also to Dorothy Gabri, who managed the rough draft in the midst of her duties as department secretary; Sharon Coyne, who retyped and edited the rough draft; and LaDonna Larrow, who typed the final revisions with dispatch.

Finally, the book would not read as concisely as I think it does without the help of Frances Bowles. Our long-range author-editor relationship was one I enjoyed. Though there were times when her editorial knife made me squirm, I ended up feeling that she was right—most of the time.

Contents

1   Supervision, Supervisors, and Teachers

In one sense this is not a book about the global practice of supervision in the schools. It does not deal, for example, with curriculum planning, in-service training, or instructional systems, or with prescriptions for organizing the supervisory substructure of school districts. It does not outline a series of supervisory functions; nor does it give attention to such concepts as "clinical supervision" or "competency-based supervision," however those notions may be variously interpreted. Depending on one's viewpoint, then, the absence of such content may place the concerns of the book beyond the mainstream of what supervisors and professors of instructional supervision discuss when they meet.

In another sense, one that in my mind cuts to the heart of the supervisory process (and thus into the mainstream, though not a publicly acknowledged one), this book is indeed about supervision. Its major concern is with what appears to be the most problematic part of the whole supervisory enterprise in the schools—the nature of the human relationships that exist between supervisors and teachers. It is a matter of some curiosity that, with a few exceptions (Mosher and Purpel, 1972; Goldhammer, 1969), a reader of supervisory texts is rarely confronted by what really seems to happen in the course of the inevitable meetings that take place between the parties to the supervisory process. Yet it is precisely at this point, if one can believe both supervisors and teachers, that most of the problems related to supervision occur. That is, if you ask a supervisor what makes his job difficult, the chances are that he

1

will talk about his relationships with teachers and not his ignorance of new curriculum materials. The content and technology of what supervisors deal with seems not to constitute a big problem for them. They seem to be well aware of methodological problems in teaching, of new curriculum thrusts, of teaching aids, resources, materials, and so forth. And they also appear to feel competent about the level of their knowledge in these various areas. The process side of the relationship is, however, another matter. The question with which they deal most often, though perhaps not consciously, is how they can get teachers to utilize supervisory resources. To put it another way, what seems to be at issue for most supervisors, in one fashion or another, are the problems that surround the establishment of productive working relationships with teachers.

The establishment of "productive working relationships" is crucial for supervisors. That this is not merely a dramatic conjecture on my part will become evident in the next several chapters, but a few bits of data at this point may serve to highlight the point. In a recent survey of teacher attitudes toward supervision (Heishberger and Young, 1975) it was reported that, while 82 percent of the respondents felt there was "a definite need for supervision and evaluation in the schools," 70 percent indicated that "the supervisor is often perceived as potentially dangerous." What a neat bind! This is almost like saying that teachers would like to eat a deliciously spicy pizza pie but they are afraid to because they think heartburn will face them in short order. If, indeed, a teacher perceives supervisors as potentially dangerous, it takes little imagination to suggest that a teacher's behavioral set toward the approach of a supervisor will be, at best, tentative if not downright defensive and avoidance oriented—and this despite the likelihood that the teacher may want, even need, help.

Another bit of data that helps to make the point. A colleague of mine, Charles Reaves of Texas Tech University, told me about a little exercise carried out in his supervision classes. He passes out to each student a card that has printed on it one or the other of the following "situations":

1. You are a teacher. You have just received notice that you will be appointed a supervisor. What is your reaction?
2. You are a teacher. You have just received notice that you will be observed by your supervisor. What is your reaction?

Representative samplings of the responses to the first situation are:
—"I'd feel that my hard work in teaching had paid off. I'd feel good."
—"I'd try to remember the good (and bad) things my supervisors had done and do the same (or avoid the same)."
—"I'd hate to leave the children, but look forward to helping other teachers."
Some typical reactions to the second situation are:
—"I'd tell the children to be on their good behavior."
—"I'd put up displays of the students' work."
—"I'd make sure my lesson plan book was up to date and my desk was neat."
—"I'd be very anxious, but after he arrived I'd probably teach a regular lesson."
—"I'd give her what she wants—individualized instruction."

My colleague went on to say that the thing that really surprised him was that, of the many times he has asked students to respond to these "situations," only three have suggested they would see the supervisor as a source of assistance. Clearly, something seems to be amiss. On the one hand, we have teachers saying they would look forward to helping other teachers. On the other hand, we have essentially the same people suggesting that they would find such encounters a somewhat unpleasant prospect—almost as if they were refusing help from themselves. I may be stretching the logic here a bit, but not overly much. Something obviously occurs, and in a systemic fashion, that interferes with the best intentions of supervisors to support and share their expertise with teachers. The responses to the second situation do, indeed, suggest defensiveness and anxiety, thereby indicating potential danger.

A third source of data reinforces this perspective. In a study of the effectiveness of feedback to teachers that was related to the source of the feedback, Tuckman and Oliver (1968) created four experimental conditions. These were feedback (a) from students only, (b) from supervisors (vice-principals) only, (c) from both students and supervisors, and (d) a no-feedback condition. The results indicated that student feedback alone produced positive change as measured by student ratings; that adding the supervisors' ideas to those of the students did not change the ratings; and that supervisory feedback alone produced a change that was the opposite of these effects when compared with the no-feedback condition. In other words, teachers seemed to react to the observations and suggestions of supervisors in a way that is opposite to what is intended by the supervisors. In their discussion of these results, the authors make the following point: "It can only be surmised that teachers are defensive toward (or even hostile to) administrators who, in the absence of much basis for judgment, attempt to tell them how to teach" (p. 300).

Do supervisors sense the same systematic set of dynamics as teachers relative to the supervisory-teacher relationship? Some data provided in later chapters suggest they do, but not in nearly so gross a manner as teachers. It appears that supervisors are more inclined to attribute the resistance and defensiveness they encounter to individual differences among teachers rather than to any type of systemic or role-induced phenomenon. There would appear to be little doubt that individual differences do come into play, but it seems reasonable to assume that, if 70 percent of a sample of teachers thought that the supervisor is often perceived as dangerous, this represents something more than the attitudes or behaviors of isolated individuals. That "something more" might include factors such as teacher autonomy, tenure, professionalism, and authority. It is as unlikely that supervisors are characterologically dangerous as it is that teachers are predisposed to be resistive and defensive. Further, for supervisors to ignore the systemic factors that are related to and impinge on their ability to function productively is folly. Problems are rarely solved by refusing to acknowledge their existence.

The character of the supervisor-teacher relationship, then, is a problematic one. Prescriptions in the literature concerning what it should be in an ideal world abound; they can also conflict. For example, Heishberger and Young report that almost two-thirds of the teachers they studied said that they would prefer a helping relationship (not defined) with their supervisor. About one-third thought in terms of a collegial (again, not defined) one. On the other hand, Kogan (1976), with specific focus on clinical supervision, suggests that the role of helper for the supervisor is inappropriate and that to put the teacher in the role of "helpee" is not conducive to professional development. He advocates collegiality. Flanders (1976) writes that the prime goal of supervision is the improvement of instruction and characterizes this task as a humanistic endeavor, but he does not label the supervisor-teacher relationship with regard to what it should or should not be. Instead, he uses several process descriptors of what may be involved in that relationship: "helping another person change his teaching behavior," "assisting a teacher to modify patterns of instruction in ways the teacher has selected," "a partnership in inquiry in which two persons compare intriguing alternatives" and in which "the supervisor is simply a person who has more experience in the conduct of the inquiry" (pp. 47-48).

The functional-process concept of an idealized image of the supervisor-teacher relationship of which Flanders writes seems to make more sense than attempts at putting labels on it. Labels, in this case, lead to meaningless argument. For example, it is of minuscule importance for the process of supervision whether you observe a supervisor's behavior and say, "Aha, now *that's* collegiality," while I observe the same behavior and say, "Aha, now *that's* helping." What is important is that, however the behavior, or role, for that matter, is labeled, it somehow encourages the partnership-inquiry process to further itself. And this point would hold whether or not the behavior in question involved a Rogerian nondirective response, a pointed question, information giving, demonstrating, or what have you.

There is, however, an earlier conceptual starting place for the focus of this book, which is an analysis of the interactive relationships between supervisors and teachers. Though it is only human to think about desired states of being, it makes sense to think first about where we are. From my own studies and those of others, from innumerable discussions with teachers and supervisors, and from many talks with colleagues—all of which come to play in this book— two general statements about supervision in the schools can be made. The first is that much of what occurs in the name of supervision in the schools (the transactions that take place between supervisor and teacher) constitutes a waste of time, *as teachers see it*. In many instances, the best evaluation that teachers give of their supervision is that it is not harmful. The second is that the character of relationships between teachers as a group and supervisors as a group can be described as somewhat of a cold war. Neither side trusts the other and each side is convinced of the correctness of its position. Supervisors seem to be saying, "If *they* would just listen to us, things would really get better." Teachers seem to be saying, "What *they* give us doesn't help. It would be better if they left us alone."

The metaphor of the cold war breaks down, of course, when one considers its dynamics and goals and compares them to the on-and-off cold wars on the international scene. There are rarely any overt threats, and neither seems to attempt to gain any obvious advantage over the other. Though I might be accused of stretching things too far, I would like to suggest that the metaphor is still appropriate. One can fantasize teachers struggling to protect their territory while supervisors struggle to gain further access to it. The primary weapons are subtle forms of strategic gamesmanship, characterized by secretiveness and defensiveness. Some of the studies mentioned in this book strongly suggest that this is a good descriptor of many, perhaps most, supervisor-teacher relationships.

This book, in part, analyzes the behavioral and organizational dimensions of this cold war, but it is not a doleful analysis. It was written in the hope that readers will be encouraged to think about change.

Though there may well be human conditions in which any type of change would be welcome, change without specific direction is usually an exercise to be avoided. The direction of change implicitly proposed here is away from a state of supervisor-teacher relations that may be closed and defensive to one in which they may be open and supportive. Should there be such a change, the nature of a supervisor's encounter with a teacher may become not a matter of, "Who will win?" but, instead, one of, "Can we solve this problem together?" Thus, the philosophical thrust of this book is strongly linked to behavioral and organizational factors that are part of Flanders' concept of supervision as "a partnership in inquiry . . . ."

Two underlying propositions, one about problematic human relationships and the other about schools as social systems, guide this book. The first is that the problems that most teachers and supervisors seem to encounter are the result of behavioral conflicts and *not* the result of personality differences. Only rarely are the people involved repelled by one another. If this were not so, the case would be hopeless. Most people can learn new behaviors. It is much more difficult—perhaps even impossible—for people to change their personalities.

The second proposition is that the norms and values of schools as social systems directly affect the relationships between supervisors and teachers, for supervisors and teachers do not interact in a social vacuum. What they do, what they say, and how they deal with each other is always, in some fashion, related to the manner in which they perceive, interpret, and react to the normative struture and role demands of the system in which they work. Thus, although this book deals mostly with issues related to interpersonal exchange, one should always bear in mind the nature of the human organization in which the exchange takes place.

2   Part of the Problem Is
in the System

My interest in the interpersonal and organizational factors that impinge on and affect the way supervisors and teachers deal with each other was stimulated some years ago when I started teaching graduate courses, not in supervision, but in interpersonal and group relationships to students who were, for the most part, public school teachers. Almost inevitably, at some time during each semester, the discussion would turn to the supervisory relationship, what it was like, and how effective it was, and each discussion was much the same. When the topic first came up, for example, smiles appeared on the faces of the students and often snickers could be heard. (Similar but more pronounced reactions occur, incidentally, when teachers are asked to talk about the faculty meetings in their schools.) On probing for the reasons for these reactions, I learned that, while a distinct minority of teachers reported satisfactory and helpful relationships with their supervisor, for most teachers this was not the case. They reacted with a sort of left-handed compliment, saying that their supervision was, at the least, not harmful. The broad consensus was that the supervision they received was ritualistic and rather a waste of time.

When the nature of my university position changed so that I had direct responsibility for teaching courses in supervision, I had the opportunity, in a different setting, to approach the circumstances of supervision in the schools in a more direct fashion. Though the setting was changed, the reactions of students had not. A fairly sizable majority continued to report that they saw the processes

9

and outcomes of the supervision they received on the job as relatively unhelpful, sometimes threatening, and frequently dull.

It is relatively easy, and also unthinking when confronted with
such reactions, to slough the problem off onto the person of the
supervisor. If supervisors can be characterized as dull, unfeeling,
unimaginative people, then there is no need to deal with the problem
openly. It comes to be tolerated as one of the lesser (or major, in
some cases) evils of the system. But supervisors are not, as a group,
any duller, more unfeeling, or more unimaginative than the rest of
us (though some must be, as are some college professors, school
principals, and teachers). The supervisory problem, then, is complex. It involves questions having to do with the way the larger
educational system behaves, organizational factors associated with
the schools, and behavioral patterns of individual supervisors that
give rise to particular interpersonal sets that may exist between
supervisors and teachers.

A reasonable place to start this inquiry is with the more global
system. In particular, the focus will be on the process by which
supervisory people come to hold their positions and on the characteristics of the supervisory substructure and function that make it
exceeding difficult to judge whether or not it is producing anything
of value.

SELECTING SUPERVISORS

There is no single process by which teachers get promoted to
the position of supervisor. In some school districts the system is
unabashedly, if covertly, political: promotion is more dependent,
assuming certification requirements have been met, on how close
one is to powerful people in the central office than anything else.
In one system I know, it apparently pays to be a member of the
"Irish Mafia" if you want to be a principal or supervisor, an allega-
tion that probably reflects the disenchantment of some who thought
themselves qualified but were not promoted. Nevertheless, whether
the particular "Mafia" be Irish, Italian, Jewish, or WASP, the point
is that, in some systems, perhaps many, in order to become promoted
to supervisory responsibility, one must have some access to, and
influence with, the power structure. One's ability to help teachers do
a better job of teaching is not at issue.

Regardless of the political processes, two major and likely fallacious assumptions undergird the system of selecting supervisors in the schools. The first is that, in order to be a good supervisor, one must have been a good teacher, however that is defined. This seems to be a reasonable point of view, but it is simply an assumption that has not been tested. It may well be that some good teachers will make more productive supervisors than some who are not so good. The roles of teachers and supervisors are quite different, however, and to predict a person's performance as a supervisor on his success as a teacher seems to be slightly out of touch with reality. If this comment appears a bit too strong, then, at the least, the doubting person would have to admit that there is no evidence to suggest that being a good teacher will quite easily enable one to function equally well when that person has to behave in ways that will help others be good teachers. In point of fact, there are examples galore (mostly by word of mouth, I must admit) of people who, being highly skilled at a job, were promoted to some sort of supervisory position and failed.

The second questionable assumption that underlies the selection of supervisors is that certification is both the prelude to, and the equivalent of, competence. You cannot become a supervisor until you receive certification and, once you have it, you are presumed to be competent. How else can we account for the major investments that school districts put into in-service training for teachers (which typically has little effect on teaching, incidentally) and the almost total lack of concern that these same districts appear to have for the continued growth and development of their supervisory personnel. Supervisors do attend curriculum workshops and so on, but one would have to look long and hard to find a system that has made any major commitment to improving supervision.

The process by which a person becomes certified as a supervisor typically involves the earning of a prescribed number of graduate credits in courses with appropriate titles. Some sort of internship may also be required. Now anyone who is even vaguely familiar with graduate training programs, particularly on the master's degree level where most certificate-bound students may be found, knows that to presume competence based on this training is sheer nonsense. Most programs leading to certification are nothing more than the accumulation of the appropriate number and kind of credit hours, period. I have the feeling that the whole certifying process, perhaps necessary to lend some order to chaos at one time in the past, exists now in self-perpetuity simply because it is there. And few people seem to be inclined to want to change that part of the system, least of all those who earn their living by "certifying" others.

THE SUPERVISORY SUBSTRUCTURE

School systems, like all other organizations, tend to develop structural patterns to deal with problems as they arise or to further organizational goals. Supervisory structures are no different. On the perfectly logical assumption that some means were necessary to maintain and enhance the quality of instruction and to eliminate ineffective teachers, two patterns seem to have developed. The first is an internal, school building notion, by which the building principal has overall responsibility for the quality of instruction in his school. In secondary schools he may delegate this function to department heads; in elementary schools, where there is no departmental organization, the principal typically assumes this function himself. The second supervisory pattern is external to the school itself, for it involves specialists in subject matter or some particular methodology (such as the teaching of reading) whose home base is the central office of the school district. Their job is to visit schools and teachers, either by request from the school or on their own initiative, visit classrooms, hold in-service meetings and, in general, try to raise the level of instruction. Sometimes they provide evaluations, at other times only consultation. The helping teacher concept is an illustration of the latter, as the person filling this role visits schools and, in essence, tries to sell the value of his services to the principal and the teachers.

Regardless of the pattern or combination of patterns a district develops, what happens is that these elements of the structure become institutionalized. Rarely is their efficiency questioned, and equally rarely are questions raised concerning whether the function for which the structure was created is being performed.

There seem to be two reasons for the unquestioning acceptance of the supervisory system as it is. First, when a particular structural pattern becomes institutionalized, it develops a power base of its own that may be informal and independent of any but the most overt constraints of the organization. Its personnel are apt to resist criticism and attempt to forestall it by communicating their successes and not their failures—if they are aware of them. This circular and self-reinforcing process is nourished by the common organizational assumption that, if a part of the structure is devoted to working on a particular problem, the level of productivity of the unit involved is satisfactory and sufficing. It seems to be only in crises that particular functions are singled out to see if they are producing the intended results. This suggests that, with the enormity of the problems facing the schools today, particularly in the large cities, the concern with budget, staffing, minority groups, and so forth may be too great for anyone to turn attention to the ways in which the quality of supervision might be improved. If such be the priority system, it is a risky one.

Second, reliable and valid measures are difficult to come by. The criteria for effective supervision are even vaguer than those for teaching. Who is to say whether or not the supervisor is doing the job? The supervisor? The teacher? The students? More than likely, as in the case of university professors, it is simply a case of assuming that things are going all right unless there are loud and insistent complaints. There are complaints, of course, but they are not noticed until the right questions are asked of the right people—in this case, the teachers. For example, some years ago I was discussing the informal communications networks that exist in schools with a group of students. Quite by accident I discovered that teachers, sometimes in collusion with their principal, tend to develop warning systems to let one another know when the central office supervisor is in the school to make classroom visits.

— In one school, the first teacher to discover the supervisor gives a particularly colored pencil to a youngster to take to the teacher in the next room. The process is repeated by the second teacher until, in very short order, the entire school is aware that the supervisor is in the building. (There are many variations on this theme: an irrelevant book, an eraser, or some other inconsequential item may serve as the alarm.)

— The supervisor, in another situation, wore loud and colorful hats. She would leave her hat on a table in the principal's office. The alarm in this case took the form of a note that circulated the building on which was written, "The Hat is on the Mat."

— Another supervisor, regarded by the teachers to be out of touch with reality, provoked a warning charade. The teacher who discovered him would stand at the door of the next classroom, catch the eye of the teacher inside, and then whirl her hand around her head to signal that "he who was way out in orbit is here." This ritual was performed throughout the school.

— In the chemistry complex of an open high school, the first teacher to learn that the supervisor is around squirts the CO_2 fire extinguisher, which makes a whooshing sound. The whoosh is repeated by each teacher until all are on their toes.

— A principal may be in collusion. When the central office supervisor starts to visit classrooms, the principal fakes a telephone call (or some other type of message) for the supervisor. He gets on the school public address system and says something like, "Will Mr. X please call the office for a message?" Thus, through the magic of electronics, the entire school is immediately alerted to the intruder.

These anecdotes, and there must be scores of similar ones, are amusing, but they are also tragic. They symbolize the distrust teachers have of the system of supervision in education, of the representatives of that system, and of individuals.

It is not my intent to hold supervisors in education up to ridicule. It is my intent, however, to suggest that the system, as a system, is not producing what it could and should. Undoubtedly there are many teachers who seek and receive help from their principal, central office supervisor, or helping teacher. But the overall feelings that develop when supervision and supervisory relationships are discussed with a group of teachers are ones of indifference or hostility; their anecdotes are laced with ridicule. Teachers who are happy about their supervision seem to constitute a definite minority.

The thesis of this chapter has been that at least part of the reason for the lack of value that most teachers seem to place on their supervisor can be found in the way the system itself seems to operate. This is particularly true with regard to an untested assumption that the system makes relative to what it takes to be a competent supervisor (the certification process) and the equally untested assumption that the structure is producing what it was intended to produce. Rational people (all of us) design rational systems, and they should work — or so we reason. And so, once having established a structure, we tend to forget about it and assume that it is working well, particularly when it is difficult to know what the product is or should be. But then, one of my own private rules of thumb is that "the road to hell is paved with untested assumptions that are acted on."

It occurs to me, finally, that I may have come across as just another educational cynic who enjoys criticizing, poking fun at, or putting down the system. Indeed, I do become depressed at what I see, and I suppose this depression emerges, at times, as cynicism. Cynicism, however, is a luxury for people who have no stake in the problem. I do have some serious questions about what transpires in education in general, and about the quality of much of the supervision that takes place. I do believe, however, that the system and the people who work in it (including myself) are capable of changing. But the changes that take place need to be based, in my judgment, not on traditional rituals of change, nor on untested assumptions about what ought to be. What is required are designs for change that are undergirded by relevant data and sound theory. It is my hope that the balance of this book will provide at least some of the data and theory.

3

The Goals and Realities:
Digging a Bit Deeper

In Chapter 2, I suggested that a way to start looking at the problem of supervision in the schools was to focus on the larger system of which the supervisory structure is a part. I also made note of some symptoms of the problem, that is, the warning systems that teachers used to alert each other that the "enemy" was on the prowl. But symptoms of a problem are simply indications that something is wrong. In this chapter and the next I probe somewhat deeper into the details of the "something" that is the major concern of this book—the character of the human relationships that develop between supervisors and teachers.

The idea that something is wrong with any system implies that there is some kind of interference occurring between what that system was intended to produce, its goals, and what it does produce. Thus, I start this inquiry with a brief discussion of what supervision is supposed to be all about as a lead into providing a bit of information on some of the sources of the frustration and conflict that teachers seem to have about their supervision and that, to some degree, are shared by their supervisors.

It is not difficult to identify the goals of supervision in education. They have been defined many times in slightly different ways, but they seem, in the final analysis, to cluster into two interdependent categories: the improvement of instruction and the enhancement of the personal and professional growth of teachers. Further, and most important to the thrust of this book, you cannot really accomplish one without paying attention to the other.

17

Supervision is an interactive affair, not only between and among people, but relative to its aims. For example, any change in a teacher's classroom behavior probably cannot be made without help being concurrently offered to the teacher as a person for problems he may have dealing with himself and other people—both adults and youngsters. Or, a supervisor's attempt to help a teacher learn radically new curriculum concepts is probably doomed to failure unless he is prepared and skilled enough to help the teacher overcome the resistance he may have to changing his way of presenting science, for example, from a didactic approach to one that is more experiential and process oriented.

Notice that the word "help" has been used in one form or another several times in the preceding paragraph. It is this word that provides a clue, to my way of thinking, to what supervision is all about. Essentially, supervision is the giving and receiving of help regarding the performance of some task or the resolution of a problem. In order for this process to be productive, three major conditions have to exist: the teacher must want help, the supervisor must have the resources to provide the kind of help required or know where the resources may be found, and the interpersonal relationships between a teacher and supervisor must enable the two to give and receive in a mutually satisfactory way.

The last point is critical, and it provides an underlying theme for much of our discussion in this and future chapters. It matters little if the teacher knows he needs help and if the supervisor has the resources to give the help required *if* each is put off by the other. For example, if a teacher is aware that he is having difficulty involving his youngsters in a particular area of study, but sees his supervisor as uncaring, not personally involved, or domineering, the chances of his seeking his supervisor out or acting on suggestions that may be unilaterally offered are minimal. If the supervisor sees the teacher resisting his suggestions or being defensive in other ways, he is quite apt to take an attitude of general negative evaluation of the teacher as a person and, behaviorally (consciously or otherwise), the supervisor may act then to increase the social distance between himself and the teacher. Thus, what occurs (and it seems to be prevalent in educational supervision) is a degenerative communications cycle that minimizes the potential helpfulness of the whole process.

SOME DISTURBING AND NEGLECTED FINDINGS

The proposition that the supervisory system in the schools seems not to be living up to the expectations held for it is not based on newly discovered facts. We have known this for some time, as the following will indicate, but we have neglected to do much about what we know.

Wiles (1953) cited a study in which it was found that only 4 percent of the teachers in Indiana felt that the quality of supervision they received was good. Data from a more recent study of teachers in the Philadelphia area (Blumberg and Amidon, 1965) reinforce that finding, suggesting that a sizable percentage of teachers considered that the time they spent with their supervisors was "utterly wasteful," while a quite small percentage perceived it to be time well spent. In yet another study reported by Wiles (1953), almost 2,500 teachers were asked about their sources for new ideas or changes in teaching practices. Only 35 (about 1.5 percent) indicated their local supervisor as a source. The picture that emerges from these studies seems to be that most teachers have a view of supervision that is incongruent with its goals. They may also see supervision as a part of the system that exists but that does not play an important role in their professional lives, almost like an organizational ritual that is no longer relevant.

Teachers' perceptions of the worth of their supervision present, of course, only one side of the coin. It will come as no surprise to anyone that supervisors see the situation differently. Unfortunately, the data we have are limited, but perhaps they are minimally sufficient to give a glimpse into the supervisor's mirror. Blumberg, Amidon, and Weber (1967) reported that supervisors, when they evaluate the effects of their efforts, take almost a polar stance to that of teachers. Most tend to view the results of their work in a very positive way, and few feel that what they do with teachers is a waste of time. Perhaps more interesting, though, are the findings of a study, published by the Department of Elementary School Principals of the National Education Association (1968) and based on reports of elementary school supervising principals. It revealed that the principals saw themselves spending about 35 percent of their time in the supervision of teachers and that the principals said they would like to increase their supervisory time by 40 percent, that is, up to about 50 percent of their total work effort.

So, we seem to be caught in a curious type of bind of which, I suspect, not many people in education have been made publicly aware. It is this. Teachers tend to say they find their supervision of little value. Supervisors say their work has a lot of value. Supervisors seem to be saying that they want to spend more time doing what their clients (the teachers) consider to be relatively useless. We seem to be involved in a circular, self-reinforcing, and, one would suspect, extremely uncommunicative system, the maintenance of which requires a large expenditure of increasingly scarce resources for an actitivy with a relatively small reward, at least from the point of view of those whom the expenditure is supposed to benefit.

Curiously enough, the potential for productive supervision in teaching is great, at least theoretically, if one were to think about the character of teaching as a work technology. Woodward (1958) identified, in industry, three kinds of production or work technologies: the *single-unit* or *small-batch* technology, which is characterized by the type of work in which a single person or a small group has most of the responsibility for seeing a job through from beginning to end; *mass production* or *assembly line* work is precisely what it says—a person doing a small part of a much larger task over which he exercises little control; *continuous process* technology is seen, for example, in oil refineries, where many workers are removed from the product itself and they merely turn valves or push the appropriate button at the right time. Relating supervision to the nature of the work technology, Woodward says that the potential for increasing production through supervision is least in a continuous process situation, somewhat more in mass production, and highest in the single-unit or small-batch category. In the continuous process technology, the worker has little or no control over his work. He does not plan events; nor is he responsible in any way that matters for the quality of the final product. His job is confined, for the most part, to seeing that the product is processed in the way called for by others. Because he is a monitor, supervision can do little to enable him to do a better, more effective job.

In mass production or assembly line work, the planning and control and the responsibility for the quality of the end product tend to be removed from the worker. Some assembly line work does call for considerable skill on the part of the individual, and it would be then that the potential for supervision to influence productivity would be greatest. This potential is, however, relatively low.

In the single-unit or small-batch technology, the worker has major, if not total, control over what he does. His are the responsibilities for planning, gathering resources, conducting his operation, initiating interactions with others, and developing quality control of the end product. It is no wonder that, under these work conditions, the potential for supervision to affect what goes on is greater. The skills required of the person in this situation are more varied, and his options for making decisions are wider and have more impact on the product.

Teaching obviously fits the description of the single-unit or small-batch work technology. Teachers as individuals or in teams have, in most cases, almost total control of planning, gathering of resources, decision making, and product evaluation in their work. The situation is ideal for productive supervision. Yet, as we have seen and shall pursue further, the gap between what could be and what is seems to be rather wide and, though the gap may not be getting greater, one is hard put to discern its narrowing.

DIGGING A LITTLE DEEPER

There certainly is a place in our society for the problem poser, that is, the person whose function it is merely, but possibly with great force, to point accusing fingers at social or institutional ills. Such, however, is not the role I wish to play in writing this book. Rather, though indeed I raise questions and, I think, serious ones about the efficacy of the supervisory system in the schools, my aim is not to be the "Grand Inquisitor" while I sit safely in my university office, far removed from the day-to-day life of supervisors and teachers. What I do want to do is to inquire into some of the circumstances that underlie problems of supervision and, perhaps in the process, to help others do the same.

A way to start is to listen to what people are saying. On a number of occasions I have started a class in supervision by asking groups of teachers and groups of supervisors (all members of the class) to discuss problems they have faced in supervision, either receiving it (the teachers) or giving it (the supervisors). These discussions are recorded and the following excerpts constitute a fair sample of the points that usually develop.

Teachers on Supervisors and Supervision

The reactions of teachers to supervisors and supervision come first, and representative comments appear below:

— An awful lot of people who are supervisors or who are called supervisors have been out of the classroom so long that they've forgotten what it's all about. They remember things from their own or other people's experience but they are no longer aware of what's really going on.

— My helping teacher would come by to observe. After the observation she would say, "Do you want any help?"—which was the extent of her help. Once in a while she would find some trivial thing to complain about to show she was on the ball. "Is your lesson plan book up to date?" or "What page are you on and how closely are you following the curriculum?" These are ridiculous questions. There was never anything about my objectives or how the kids are coming along.

— I've had one very poor experience and one extremely good one. When I was a new teacher my supervisor would come in once a month. The only comment I ever received was "very nice." That's all. I knew there had to be some criticism, and I wanted to know so I could improve. But the only other comment I received was, "You have to cover five more units." The good experience was completely different. My supervisor observed and we talked. She got me to observe other teachers and other teachers came in to observe me. She made materials available to me and encouraged me to go to workshops.

— I've had a very positive experience with supervision. My supervisor really helps. He doesn't ask petty questions, but gets directly to the point. He simply says "What can I do to help?" He involves us in solving problems.

— So many supervisors just don't seem to like people.

— We have a supervisor who comes around on what he calls his "pop-in" visits. He blasts in the door, sits for fifteen or twenty minutes, and then leaves. Later he tells you that you don't erase the boards enough or that the shades aren't even. Or you shouldn't have scolded so loudly because there may be another kid in the classroom with an emotional instability and you might shake him up. And this stuff actually appeared on the report.

—In my first year of teaching I was observed once and evaluated on the last day of school in a meeting with my principal and my supervisor. The meeting lasted two minutes and fifty seconds. This is how it took place. Three forms, all the same, were passed out. Each of us signed one, and then one was filled out in this manner: The principal said, "We'll put a few E's in there and a few S's in there. That means excellent and satisfactory. Is that all right with you?" And then I signed it.

—I get the picture that supervisors say, "I want the teachers to develop their way of doing things. I want them to be free to do it. But I want them to do it *this* way."

—With the competitiveness, threat, artificiality, and so on, I don't get the feeling we're talking about real people. It's just people to be manipulated or goals to be accomplished.

—Part of the artificiality of the supervisory situation is the kids. If you let them know you're going to be observed, they say, in effect, "Don't worry, teach, we'll take care of you."

Most of these comments are negative and somewhat derisive. Issues that teachers raise and that seem to account for their negativism include the notion that supervisors seem to be out of touch with the classroom. Though they see many teachers in action, they are out of the action and, thus, do not understand what is going on. Their lack of understanding blocks them from real communication with teachers and prevents them from being helpful.

Much of what gets communicated from supervisors to teachers is perceived by teachers to be procedural trivia and not a concern with problems of teaching. Teachers are hard put, and quite understandably so, to find the relationship between the evenness with which the window shades are drawn and questions of teaching and learning. And, though it may be important to have an up-to-date lesson plan book, it is probably true that there is little relationship between such currency and the nature of the teaching-learning processes that occur in a classroom.

Teachers also seem to read a sort of insecurity into what they see as supervisors' avoiding them. The inference being drawn is that supervisors feel uncomfortable and unsure of themselves in their role. Whether or not this inference is valid is not at issue; the fact that such an interpretation is made is. Probably related to the supervisors' apparent insecurity and subsequent evasion is the teachers' feeling that supervisors do not seem to like people. In all likelihood, that is not the case; supervisors, as a group, probably like people neither more nor less than teachers. But whether or not they do is less important than how they are seen. And, as seems likely, teachers tend to reciprocate in kind by avoiding the supervisors.

Still another avoidance mechanism can be inferred from the teacher's feeling that the whole process of supervision is not taken seriously. When, at the end of a year, the principal and supervisor say, "We'll put a few E's in there and a few S's in there," they cannot help, though their motivation may be quite different, communicating that the whole business is a matter of "going through the motions." Teachers would certainly respond in similar fashion and devalue the potential help they might receive in the future.

Some teachers perceive that their supervisors play a democratic game. On the one hand, they are seen as communicating an interest in the teacher's self-development and the creative solution of his problems. On the other hand, perhaps when the chips are down, it turns out that the "creative solution of problems" is really the supervisor's solution. It is a bit like an experience I once had with a management consultant who told me about his firm's "Guided Discussion Leadership Training Program." The goal was to train managers to lead discussions so that the group arrived at decisions that they thought were theirs, but that were really the ones he wanted them to make in the first place. When a teacher experiences this kind of situation, the chances of his being willing to involve himself with his supervisor the next time around become drastically diminished.

Finally, we come to the point of artificiality. Teachers seem to be saying that the whole process is like a game. It is, perhaps, analogous to the situation that develops when a person goes to buy a car. There is a list price on the car. The salesman gives the price, but he knows he will not get it. The buyer offers a price, but he knows that he will pay more. Each side is aware of the game, and it frequently gets played out to the end with each party feeling that he won. In supervision, it seems, games also get played. The teacher knows he is going to be observed and evaluated. He tells his students. If they like the teacher, they "take care of him," and the supervisor, who possibly went through the same process as a beginning teacher, observes a good lesson. The teacher gets what he wants, and the supervisor gets what he wants. And the game is over. But nothing really happens.

The different reactions of the few teachers who view their supervisory experiences as productive are interesting. Their supervisors communicated a willingness to engage with them; they dealt with problems of teaching and learning; they had resources that were made available; the image they presented to the teacher was that of a human being first and a supervisor second.

There is another type of information that becomes available, in my experience, when a group of teachers from different schools and systems sits down to talk about their reactions to their supervision. It has to do with the processes and reactions that develop among the teachers who are talking as well as those who are observing. No one is prompted. People simply talk to each other. What seems to happen is, to my way of thinking, rather striking. As soon as they start, it becomes evident that what the discussants are saying echoes the feelings of others in the room. There is much laughter and nodding of agreement and, after the formal part of the exercise has terminated, frequent interjection of corroborative experiences. The point is that the way people behave in these situations lends credence to what they say. Finally, I must admit I experience no surprises from these discussions. It is all, unfortunately, quite predictable.

Supervisors on Teachers and Supervision

Supervisors, too, have perceptions and feelings. What follows is a fair sample of the way they describe their problems:

—The major problem I have is my frustration because the problems I confront with teachers are so profound that they're beyond my power to help. The bureaucracy gets in the way, particularly in the disciplinary cases.

—It seems to me that teachers want their supervisors to give them easy solutions to all their problems.

—Too many times the teacher takes things for granted. That is, the teacher figures the supervisor will come in to help. The supervisor figures the teacher will ask. But nothing happens. There's no communication, at least as far as asking for help is concerned.

—The big problem for me is the older teachers and change. They have a tough time adjusting to it. They've been in this rut year after year. I don't worry so much about the younger teachers, but I sure do about the older ones.

—I focus on the older teachers because I know them. I pass over the new teachers and make excuses for them. It's really touchy to say to a teacher who's been in a school for fifteen or twenty years, "I'd like you to start thus and so . . . ."

—The degree of cooperation you get from a teacher is directly proportional to the degree of security [he has] in the classroom. But it's also related to the security of the supervisor. If you're unwilling to engage the teacher at an early level of planning, the success of any program will be affected.

—It seems to me that the basic problem is that new teachers tighten up. They don't trust the situation. They react differently in the classroom when you're there. You don't get a true picture of what's happening. You write up an observation, and you know darn well it's not the way the teacher really operates. I don't seem to be able to overcome it, and neither do they.

—I know that I pose a threat as an authority figure. And I also know that teachers question my experience and skill. I frequently get the feeling that, when I criticize what a teacher is doing, the unspoken response is, "If you're so smart, do it yourself."

Supervisors' reactions to their jobs and the problems they have with teachers have some parallels with, but also some differences from, teachers' reactions.

The bureaucracy of school system organizations apparently has the effect of blocking and frustrating some supervisors in their efforts to deal with classroom problems and thus present a helpful image to teachers. For example, both a teacher and a supervisor might agree that a particular youngster's behavior is so disruptive to a class that he should be moved, but bureaucratic functioning makes the process intolerably slow or, perhpas, impossible. It is possible that the system gets blamed for the supervisor's inability to be more helpful. Nevertheless, there is undoubtedly an element of truth in the supervisor's complaint. And the result of the supervisor's inability to influence the system—a degeneration of the relationship between supervisor and teacher—is to be expected. Earlier research (Pelz, 1952) in an industrial setting has indicated that one of the critical factors that affects subordinates' ratings of productive supervision is the belief that supervisors are able to influence decisions at upper levels of the organizational hierarchy. The fit in this case is good, and, if it is true that supervisors feel stymied by the organization, particularly on issues important to the teacher, one would be inclined to predict negative outcomes in the supervisory relationship.

A supervisor's perception of teachers' overdependence will create problems. Such overdependence conflicts with the way in which the supervisor sees his role. A supervisor sees himself as willing and able to help a teacher solve a teaching problem. The teacher, at least from where the supervisor sits, says, in effect, "Please don't bother with this problem-solving stuff. Just tell me what to do." There are certainly situations in which direct telling is all that is needed. It is probably true, however, that most classroom or teaching problems do not have simple solutions. They require thought, analysis, and solution testing. Where the supervisor considers discussion necessary but the teacher demands a quick, easy answer, it is not difficult to picture the bind in which the supervisor is caught. He wants to develop and maintain good relations with the teacher. In order to do this, he must be helpful. Yet, the teacher is asking for the kind of help the supervisor feels will be unproductive. What should he do? He is damned if he does and damned if he does not. In many cases, an uneasy disengagement is all that results.

As we consider the comment, "The teacher figures the supervisor will come in to help, the supervisor figures the teacher will ask, but nothing happens," we can see the roles conflicting even more. The image I fantasize from this is that of a boy and a girl, attracted to each other, wanting each other, but neither being sure who should make the first move nor how it should be made. Communication does not occur unless one of the two takes a risk or, perhaps, a matchmaker arrives on the scene. The analogy is not so farfetched. It should be apparent that a good bit of tension surrounds the whole question of supervision in education. It is not unusual for teachers to say that a request for help is regarded as a sign of incompetence, and who wants to be perceived as incompetent? Conversely, supervisors are leery of being unwelcome intruders. They have been rejected enough, and it is not pleasant. Caution being the better part of valor, they wait for requests for help that do not come, an uneasy situation to say the least.

Supervisors express a great deal of concern about the problems of working with older teachers, typically those who have been teaching for ten years or more. It is a complex problem. Older teachers have tenure; they are untouchable in the sense that their tenure deprives the supervisor of any direct source of influence; they can, and sometimes literally do, tell the supervisor to go "peddle his papers someplace else." To the supervisors these teachers frequently seem to be in ruts, dealing with the same subject matter and using the same methods, procedures, and rituals year after year. The old saw, "Has he been teaching for thirty years or for one year thirty times?" holds here. If it is the latter, supervisors tend to become concerned and quite properly so. One can hear a supervisor, especially a younger one, ask and then answer the question, "In the face of tenure, difference in age, and all that goes with it, how can I work with that teacher? I can't. I won't." The frustrations that develop from these circumstances are not hard to picture. Probably foremost among them would be the supervisor's sense of his own impotence in the face of a system that he supports but that gets in his way.

A clue that some supervisors are aware and concerned about their relationships with teachers is provided when their attention turns to the teacher's security in his role and the supervisor's in his. One might hypothesize that, the more secure the teacher is as a teacher, the easier it will be for a supervisor to intervene, communicate, and help. And, the more secure a supervisor is as a supervisor, the more able he will be to initiate problem solving with the teacher. The second hypothesis suggests that the security of the supervisor will be related to the ease with which he can test the quality of his relationship with the teacher. This point can be seen, inferentially, as the starting place for engaging the teacher in collaborative planning.

What contributes to a supervisor's role security? In addition to confidence in his planning and curricular skills, the supervisor's security might depend on a variety of less obvious conditions, such as interpersonal needs for control or closeness or a sense of one's ability to communicate empathically. One such condition came to light in the behavior of a participant (a teacher who wanted to be an administrator) in a human-relations-training group. Throughout the program he had been rather quiet and had resisted initiating action with others. He had also resisted attempts on the part of others to engage him. Most of the group saw him as the person from whom they would be least willing to accept influence. In a discussion with me after the program, his conflicts surfaced. He saw himself as an assertive person who had no trouble with youngsters. But his relationships with adults had been clouded by his concept of something called "democratic leadership": in order to be a democratic leader (supervisor) you do not try to exert influence. You let things happen. It is not hard to envision his future relationships with teachers if he were to maintain this stance. He might well be the supervisory type about whom it was remarked, "After the observation she would say, 'Do you want any help?'—which was the extent of her help."

Supervisors, as well as teachers, refer to the artificiality of the typical supervisory situation, particularly as it applies to new teachers. Much as the teachers are aware that they and their students are "putting on a show" for the supervisor, so the supervisor is aware that he has an orchestra seat, front row center. At issue is the level of trust between the supervisor and the teacher, which probably bears a direct relationship to the level of threat the teacher perceives in the situation. The new teacher may think, "The supervisor, his observations, and evaluation represent a threat to me. I cannot talk about it with him. The only way I can deal with the situation is to play a game and hope he doesn't find out." The supervisor seems to be saying, "This is a game. I cannot talk about it with him. The only way I can deal with it is to play along but pretend I'm not playing." Thus, in many cases, the supervisor and the teacher get caught in a degenerative charade that has no real winners. It becomes a tie, with the exception that the third and sometimes unwitting party to the game—the youngsters—may ultimately lose.

When situations such as this develop, I would guess that only rarely is the supervisor as a person the issue. Rather, it is what he represents that both he and the teacher find difficult. He is one of "them" and, as such, is seen, frequently, not as an understanding helper but only as the establishment representative who holds power to reward or to punish. So there is a tendency for supervisors and teachers to avoid one another as people and to construct sometimes elaborate games in which both engage.

The organizational "we-they" conflict is reflected in the supervisor's reaction, "I frequently get the feeling that, when I criticize what a teacher is doing, the unspoken response is, 'If you're so smart, do it yourself.'" Most teachers, young or old, are sincerely interested in becoming better and more skilled at their craft. Why, then, should they reject, verbally or nonverbally, help when it is offered? One reason is that the help, or the way in which it is offered, may be seen as irrelevant or offensive. Another reason is that such rejection may be symbolic of the continuing battle that is waged in practically every organization between those who are "getting their hands dirty" and those whose job is managing, planning, organizing, training, and so forth.

There is a certain, perhaps considerable, validity to the feeling that one who is organizationally removed from the job being done does not really understand its problems and requirements. There is also a good bit of truth in the notion that a skilled third party (a supervisor) can observe things about the job and the way it is being done of which the primary actor (the teacher) is not aware, and can offer helpful suggestions or criticisms. These points are all quite rational and the problem at hand—the "we-they" conflict—has a great deal of emotionality at its base that is rarely discussed. Further, when conflicts that have both rational and emotional sides develop in a person, they are typically resolved in the direction of emotionality. So that, even if a teacher were confronted with the rational point of view about the potential value of a skilled third party, he might well counter with "Yes, but . . ." or "There are always exceptions," or "Some of my best friends . . . ."

That relationships should exist between organizational character and the behavior of the people who work in organizations should come as a surprise to no one. What is at least somewhat surprising is the apparent lack of concern on the part of school administrators about the relationships. While we can do little in this book about telling a school administrator where he should or should not focus his energies, there is no way to discuss the behavior of supervisors without first examining schools as a particular organizational type. The focus in Chapter 5 is on the manner in which some of the particular organizational characteristics of schools bear on the nature of supervisor-teacher relationships. Before that, however, supervisor-teacher relationships are viewed through the medium of fantasy in Chapter 4.

4   Some Fantasies about Supervisors and Teachers

The data most typically used in the behavioral sciences to assess a situation and to generate or test hypotheses is of the paper-and-pencil survey variety. Occasionally and, fortunately more frequently, data are also gathered as a result of direct observation of behavior. In addition, we rely heavily on self-reports of the people involved for our situational analyses. We then engage in content analysis of these reports. Depending on the rigorousness of the study design, each of these types of data has unquestioned value. What I have come to realize, however, is that, perhaps motivated by the search for rigor, some of the intensely human perspectives on interpersonal, group, and organizational life get left by the wayside. That is, I sometimes feel that, in our rush to be "scientific," we may misunderstand what the human enterprise is all about—or a good part of it. We may miss the beauty marks as well as the warts. We may also miss part of our essential humanity.

Several chapters further on in this book the supervisor-teacher relationship is examined in a fairly systematic and quantifiable way. This chapter approaches the relationship through the medium of fantasy. With the exception of some professionals engaged in the practice of psychotherapy or psychotherapeutic research, the use of a person's fantasies as a source of descriptive and diagnostic data has largely been neglected by both social and behavioral scientists, certainly those involved in the field of education. This chapter is not a major effort to rectify that situation, but it does present, in my opinion, a way of understanding supervision from the teachers' point of view that might not be obtainable through more traditional research methodology.

The particular way of collecting data about a person's fantasy life that forms the basis for this chapter is based on the following notion: As we come to know a person or group, as we have experiences with people occupying particular organizational positions, we start to categorize them and to assign characteristics and some-times stereotypical behavioral patterns to them. Frequently we attribute motivations to them, even though this can be risky in the absence of more direct data. Given this categorization, characterization of behavior, and attribution of motives, it becomes possible to construct a fantasy concerning the nature of the house in which that person or group lives. Sometimes this fantasizing almost takes the form of a party game in which many of us have engaged from time to time. That is, we play at creating fantasies of people's homes based on our experience with the people.

A brief example will help to clarify my point. A few years ago I was asked, as a consultant, to spend some time with the social studies and English departments of a high school that were experiencing difficulties in their ability to work together. In order to collect some data, I asked each department to imagine the house they saw the other living in. The data, of course, were to be shared. Two parts of the house that the English department constructed for the social studies department have remained in my mind. First, there was a large picture window in the house, *but you could only see through it one way*—from the house to the outside. This made the picture window a one-way mirror. Second, the house was situated on a high hill, and it had a swimming pool and a snack bar. But a sign at the pool entrance read, *"Admission by Invitation Only."* The imagery was sharp. These two points provided much more "meaty" and powerful information than the English department had provided via rating scales or other means. The English department evidently felt that the social studies department did not readily see points of view other than their own; nor was it easy to enter into their communications system. Further, and as an unanticipated by-product of the exercise, both groups had fun performing the task, and the feedback was received in an open, rather relaxed manner. Both groups actually seemed to look forward to hearing what kind of house the other fantasized them occupying. The tension usually associated with such sessions was absent.

So much for creating fantasy houses. What follows are descriptions of such "houses" as they were developed by four groups of teachers. There were four teachers in each group. Two of the groups were asked to fantasize the houses that they saw supervisors living in at the time, and two were asked to fantasize what a supervisor's house might be like in the future. I do not pretend that the results are generalizable. The descriptions that follow seem, however, clearly to build on the discussion in the preceding chapter, and they do this in a rich and provocative way.

TWO DESCRIPTIONS OF FANTASIZED HOUSES IN WHICH SUPERVISORS NOW LIVE

1. One approaches the house via a long, winding driveway. You cannot see the house from the road. The lawn surrounding the house is very green because it is made of astroturf. The house itself is square and has a flat roof. There is nothing romantic about it. There are no windows in the house. A number of things strike you as you enter. Everything is in its place. The furniture is very austere, and it is nailed to the floor. There is a picture on the wall that is a flowchart, in color, of administrative positions. Diplomas hang next to the flowchart. There are floral arrangements composed of artificial flowers. The lighting system is stark and very bright. The house is very clean. It has a central cleaning system with vacuums in the walls. In the house are janitorial supplies and textbooks. There are also disconnected bodies sitting in straight rows.

2. The house is located in the suburbs on a large plot. It is very distant from the road, thus seeming to convey a need for privacy. Inside the house there is a "receiving place" for people who enter. There also seems to be a "safe place" that the occupant uses for retreating. There are lots of mailboxes and mail chutes. Piles of mail are constantly forming in big bins which must be filled by 3 p.m. The library has floor-to-ceiling book cases. But the books are not accessible because the bottom shelves are empty. The books are not sorted. There is a medicine cabinet that is filled with Band-Aids, assorted remedies, and lots of Kleenex. There is also a telescope in the house, but it is very narrow, enabling the viewer to see only a little bit of the scene at any one time. There is a conference room in the house and also a coffee urn, but the urn is in a different room. In the conference room there are pictures of the supervisor's family and his/her diplomas. There is a picture of the graduation when the diplomas were awarded. These pictures are well lighted. There are also framed testimonials and autographed pictures of previous clients. Curiously, the clients of the supervisor don't have ears, so there is a megaphone at the supervisor's place at the conference table.

TWO DESCRIPTIONS OF FANTASIZED HOUSES IN WHICH
SUPERVISORS MIGHT LIVE IN THE FUTURE

1. The house is a round one. There are lots of two-way windows. It is located in sort
of a parklike atmosphere. The house seems friendly and can be expanded. It is all
on one floor and has a large revolving entrance door making it easy to enter or
leave. The fact that it is round and on one floor conveys an egalitarian, not bureaucratic, atmosphere where all resources have equal input. In the inside, around the
wall, there are lots of partitioned enclosures, each with a revolving door. The partitions separate the enclosures from a "commons" area, but do not totally enclose
them. The "commons" is used for discussions between the occupant of the house
and visitors.

2. The house is in the country with two acres of land around it. It is an older house
and is painted white with green trim. The doors are never locked. On the outside
there is a "fun" garden where people can gather for a party. The house is furnished
very comfortably. There is a fireplace, and furniture you can sink into. There are
many guest rooms and a large kitchen with a big table. The walls in the kitchen are
made of brick and are decorated with many pots and pans. The coffeepot is always
on. The stairwell leading to the guest rooms is very large. There are French doors
that open onto the garden. The house conveys a style of Old America.

As I read and reread the descriptions of these fantasized houses,
I was struck by the fact that almost every sentence contains meaningful messages relative to the supervisor's role and function.
Further, they are phrased in ways that would enable most people
to relate to, understand, and interpret them. Interpretations will
certainly vary, but one does not have to be a trained psychodiag-
nostician to make sense of the fantasized houses. My own sense of
it all follows.

THE SUPERVISOR'S HOUSE TODAY

An impression that quickly becomes clear is that the teachers
saw supervisors as *distant*. "You cannot see the house from the
road." "It is very distant from the road, thus seeming to convey the
need for privacy." The teachers also seem to be saying that they
see their supervisors conveying a climate of *artificiality*, being *unimaginative*, and rather *closed* to new ideas. Note the following:
"The lawn surrounding the house is very green because it is made of
astroturf. The house itself is square and has a flat roof. There is
nothing romantic about it. There are no windows in the house."
Thus, an image starts to emerge before we enter. What has happened

is that the teachers who "built" these houses have focused first on external factors related to their ability to approach their supervisors. And the feeling that one gets is that of difficulty of approach, an approach that is hindered by perceptions of distance, artificiality, and closedness. It is almost as though the supervisor, possibly hindered by organizational trappings and procedures, becomes cloaked in bureaucratic formalities that serve to reinforce precisely those factors that block the help a supervisor may have to give a teacher.

As we enter the house (or, as supervisor and teacher start to interact), other patterns of "living" develop that seem to reinforce the images created from the outside. The artificiality that seems implicit in a lawn made of astroturf is confronted directly in the house by reference to "floral arrangements composed of artificial flowers." New features, however, enter the situation. *Neatness, order,* and *rigidity* are apparent. "Everything is in its place. The furniture is very austere and is nailed to the floor." *Formality* and *defensiveness* are present: "There is a 'receiving place' for people who enter," and "There also seems to be a 'safe place' that the occupant uses for retreating." Formality and a *procedural* emphasis is supported by the statement that, "There is a picture on the wall that is a flowchart, in color, of administrative positions."

Obvious perceived *needs for status*, supporting once more the formality and bureaucratic emphasis, are present in both houses. In one, "Diplomas hang next to the flowchart." In the other, "In the conference room there are pictures of the graduation when the diplomas were awarded. These pictures are well lighted. There are also framed testimonials and autographed pictures of previous clients." Other factors, however, intrude subtly into the situation as presented by the pictures. For example, the picture of the supervisor's family seems to be saying, "But I am human, after all. Look, I have a family!" And, in addition, the framed testimonials convey to me, at least, the supervisor's need to let teachers know that, despite all the organizational and interpersonal encumbrances that are present, other teachers have found it helpful to work with the supervisor. It almost seems to be a frustrated and plaintive cry to "Try me."

The image of supervisors having to deal with a great deal of *routine administrative busywork* is graphically presented in the second house. "There are lots of mailboxes and mail chutes. Piles of mail are constantly forming in big bins which must be filled by 3 p.m." The need to have the mail bins filled by 3 p.m. reflects, perhaps, the perception of teachers that supervisors see their effectiveness measured by the quantity of busywork they accomplish each day. Another interpretation is that teachers perceive supervisors using the large quantity of administrative work they do as an excuse for not interacting more with teachers.

Reference is made in both houses to the supervisor as a person with *material and technological resources*. There are, for example, janitorial supplies and textbooks in the first house. In the second house, however, we see a curious twist. "The library has floor-to-ceiling book cases. But the books are not accessible because the bottom shelves are empty." In other words, supervisors do have lots of resources available, but they are not easy to get. One has to be able to reach to the upper shelves, and, even if one does, it is hard to use them because "The books are not sorted." Material and technological resources are not the only help available, however, because, "There is a medicine cabinet filled with Band-Aids, assorted remedies, and lots of Kleenex." Part of the supervisor's role, then, is to help the teacher overcome some of the emotional trauma that may develop in the course of teaching. The supervisor, in a sense, *administers first aid* and *provides comfort*.

Some teachers appear to see supervisors as *separating task behavior quite distinctly from positive social-emotional behavior*. "There is a conference room in the house and also a coffee urn, but the urn is in a different room." In addition, the work in which supervisor and teacher engage tends to *deal with isolated fragments of the problem and not the total problem* as we read, "There is also a telescope in the house, but it is very narrow, enabling the viewer to see only a little bit of the scene at any one time." An inference can be made from other parts of the houses that it is the supervisor who manipulates the telescope.

Finally, and what in my mind is very striking, is the fact that in the descriptions of both houses and the people who go into them, there is reference to people who have some sort of physical impairment. In the first house "There are also disconnected bodies sitting in straight rows." In the second, "Curiously, the clients of the supervisor don't have ears, so there is a megaphone at the supervisor's place at the conference table." Interpretation of these comments will surely differ. I offer two, tentatively. The disconnected bodies seem to suggest that the teachers feel that supervisors work with them in a fragmented way that denies their humanity. Disconnected bodies are not living. The reference to clients without ears calls for a different view. What it says to me is that teachers tend not to listen to supervisors. They turn them off, and supervisors are aware of this, which leads to the supervisor's need for the megaphone.

It is also curious that reference to people who are physically impaired came last in the fantasies of both houses. Perhaps, in a way, the teachers who built these psychological houses felt that the nature of what they had fantasized led to impaired human relationships between supervisors and teachers.

THE SUPERVISOR'S HOUSE IN THE FUTURE

The houses that teachers fantasized supervisors might eventually live in are radically different from those of the present. And, interestingly, though the two houses are architecturally different, they convey many similar impressions. Two points seem to stand out quickly. One is the factor of *openness* and *accessibility*. "There are lots of two-way windows" and "a large revolving entrance door making it easy to enter or leave." "The doors are never locked." The second factor seems to be one of *comfort*. "It is located sort of in a parklike atmosphere. The house seems friendly and can be expanded." "The house is furnished very comfortably. There is a fireplace, and furniture you can sink into."

The roundness of the first house takes on a distinct meaning in contrast to the traditional mode of the second. Being round and on one floor "conveys an egalitarian, not bureaucratic, atmosphere where all resources have equal input." Teachers, by constructing this house, are saying that their ideas have merit, too, and that they want to be heard. Ideas should be considered for their worth, not because of who had them. On the other hand, the style of "Old American" of the second house seems to suggest something solid and a situation in which old values are not cast aside simply because they are old. The impression of something solid is supported by, "The walls in the kitchen are made of brick . . . ."

The availability of resources is dealt with in different ways. In the first house, "around the wall, there are lots of partitioned enclosures, each with a revolving door. The partitions separate the enclosures from a 'commons' area, but do not totally enclose them. The 'commons' is used for discussion between the occupant of the house and visitors." Resources, in this house, then, are easily accessible. Visitors can wander from one resource area to the next, apparently under no pressure. The situation seems like the "easy-off" and "easy-on" signs one sees on the freeways as a driver is solicited by roadside filling stations. The role of the supervisor (occupant) is that of a consultant, it appears, to be used by teachers at their choice—again with easy access to resources.

In the second house, the location of resources is of interest. That is, the pots and pans are on the brick walls in the kitchen. A teacher can take whatever utensil is needed, depending upon what that teacher wants to cook. That is, the supervisor, who stands solid, has much to offer the teacher, depending on what it is the teacher wants to do.

Finally, the fantasy of the second house seems to give much more attention to warmth and conviviality than that of the first, which gives a very businesslike yet relaxed impression. "There is a 'fun' garden where people can gather for a party. The coffeepot is always on. The stairwell leading to the guest rooms is very large. There are French doors that open onto the garden."

It would be tempting, if one were cynically inclined, to seize on the fantasies that have just been discussed as proof that supervisors are ignorant or ill-motivated people who do little but harm to teachers. In point of fact, of course, the "houses" are proof of nothing. What they do provide, it seems to me, is some confirmation and elaboration of the nature of the problem introduced in earlier chapters that surrounds the interaction of supervisors and teachers. The discussion that follows, then, should be treated as a sort of descriptive and diagnostic hypothesis, and not a statement of fact.

The image of supervisor-teacher relationships that is implicit in the "now" houses seems to be one of strain, tension, and uneasiness. Supervisors are difficult for teachers to approach. They are seen as distant, or their behavior conveys to teachers that they desire distance. This view may be related to perceptions by teachers that supervisors are closed to the ideas and feelings of teachers and to the notion that much of what goes on in supervision is artificial, a sort of unreal ritual.

If teachers see supervisors in this light, then the chances are good that these perceptions will be communicated to the supervisors, if not by words, then by behavior. From my own research and experience, the primary mode that teachers use to react to supervisors is that of avoidance. But the supervisors sense the avoidance and, of course, they must deal with it. To be avoided by someone is not a particularly ego-enhancing experience. In order to counter the deflationary effect of teacher avoidance, it may well be that supervisors engage in various status-building efforts. Recall the diplomas, the testimonials, and the organizational flowchart that had to picture, one suspects, the supervisor in a position of relatively high status *and* with direct access to people in the system with *higher* status. But that is not all, as one can visualize supervisors saying, "They wouldn't avoid me if they knew I really was a human being who wanted to be helpful and not just a bureaucrat who supports the system." That is why we have the picture of the supervisor's family in one house and the variety of resources that are available. But apparently the resources are not readily available in all cases. In the second house the books could not be reached, the implication being that a teacher would have to ask. Encouraging this kind of dependency among adults frequently has the unanticipated consequence of creating hostility and leading to further avoidance.

The spiral is reinforcing and downward in each of the two cases that were examined. The teachers see themselves being treated as people who have something wrong with them, either disconnected bodies (leading to fragmented interaction and problem solving) or earless (suggesting that teachers feel that supervisors think they must resort to power, symbolized by the megaphone, in order to be heard).

This is not a pretty picture and, of course, it is not meant to describe every supervisory situation. Nor, as I noted earlier, is it meant to characterize supervisors as bad or evil people. It is also clear that the picture is not complete because there is not an adequate sampling and because we do not have the houses that supervisors might fantasize for teachers. Nonetheless, given the fact that the teachers worked together to fantasize the houses and that each was reacting to his own experience, both the nature of the data and the similarities between the houses lend some credence to the presentation and to the inferences that have been made.

The futuristic "houses" that were fantasized exhibit much less personalized detail, it seems, than those of the present. Why this is so is a matter for the futurists to research. A reasonable hypothesis might be that, as people think about the future, they tend to focus on general environmental conditions rather than on personal or interpersonal specifics. At any rate, it can be seen that the houses in which supervisors might live one day contain practically no specific reference to the supervisor as a person, except by indirect inference from design and furnishings. There are, for example, no diplomas or pictures of the supervisor's family on the walls.

The vision of supervisor-teacher relations in the future that is contained in the fantasies seems to be predominantly marked by several conditions that are in contradistinction to the present. They are marked by openness and nearness, as opposed to closedness and remoteness; comfort and warmth, as opposed to tension and coolness; easy, rather than difficult access to resources; humanism and flexibility, rather than mechanism and rigidity; and a collaborative problem-solving climate, rather than what appears to be a climate that focuses on procedures and form. One may also infer that, though the future might, indeed, be different, it does not abandon the stability and tradition of the past. The baby is not being thrown out with the bath.

It has been my intent to create for the reader a data-based sense of the issues and problems that seem to be involved in the interaction, or lack of it, that occurs between supervisors and teachers. The data presented have, for the most part, been casually collected. But they come from a variety of sources and were obtained over a rather long period—more than fifteen years. It is this similarity of attitude over time that strengthens the argument on which this book is based: that a sort of stalemated cold war tends to exist in the schools between the supervisory system and the instructional system. I hasten to add that it does not exist between all individual supervisors and teachers.

At the risk of some repetition, my summary thinking about the situation is this: What transpires today under the banner of supervision, if we are to believe our data, is not a function of evil or ignorance. Rather, I see it as resulting from a tendency common to much thinking in education. We create a structure for a job, specify functions, and then assume it will work, merely because it is rational.

This has marked innumerable innovative attempts and has been specifically documented by Sarason (1971), using as his reference the introduction of the "new math." And so it is with supervision. Reasonable people would say that the supervisory system should work and work well. But it seems not to because, I think, in our rationality we neglect the individual, group, and organizational dynamics of the system. We ignore the hopes and fears of teachers *and* supervisors. We do not think about the unintended consequences of evaluation systems, of tenure systems, of certification systems. We neglect strategies of maintaining open communications linkages and avoid the problems that have historically developed between those who are supposed to know how to do things and those who "get their hands dirty" doing them. Instead, we do what comes naturally, perhaps. We assume things will work, because, after all, they should. In this case, as in many others, however, they have not, or at least so it appears. And, if what has occurred in the past is the best predictor of the future, one would sadly predict that the data about supervisors and teachers will be neglected. After all, teachers have not occupied any central offices in sit-in fashion to protest supervision. They show their dissatisfaction, typically, by engaging in avoidance behavior.

5 The Organizational Environment of Supervision

Sometimes explicitly, but more often implicitly, a thread that has run through the preceding chapters is that we really cannot understand supervisor-teacher relationships unless we also understand something about schools as organizations. The argument is a relatively simple one. People working in organizations do not behave in a vacuum. Much of what we do and our particular behavioral styles reflect the norms, values, and organization of the social system in which we are employed. Organizations, by their very being, develop frames of reference within which people behave and interact. And, in interactive fashion, these frames of reference are changed over time by the behavior of the people who work in the organizations. In schools the most obvious recent example of this change is the way in which the development of militant teachers' organizations has affected the attitudes of administrators and school boards.

This chapter does not constitute a thoroughgoing theoretical discussion of organizational theory as it may apply to schools. (For the reader who is interested in pursuing an inquiry into the more academic side of the organizational behavior of schools I suggest starting with Bidwell's (1965) "The School as a Formal Organization.") Rather, I shall be describing some of the elements of school organizational life, some subtle and some obvious, that seem to bear on the nature of the interaction between a teacher and supervisor. These elements are concerned with the autonomy of the school, the autonomy of the teacher, tenure and the presumption of competence, the productivity of teaching, aspiration levels of teachers, and the issues of professionalism and bureaucracy.

43

THE AUTONOMY OF THE SCHOOL

School systems seem to me to resemble, in some ways, a feudal kingdom. The central office resembles the palace; the individual schools, the various baronial estates. The central office gives certain things to the schools, lays down broad policies, and, in return, expects allegiance from the schools. Schools are free to develop and maintain their own internal affairs and structure so long as these don't violate the broad, systemwide policy. Besides its allegiance to the central office, the school is most held accountable for keeping the peace within its own territory, which includes not only the school itself but also the community it serves. The most severe indictment that a school principal or teacher can receive, for example, typically has little to do with problems of educational leadership or teaching ability and far more to do with whether the principal can control the school and the teacher the classroom.

Visitors from the central office, be they supervisors, staff specialists, the superintendent, or his assistants, tend to be treated with suspicion and mistrust. When these visits occur, most of the personnel in the school are concerned about having things look good. If they do, to continue the feudal analogy, the visitor from the central office will have "collected his taxes," departed, and left the school in peace to continue its own business.

There are many ways in which the analogy breaks down. Clear subservience, for example, probably exists only rarely. The superintendent has many constraints operating on him that limit his prerogatives, though it is probably true that some superintendents appear to act under their own concept of "the divine right of Kings." There are certainly many principals and teachers who hold the central office in a good deal less than awe and fear. Nevertheless, there seems to be enough similarity between the schools and the feudal system to be fascinating to a student of behavior in organizations. The issue is not, however, to poke fun at the way school systems are organized, but to inquire into the manner in which the character of the system—the operational autonomy combined with what appears to be hygienic accountability (keeping things cool)—affects supervisors and teachers.

The most immediate result of the quasi-autonomous relationship between schools and the central office is that, for personnel from "downtown," barriers are constructed around the school. For the most part this is not planned. More likely, it is part of the mores of the subculture known as a school. New teachers are cued in by the old-timers, and the system of beliefs perpetuates itself. Supervisors, despite the fact that they may have many valuable resources to offer teachers, tend to get treated as intruders. The teachers' game plan involves keeping things close to the vest, not revealing any weaknesses, and, or so it seems, playing neither to win nor lose, but for a draw. The supervisor can hardly fail to sense the attitude and formulate his own strategy, which from my observations, involves, first of all, *not* dealing with any relationship issue with the teacher, either of an interpersonal or organizational variety. It is only rarely that one hears either a teacher or a supervisor say that he will discuss his relations with and reactions to the other or the system. Quite the contrary, it almost seems as though the supervisor refuses to deal with behavioral or relationship issues and will focus only on matter-of-fact, ritualistic kinds of things. Sometimes, for example, as I listen to tape recordings of supervisors and teachers, I get almost an Alphonse-Gaston reaction. The supervisor makes a comment, offers criticism cautiously, and throws in a little praise; the teacher says "thank you" and notes that the pupils are bright and interested. It is almost as though the two people were not human.

Without a doubt, there are supervisors who have been able to overcome the barriers between the school and the central office. There are probably some school organizations where the barrier, the "we-they" gulf does not exist or has a minimal effect. The larger problem—that schools tend to ward off intruders, even though they are "their own"—remains, and it does not go away by pretending it is not there.

THE AUTONOMY OF THE TEACHER

There are striking similarities between the relationships of a school and the central office and those of the school and its teachers. Much as the schools in a district tend to resemble a federation of loosely allied states (our feudal analogy), individual teachers are usually autonomous in their classrooms. The principal expects of the teacher allegiance to the school and a smoothly running classroom about which neither the students nor the parents complain.

If the teacher meets these two criteria, he is able to make demands of the principal, primarily that he not interfere in the classroom. "If I am loyal to the school and if neither the kids nor their parents raise any fuss, there is little for the principal or other supervisory personnel to be concerned about." It is not uncommon to hear teachers say that they like their principal because he leaves them alone.

It is also true that there is a "we-they" gulf in schools between teachers and their administrative staff. I have observed this in buildings where, from my viewpoint, the level and quality of communication between teachers and principal was high, as well as in buildings in which the opposite condition holds. It is as though subtle and covert ways are developed by teachers to keep the principal in his office "where he belongs" and "leave the teaching to us." "Principals get paid to administrate and teachers get paid to teach and there is no necessary connection between the two" is the way the feeling is usually expressed.

There certainly are some principals who have easy psychological access to classrooms, who are seen by teachers as being relatively unthreatening, and whose contributions to teaching are considered helpful. Usually, however, the talk between principal and teacher tends to be restrained, matter of fact, and rather dull. It appears ritualistic: criticisms are tentatively made, and interviews frequently end with reassurance from the principal that the teacher is doing a fine job.

Such attitudes often prevail, even in schools with team teaching or open classrooms. The symptoms may not be as evident; the emotions seem to prevail. Outsiders, be they from the central office or the principal's office, tend to be unwelcome. These reactions are typically not related to individual personality. They stem from organizational culture and the role expectations and demands that emerge from that culture.

TENURE AND THE PRESUMPTION OF COMPETENCE

In Chapter 13, I discuss in detail the relationship of the tenured teacher and the supervisor. In this section tenure is treated as an organizational variable. Quite clearly, the system of tenure under which schools operate, though its specific provisions may vary a bit from state to state, affects supervisors and supervision. Though I do not argue against tenure, I must admit that any system that puts a stamp of lifelong competence and, in a sense, untouchability on a person after three years or so of work must necessarily develop some problems that stem directly from that system. (I also believe that the tenure system in universities is as fraught, perhaps more so, with the problems of the public school system.) Though the tenure system may have been designed to protect teachers from administrative whims, to assure some organizational stability, and, perhaps, to offer a security to compensate for relatively low salaries, it has also had some unexpected results for schools in general and supervision in particular. A teacher who has been granted tenure has at his disposal a formidable device with which to insulate himself from the pressures of other teachers or his supervisor. This is not to suggest that he always does this, but he can, and at times and places of his own choosing. Thus, if he wishes to engage seriously with a supervisor, he may, or he may simply go through the motions of discussion and forget about it after the supervisor leaves. By the same reasoning, tenured teachers seem frequently, though they may be physically present, to absent themselves psychologically from in-service programs, regardless of their potential value.

The tenure system carries with it a tacit message: "We grant you a lifetime position and we have confidence that you, as a professional person, will keep current with changes in education and that you will continue to grow and develop as a teacher." Without doubt, there are thousands of teachers who do just that. There are also untold numbers who do not, but who are, nevertheless, protected from organizational sanctions. They may not be granted merit raises, but, in these days of militant teachers' unions, this seems not to be such a problem.

The insularity that a tenured teacher is able to maintain is reinforced by something unrelated to the system. Teaching is highly personal and very much governed by one's preferred ways of relating to other people. One's teaching style is more than a matter of mechanical method or behavior. It constitutes a sort of world view of people and learning. The longer it is maintained, the larger is the teacher's stake in it, and the more impervious it is to outside influence from, for example, a supervisor. We are confronted with a situation where, willy-nilly, the system seems to reinforce what comes naturally to an individual teacher. Tenure gives a teacher the time to solidify what he does and protects him from the necessity of having to change.

Under these conditions, it is not difficult to understand that supervisors might have a difficult time with tenured teachers. It is a problem of entry into the teacher's "system." When a teacher is not on tenure, entry is assured even if influence is not. When a teacher is on tenure, gaining even physical entry into his system is not at all assured, much less the chance of effecting any influence.

This set of circumstances is necessarily important for the supervisor who wishes to work with and help a tenured teacher. First of all, the chances of his being asked for help by the teacher are minimal. The overture, then, needs to be made by the supervisor, and, if it is to be effective, has to be more than, "I'd like to sit in on your class and see if I can offer any help." The unspoken response is quite apt to be, "Who needs you?" In short, then, the supervisor needs to have something to offer—perhaps new curriculum materials or a channel to classroom materials that are in short supply. (I know of a school in which the only reason that resource teachers (central office people) were paid any heed at all was that they were the best source of classroom supplies. If a teacher agreed to work with them, the supplies were forthcoming; otherwise, no such luck.)

THE PRODUCTIVITY OF TEACHING

With some exceptions, for instance, if a class does not learn to read or if a particular teacher's students do not do well on achievement tests, it is difficult to measure a teacher's productivity. By their very nature, the schools are engaged in a task that is ill suited to precise measurement—the task of helping to develop young people into thinking and growing human beings, as well as that of teaching them certain basic skills. Not only is it difficult to measure the degree to which the goal is being achieved, but it is also hard to identify what a teacher is doing that may help or impede the students' progress. It is not as if we were dealing with the manufacture of television sets in which, if a wire is hooked to another in one way, it is a correct linkage; otherwise, it is not. The problem in education, as any teacher or supervisor knows, is infinitely more complex.

How, then, can supervisors help someone else be productive in a situation where the measures of being productive are not clear? It may well be that this question is rarely raised by supervisors or teachers. Yet it is there, persistently, and I suspect that it is supplanted, perhaps unconsciously, by a preoccupation with matters of lesson presentation or the appropriate use of audiovisual aids. This, too, is understandable because supervisors and teachers seem to be most at home with methods and materials. In the final analysis, however, it may be that the two will have to sit down and deal with the questions: "What does it mean for me, as a teacher, to be productive?" "What is it that you, the supervisor, can do to help?"

Not Asking for Help

Teachers, with the possible exception of beginning ones, typically do not ask for help with their teaching problems, either from other teachers or from supervisors. The reasons for this have not been adequately investigated, but a couple of tentative explanations are plausible, even in the absence of rigorous inquiry. There is, for example, the problem imposed by what has been called "the tyranny of the schedule." A teacher's life in schools, particularly secondary schools, is rather severely ordered by time. Most of it, about 85 percent, is spent in the classroom. This leaves precious little time during the course of a school day when teachers can consult with each other, even if they wanted to. Two pieces of research are relevant here. In an unpublished study of teacher interaction with other adults during the course of a typical day at school (DeSanctis and Blumberg, 1979), it developed that the average length of time teachers spent with each other in any one discussion was about five minutes, hardly time enough, one would suspect, to give serious problems of teaching more than a cursory "hello." This inference is reinforced by a finding in a study by Millikan (1979). One of the strongest barriers preventing teachers from requesting consultative help, or so teachers have said, is time. Teachers simply do not have the unstructured time available that professors or corporate managers have to wander down to the office of a colleague and discuss a pressing problem. Further, even during planning periods available to teachers, the chances are good that the person who could help them is engaged in teaching and thus unavailable. Such, once more, are the effects of schedule tyranny.

Another explanation for the seeming lack of help-seeking behavior on the part of teachers takes the form of a hypothesis I hold that is reinforced whenever I raise the question. It seems that for a teacher to ask for help is tantamount to a confession of incompetence, particularly if he is tenured. The conflict is evident. Tenure implies competence; asking for help implies that a teacher cannot deal with the situation with his own resources and is, therefore, incompetent. The two cannot exist side by side in any comfort, so the way out is not to ask. I have been told by untenured teachers that they do ask for help, but they are careful not to make their requests too frequent or pressing, lest they communicate to other teachers or to the supervisor that taking charge of a classroom is simply too difficult.

The most obvious problem that the reluctance to ask for help creates for a supervisor is concerned with his entry into the teacher's "system" and the resulting productivity that can be expected from the manner in which he does gain entry. The history of productive helping relationships, going all the way from psychotherapy to large organizational consultation, suggests clearly that help is best used when it is sought. But teachers do not seek help from supervisors. This puts the supervisor in a bind. How does he start to work with a teacher so that he makes himself of value—in his own eyes, if not those of the teacher?

Two approaches seem to be in vogue. One, already mentioned, is to come bearing gifts, the unspoken contract being "I will give or make available to you these opportunities; in return, I expect you to let me into your system so that you become a client of mine." The second, perhaps the more common, approach is simply to observe a teacher in action and offer some comments, either in discussion or in writing after the class.

Problems exist with both methods. As for the gift bearer, what has been given can be taken away or denied in the future. That is, when rewards are used as a basis of influence (French and Raven, 1959), the message is that the rewards will be forthcoming as long as the recipient continues to behave in a manner satisfactory to the giver. Dependency on the giver tends to develop although, in our case, one might suspect the teachers of unilateral game playing or going through the motions of working with the supervisor without becoming involved in order to get what they want. The exchange continues as long as the teacher can pay the price without too much damage to his self-esteem or too much pressure from his peers.

Several problems accompany unsought help given through classroom observation. Primarily, few people like to be intruded upon, and fewer still like intrusion when the system creates an aura of suspicion almost regardless of who the outsider is and what he has to offer. When these circumstances are coupled with what appears to be a derogation of the supervisor's skills and his ability to be of help, it is not hard to see why there can seldom be a productive working relationship with the teacher.

TEACHERS' ASPIRATION LEVELS

One aspect of supervision in education that clearly differentiates it from supervision in most other organizations is the concept of teaching as a profession and the manner in which this concept is related to the aspirations of teachers. We can make some comparisons to both private industry and governmental agencies.

A college graduate hired by a large corporation or a governmental organization at a salary of $12,000 a year would be unlikely to want to stay in whatever job he was hired for, perhaps receiving some salary increases, until he retired. A person's initial job in such organizations is seen as getting a foot in the door before moving on to bigger and better things; such as hierarchical advancement, more authority and responsibility, and a higher salary. Sometimes advancement involves staying within the subsystem where one was first employed, becoming knowledgeable and effective, and waiting for promotion to the next level when there is an opening. Sometimes it involves a series of lateral moves in the organization that may not involve the immediate assumption of greater responsibility, but that expose one to a variety of work experiences, as well as to a variety of upper-level decision makers. When higher-level openings do occur, the individual is in a better position to compete with his peers.

This whole process is likely to consume a number of years and require that one be aware of the opportunities for and demands of higher management. Lower or middle managers without this awareness tend not to be viewed too favorably by their bosses. When a manager is asked what he wants to become in an organization, it is usually pretty important for him to say, "I'd like to have your job" or "I want to be Vice-President of Marketing." Private industry, and perhaps to a somewhat lesser extent governmental organizations, places a high value on upward organizational aspirations. To be satisfied with one's position, authority, and responsibility is an in- dication that a person has "run out of steam" or that "the next level kitchen is too hot." Neither of these labels is one that most managers would particularly care for. Once they develop such a reputation, it usually sticks and promotion and all that goes with it tends to be foreclosed.

The advancement and aspiration level of teachers is vastly dif- ferent from those of managers. Reasons for the difference are not hard to find. Casual discussions with a number of teachers over the years seem to indicate that they wanted to be a teacher, to be a teacher, to be a teacher. The idea of becoming a superintendent, a principal, or a central office supervisor is usually not part of the ambition of most beginning teachers, though some, judging from the age of my graduate students, develop it after a couple of years of teaching.

Three primary reasons seem to account for the motivation of teachers to move to more influential positions within the system. One is a genuine desire to be in a position where, theoretically, at least, a person can influence the quality of education in a more global manner than through the vehicle of being a classroom teacher. Then there is the desire for the higher salary that accompanies supervisory or administrative positions. And, finally, there is what appears to be an increasingly prevalent phenomenon—or perhaps it is just now being publicly recognized—of teachers "burning out." That is, work in the classroom becomes, for many teachers, a psy- chologically debilitating experience. One way out is to move into an administrative or supervisory position. For most teachers, how- ever, the issue of moving out of the classroom either does not arise or it is not translated into action: simply being a teacher may con- tain enough fulfillment potential to obviate concerns about becom- ing something else. Or, even if teachers do have these concerns, they decide to live with the situation as it is. This would be par- ticularly true in these days of declining enrollments when many administrative and supervisory positions are being eliminated.

Two other points need to be made to help us understand teachers' apparent lack of concern about upward movement in the organiza- tion. First, there are many women in teaching. This is not to say that women do not or would not make good supervisors or administrators, but it is probably true that most female teachers do not see their future as managing or supervising the future of education. To explain why this seems to be the case would require a discussion of the role of women in society and sexism, neither of which is our focus here. This seems to be changing a bit, but the role of women in education has historically been associated with that of the teacher. And I must say that men cannot deny a conscious culpability regarding this notion. When I was in graduate school, for example, it was a well-known if not formal policy that women were discouraged from matriculating in educational administration.

The second point, clearly an organizational factor, is that the positional hierarchy of schools and school systems is extremely flat compared to that of a comparable-sized corporation or governmental institution. In industrial concerns, for example, there are usually between seven and nine hierarchical steps from the bottom of the ladder to the top. Except, perhaps, in the very largest of school systems, we have in most schools an extraordinarily large number of production people (teachers) who are managed, supervised, and offered staff services by a small number of people. In the direct line between teacher and superintendent, there are probably not more than three or four positions and even fewer in the line from teacher to a staff position such as a central office supervisor.

To be more explicit, in Syracuse, New York, a medium-sized city, there are approximately 1,100 teachers in 35 schools. Each school has a principal and some have one or more vice-principals. High schools and junior high schools have guidance counselors, as do a few elementary schools. The central office has about 25 professional staff members. Thus, we have an organization of about 1,250 professional people with about 150 administrative or staff positions of all types. Since, with the exception of superintendents, the geographical mobility of people in public education is low, a teacher does not have too much room to move upward in the hierarchy. The system does not permit rapid advancement except for those in it who may be atypically aggressive and thus seek situations elsewhere. The rest teach and wait as they accumulate credentials and, possibly, political influence.

The whole issue of aspiration level and limited opportunity for moving upward in the organization effectively removes modeling as a potential source of influence by the supervisor, unless he happens to be an excellent teacher who is able to relate well to the people he is supervising. In organizations where hierarchical advancement is an important motivator, lower and middle managers typically take their behavioral and stylistic cues from the people one or two levels above them. "After all, my boss or his boss got where they are by behaving and holding the attitudes they do. The organization evidently rewards their styles. I can do that, too." This makes sense for the person who wants to move up. Organizations do have values related to managerial style, and they do reward people whose styles reinforce those values. It is thus relatively easy for an industrial manager to influence, subtly or overtly, the behavior of his upwardly mobile subordinate.

There is no particular organizational reward for a teacher to model a supervisor's classroom behavior. There may be a reward if the teacher finds the modeling behavior of intrinsic worth to himself, but this, apparently, is not common. Whatever the reason, the teaching ability of supervisors appears to be devalued by teachers. Taking this all a step further, effective modeling of teaching behavior is more apt to take place between teachers than between a supervisor and a teacher because a teacher's ideal role model is linked more to being an effective teacher than a supervisor. He would be more likely to seek out an experienced and skilled peer from whom to learn than a supervisor.

TEACHERS AS PROFESSIONALS AND
SUPERVISORS AS BUREAUCRATS

Tied to organizational position and advancement is the conflict between the teacher as a professional and the supervisor as a bureaucrat. This was expressed to me by a graduate student in the following terms:

The problem is that we teachers see ourselves as professional people devoting our time to improving what we do in the classroom and the school. We see the supervisor as having, in a sense, forsaken professionalism for a role in the bureaucracy with the major function of protecting and maintaining organization norms and values.

The development of this kind of a situation is not unusual. It has its parallels in other professional organizations, for example, the research and development divisions of industrial concerns. There are, or lip service is given to, two ladders of advancement, scientific and management. Frequently, a scientist who moves to a managerial position where his primary job takes the form of planning and decision making devotes progressively less time to research. Unless he is an extraordinarily talented scientist, his former colleagues tend to look at him somewhat askance. He has forsaken that for which he was trained for the benefits and prerogatives of being a manager; he is no longer one of them. His primary referent becomes the organization, or so it is perceived, and he is seen as not understanding what is going on where the real work is being done.

There is a similar set of circumstances in social service organizations when a social worker moves into a supervisory or management position. The person is then perceived as being removed from the action, not centrally concerned with the job to be done, and representing the system.

The attitudinal changes that colleagues perceive as one advances through an organization are not figments of their imagination. As a person moves out of one organizational role and into another, his primary reference group changes and, with it, his attitudes (Siegel and Siegel, 1957). The new role holder starts to assume the attitudes of the group to which he is most closely attached. Thus, when a teacher becomes a supervisor he starts to think and act on a different set of assumptions. Protestations to the contrary, the teacher turned supervisor is no longer "just a teacher like the rest of you."

These circumstances are not bad. They are facts of organizational life. They do, however, have unintended consequences, among which are the communications problems that seem to arise as the teacher perceives the supervisor to be mostly concerned with maintaining bureaucratic values while he, the teacher, is concerned with professional problems.

I must confess that much of what I have been saying sounds gloomy. This is not a reflection of any particular hypercritical bent or a doomsday philosophy; it is simply a statement of the case as I have observed it and as teachers have talked about it.

A BROADER PERSPECTIVE

Given the conditions of life in the school organization as they have been discussed, the reader is entitled to say, "So what?" "So what" in this case leads to an inquiry of effects of these conditions on interaction between supervisors and teachers. The process of interaction may be illustrated by a scheme known as the Circular Process of Communication Model (Figure 5.1). The model suggests that when A (the supervisor) and B (the teacher) start to interact, the following takes place:

1. The supervisor has some ideas, attitudes, or feelings that he wishes to communicate.
2. He communicates to the teacher either verbally or nonverbally. (It is possible to conceive of a supervisor letting a teacher know that it has been a tough class to deal with by an emphatic mopping of his brow.)
3. The supervisor's behavior travels toward the teacher, but on its way it has to cross the teacher's perceptual screen, which consists primarily of the teacher's perception of himself, his perceptions of the supervisor, and his perceptions of what the supervisor thinks he (the teacher) thinks (Laing, Phillipson, and Lee, 1966) — this last point may seem a little involved, but the more one thinks about it, the clearer and more important it will become. The teacher's perceptual screen provides the cues by which he experiences the behavior of the supervisor.
4. The teacher digests and interprets his experience of the supervisor's behavior, a process that provides the ground upon which he decides what he will say and do.
5. The teacher communicates his ideas, attitudes, or feelings (which may have been modified by his experiencing of the supervisor) to the supervisor.
6. The teacher's behavior travels to the supervisor, and it, too, crosses a perceptual screen, this time the supervisor's.
7. The supervisor thus experiences the teacher through his screen, digests and interprets his experience, and the whole process continues.

Apart from the subjective elements listed in step three, above, the perceptual screens of both teacher and supervisor will be affected

FIGURE 5.1   Circular Process of Communication

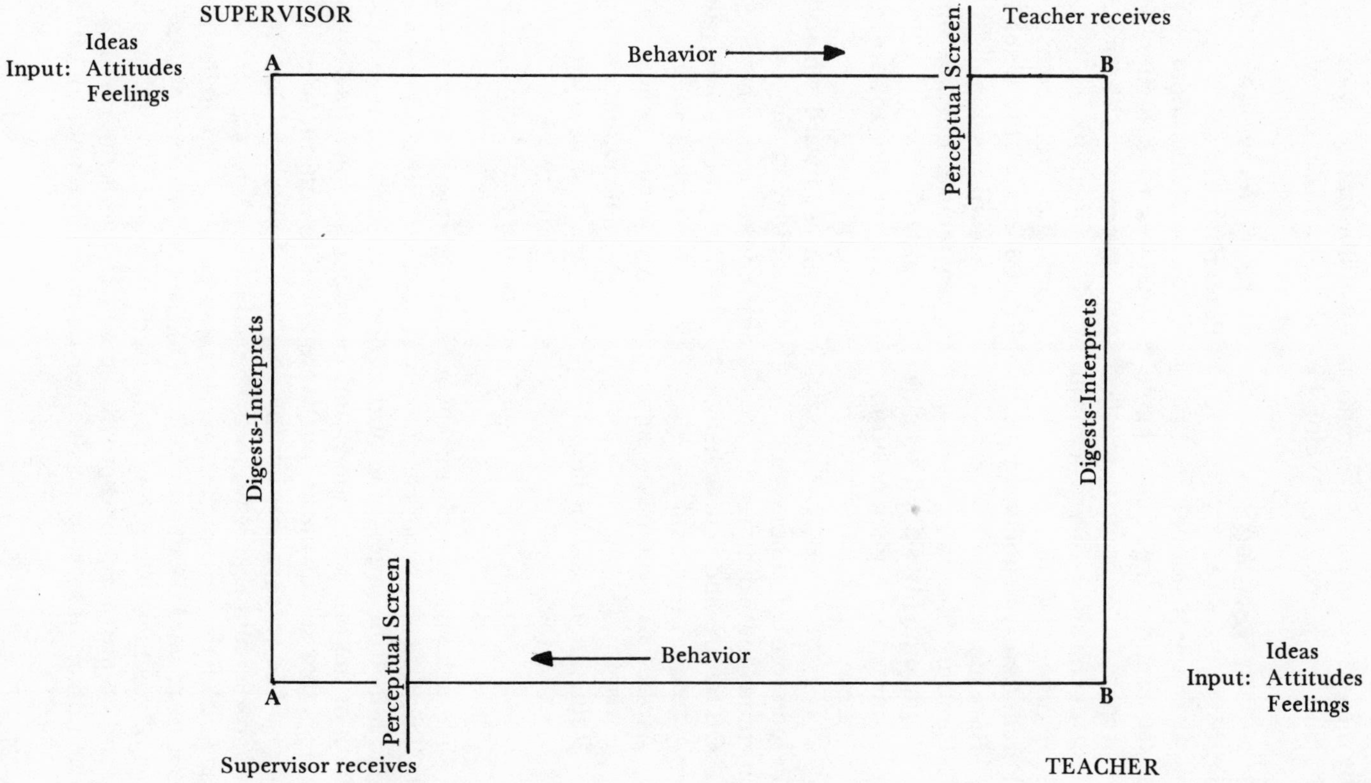

SUPERVISOR

Input: Ideas
       Attitudes
       Feelings

A ————————————————————————————— A
Digests-Interprets

Perceptual Screen
Supervisor receives

Behavior →

Behavior ↓

Perceptual Screen
Teacher receives

B ————————————————————————————— B
Digests-Interprets

TEACHER

Input: Ideas
       Attitudes
       Feelings

by the environment of the schools. I will illustrate only one possibility and let the reader develop his own from his experience.

Teacher	*Supervisor*
Perceptions of self	Perceptions of self
A true professional	A true professional
On tenure, thus untouchable	Aspires to a higher position
Aspires to remain a teacher	Concerned with measuring
Antagonistic toward central	productivity
office	A helper from central office
Perceptions of supervisor	Perceptions of the teacher
Bureaucratic	A true professional
Central office spy	On tenure, but *not* untouch-
A once highly skilled teacher	able
Aspires to a higher position	Antagonistic toward central
	office
	Aspires toward supervision
Perceptions of supervisor's	Perceptions of the teacher's
attitudes toward him	attitude toward him
On tenure and untouchable	A true professional, caught in
A true professional	the bureaucracy
Aspires to become a super-	Only really concerned with
visor	helping untenured teachers
Reluctant to ask for help	Overconcerned with pro-
	ductivity
	A source of help

Though this example may be a bit exaggerated, it is that way only to illustrate how some elements of school organization intrude upon and affect the interaction of the supervisor and the teacher. As we look at the self-perceptions and cross perceptions, one of the first things that stands out is that there are both congruencies and conflicts. The teacher sees himself as a true professional and the supervisor sees him that way, too. The supervisor's aspirations are seen accurately by the teacher, and both agree that the teacher is antagonistic toward the central office. (These congruencies of perception, or of conflict, are rarely verbalized; they are simply there.) The conflicts are more widespread. These two people do not understand each other, at least as far as their work environment and its effects are concerned. The teacher wants to remain a teacher; the supervisor does not see it that way. The supervisor sees himself as a helper; the teacher sees him as a bureaucratic spy. The teacher thinks the supervisor sees him as untouchable; the supervisor sees him as not untouchable.

If we transpose this hypothetical situation into the Circular Process of Communication Model, it becomes possible to speculate on what might transpire if the supervisor and teacher were to sit down to discuss what had happened in a class. The supervisor might open with a pleasantry, offer a bit of praise, and then ask the teacher if he were familiar with XYZ materials, newly published, which might be pertinent to the problem the class was working on. The supervisor's motivations are pure. He wants to help. The teacher, experiencing the supervisor through his perceptual screen, regards the praise as a "buttering-up" process and the comment about newly published materials as one-upmanship. How else, after all, do once competent professionals behave once they have become acculturated in the bureaucracy? The teacher then comments that, though he has not seen the new materials, he is really becoming tired of the unending gimmicks that are being produced ("that will teach him to play his game with me"). According to our model, the supervisor screens this comment ("tenured teachers are all alike, but I thought this one was different"). The cycle continues, becoming a game of parry and thrust, but no one really wins, except perhaps in his own eyes.

This example could be infinitely varied. The point has not been to specify the precise derivation of communications conflicts between supervisors and teachers, but, instead, to help the antagonists deal with the reality of their interaction. The focal point for thought and action is that the nature of environmental systems leads people in all roles to make frequently untested assumptions about the attitudes and motivations of others. Thus, the teacher assumes that the supervisor is a central office spy and reacts to this assumption as would anyone else, with caution and suspicion. The supervisor, having made some assumptions of his own about the teacher but not having tested them, reacts in kind. Behavior tends to beget like behavior. It seems clear to me that, if supervision in the schools is to perform the function for which it is intended—to help teachers upgrade the quality of instruction—the cycle of acting and reacting on untested assumptions must be broken.

There is a concluding point to be made in this discussion of the organizational environment of supervision. It has to do with a thread that has been implicit throughout the chapter, the nature of the authority-influence linkages that exist between supervisors and teachers. Everyday thinking has it that the schools, like most other organizations, are rather standard bureaucracies and that the people who work in them behave and relate to each other in bureaucratic fashion. That is, they follow orders, pay attention to the chain of command, and operate with fairly limited freedom relative to the decisions they make.

Schools, indeed, do have bureaucratic characteristics, but there is a growing pattern of thought that, rather than being in the mold of rational, tightly woven bureaucracies, they are much more "loosely coupled" (Weick, 1976). This position suggests that the organizational character of a school is much more like a rather loose confederation of people and positions, related to each other structurally but not functionally in a continuing, interdependent manner. If this notion has credence, and I believe it does, there are important implications for supervision, particularly with regard to influence. The point is that the job of the supervisor is only loosely coupled with that of the teacher. The teacher, in point of fact, can do his job for the most part without the supervisor. But the opposite does not hold: the supervisor cannot do his job without the teacher. In a curious fashion, the teacher, who is organizationally subordinate to the supervisor has a controlling influence that one would be unlikely to observe in superior-subordinate relationships characteristic of more tightly woven bureaucratic organizations.

What is at issue here, then, is related to a comment I made in Chapter 1 concerning the ingredients of a helping relationship—the teacher must want to be helped. Transposed into the current context, the teacher must want to be influenced by the supervisor before the loose coupling that exists between the two can become more tightly woven.

6 Supervisors' Styles of Behavior

In the first five chapters of this book, I have been setting the stage and, I hope, conveying that all is not well in the world of supervision. Supervision is not a matter of creating an organizational structure and then assuming it will work.

So far, our picture of supervision in education has been global, and, incidentally, valid if one can judge from the reactions of teachers who have read the previous chapters. The usefulness of global pictures, however, is limited; they tend not to be terribly helpful when it comes to enabling people to take hold of situations in an effort to change them. A similar broad and critical view is offered in a sensitivity-training group when one person says to another, "There's something about you that makes me defensive." Such a global picture may make the recipient sit up and take notice, but it does not help him answer the question, "What should I do differently?" It offers no handles for change.

The next six chapters, then, sketch in the details of the inter-action between supervisors and teachers. These details will take the form of a discussion of the results of research on specific percep-tions that teachers and supervisors have of supervision and research on motivating factors in supervision.

First, though, we turn briefly to a concern with what supervisors and teachers discuss with each other. This provides a substantive context for our major concern: how things get talked about between supervisors and teachers. Part of a larger study on teacher role preferences for supervisors (Blumberg, Loehr, and Goldstein, 1978) focused directly on the substance of supervisor-teacher interaction. A sample of 60 teachers was asked to indicate in writing all of the different kinds of things discussed in conferences with their supervisors. Their responses, which were content analyzed, yielded five rather discreet categories of substance: general school or department matters, individuated teacher concerns with self, classroom environment and behavior, individual student problems, and socializing.

To determine the relative emphasis that was placed on these categories in the course of conferences, we created a checklist of items associated with each category and asked a different group of 150 teachers to indicate every item on the checklist that, in their experience, was discussed with their supervisor. A ranking system was created to analyze the data, and, in descending order of emphasis, the ranking of categories was individual student problems, classroom environment and behavior, general school or department matters, individuated teacher concerns with self, and socializing. Problems relating to individual students take precedence, according to our data by a rather wide margin, over other issues when teachers and supervisors talk with each other. This was not an unexpected finding given the current and widespread concern with student behavior and discipline. What was a little surprising was that the rank of individuated teacher concerns was so low. One interpretation we make, which is inferentially substantiated in this and the following chapter, is that the communication system between supervisors and teachers sanctions discussion of problems removed from the person of either party but that it is much more constrained with regard to issues related to the self. This somewhat hidden piece of data, then, lends credence to the main argument of this book: that, when we consider problems associated with supervision in the schools, the crucial issues are those that pertain to the quality of the interaction and relationships that develop between supervisor and teacher.

The studies that will be discussed in this and the next chapter are based on perceptions of behavior and not on behavior itself. We will be talking, for example, about how teachers perceive the behavior of supervisors and not about the supervisors' actual behavior. This is an important difference, for it is quite possible that discrepancies exist between behavior itself and how it is perceived. Such discrepancies may arise from, among other things, organizational role differences, conflicts in expectations between the parties involved, and unmet needs.

Here is an example of just such a situation that developed in one of my classes. Unprompted, one of my students said that he saw me as uncaring, unsupportive, not listening and, all in all, not very helpful. He was so upset with what he saw as my lack of concern for students that he came close to dropping the course. Another student in the same class perceived and interpreted my behavior in almost a polar opposite manner from the first: as encouraging, concerned, supportive, and empathic. These discrepancies should not be surprising to any teacher. The surprise would be if our behavior were experienced and interpreted by all of our students in a similar, not a different, way. It would probably mean that the students had ceased to consider themselves as human, a situation hard to conceive.

The first student, it turned out when we talked, was screening my behavior through his high need for structure. The class was relatively unstructured. It was not a lecture; requirements were purposely vague and open ended; many discussions were deliberately ended without conclusion. His needs for direction and his expectations about how professors should behave and structure a class were clearly not being met. Psychologically, he was experiencing a large amount of cognitive dissonance (Festinger, 1957), a condition that obtains when a person's expectations about a situation are not matched by his perceptions of what is happening. Such a situation is uncomfortable for a person to live with, and it becomes necessary for him to try and ameliorate it. This student chose to reduce his dissonance by categorizing me as uncaring and unsupportive, a choice that relieved him of the responsibility of dealing with himself or with me.

The second student screened my behavior through a different set of needs; he required a minimum amount of structure in a learning environment. Not feeling any dissonance, he saw my behavior in a very different way: I was giving him what he wanted; I cared; I was supportive.

In many respects, how a person perceives the behavior of another is much more important than the behavior itself. For the first student, it was unimportant whether an objective observer might have categorized my behavior as supportive. As far as he was concerned, this was not the case, and a rational explanation of things would not have changed his mind. A person's perceptions of another's behavior play a large part in his reactions to and feelings about that person. I suspect that this sequence of perception, feeling, and reaction is in good measure responsible for experiences that surely all of us have had—being on the receiving end of behavior that is completely mystifying to us, motives attributed to us that simply do not exist. This is why we are concerned with studying the perceptions that teachers have of supervisor behavior and the interaction between supervisors and teachers.

When a supervisor and a teacher meet, the two of them form a temporary, miniature social system. It is not simply a matter of two people meeting to solve a problem, nice as that situation might be to contemplate. It is not an egalitarian situation. It is not free from authority, power, or influence. What actually occurs is that two role holders meet, and one of them, typically, is the control figure by virtue of his wisdom or of his authority. Our research concentrated on the supervisor as a control figure.

We have assumed that it is the supervisor, because he is the control agent, whose behavior sets the tone for the interaction. The supervisor is not responsible for the behavior and attitudes of the teacher. No one is *responsible* for the behavior of others in the sense of exercising direct control. However, because the supervisor is in control, represents the larger system, and may have an evaluative role, his behavior sends off the social and emotional messages that set the climate and must be considered by the teacher. This is certainly not a new discovery. But it is a condition, I think, that those of us in education must continue to rediscover. My hunch is that there is scarcely a teacher among us who, at one time or another, has not said, "What a dull, unresponsive class!" when, if the truth be known, something about our behavior made them dull and unresponsive. So it is with supervision: cues come from the supervisor; the teacher picks them up and responds in kind. The interactive tone is reinforced, and the roles are played. Any change usually emanates from the supervisor.

Our first study of interaction between supervisors and teachers (Blumberg and Amidon, 1965) was aimed at trying to answer two questions: Would teachers be able to discriminate among various types of behavior engaged in by their supervisor, or would they tend to describe the behavior of the supervisor in a rather homogeneous fashion? And, if they were able to discriminate, would the teachers' differing perceptions of the supervisor's behavior be related to such factors as the teacher's learning about his behavior as a teacher or a person, the level of communicative supportiveness in the teacher's conferences with his supervisor, the teacher's perceptions of the productivity of his conferences with his supervisor, or whether any significant discrepancies existed between the way in which teachers perceived their supervisor's behavior and the way in which they would have him behave?

These questions provided the dependent variables of the study. The independent variable was teachers' perceptions of the behavioral style of their supervisor. To ascertain the perceptions systematically, we used a rating scale based on a concept of direct and indirect behavior (Flanders, 1960). The scale was composed of eight items: three dealing with direct, and five with indirect behavior. The scales were not evaluative. The teachers were not asked to rate each type of behavior as good or bad, but simply to rate the emphasis that they perceived the supervisor as putting on each type of behavior.

The dependent variables were also measured by rating scales. Central to the development of these scales was the issue of communicative freedom. Rather than asking one simple question, we derived a number of items from Gibb's work (1961) on defensive communication. Gibb developed a scheme that differentiated six bipolar communicative orientations, which were either support inducing or defense inducing.

Behavior is support inducing if it is oriented toward:	*Behavior is defense inducing if it is oriented toward:*
Problem solving	Control
Spontaneity	Strategy
Equality	Superiority
Provisionalism	Certainty
Empathy	Neutrality
Description	Evaluation

Other items about the nature of a teacher's learning from supervision and an item on the teacher's general feelings about the productivity of his interaction with his supervisor were also included.

The instrument was administered to 166 teachers from all walks of educational life, from secondary and elementary schools, from urban, rural, and suburban school districts. Though no attempt was made to develop a systematic random sample, we felt we had enough of a cross section to make the results creditable. After the teachers completed the questionnaire, they were asked to review their ratings of their supervisor's behavior (the independent variable) and indicate the amount of emphasis they *wished* he would put on each type of behavior. Thereby we could determine whether certain behavioral styles generate larger discrepancies between what is perceived and what is desired than others.

In analyzing the data, we were struck by the inadequacy of our own concept of behavioral styles. We had "grown-up" learning about one-dimensional styles that turned out to be overly simplistic. We had learned about democratic, autocratic, direct, and indirect behavior, but such categories, quite correctly, did not fit neatly into what we were trying to do. Life is not one dimensional; nor can behavior be so categorized. Behavioral styles are combinations of patterns that, taken together, produce some predominant theme. And so, from the data, we inductively developed a set of supervisory behavioral styles that has characterized the rest of our work:

Style A	High direct, high indirect	The teacher sees the supervisor emphasizing both direct and indirect behavior: he tells and criticizes, but he also asks and listens.
Style B	High direct, low indirect	The teacher perceives the supervisor as doing a great deal of telling and criticizing but very little asking or listening.
Style C	Low direct, high indirect	The supervisor's behavior is rarely direct (telling, criticizing, and so forth); instead, he puts a lot of emphasis on asking questions, listening, and reflecting back the teacher's ideas and feelings.
Style D	Low direct, low indirect	The teacher sees the supervisor as passive, not doing much of anything. Our hunch is that some supervisors may appear passive as they try to engage in a rather misguided democratic role.

This typology of supervisory behavioral styles is not the last word. It does, however, go beyond the problems created by one-dimensional concepts. It also makes sense, conceptually and practically, of our data.

We devised a weighting system that enabled us to distinguish four groups of teachers in our study population that corresponded to the four behavioral styles. Thus, we answered our first question. It became clear that teachers were not insensitive to the behavioral styles of their supervisors. They could and did discriminate specific behavioral patterns in which their supervisor engaged. Did their discrimination make a difference? Would teachers who described their supervisor's style as high direct, low indirect, for example, differ in the way they described the communicative freedom of their interaction from teachers who perceived their supervisors as low direct, high indirect?

In order to answer questions such as this, the data were subjected to an analysis of variance. The results indicated that indeed there were differences. On every item tested, it became clear that the different responses were related to the manner in which the teachers perceived their supervisor's behavior.   ʼ

Our next step was to see if any consistent patterns developed. We found they did. Teachers seemed to be saying that the more their supervisor came across in an indirect manner the more they were able to get insight into themselves, both into their teacher role and as a person—a pattern of A, C, B, D. It appeared that the way in which the supervisor could be most helpful on this level of operation was to combine a relatively heavy emphasis on direct behavior with his indirect behavior (A). This finding suggests that hearing about oneself is probably most productive, not only when the supervisor (or other helping agent) questions, listens, and reflects back what he hears, but also when he does a bit of telling and gives feedback. Behavioral styles D and B seemed to provide the teacher with relatively little learning about himself. In D, one would suspect that nothing seems to happen; in B, though there may be feedback, it is apparently rejected by the teacher because there is relatively little indirect behavior to bolster the relationship, to enable the teacher to feel that he is being listened to and is a person of worth, not merely an object to be told something.

Analyzing the communicative supportiveness that the teachers perceived in their supervisors' behavior, we found that supervisors were perceived by teachers to be most *control oriented* as opposed to *problem oriented* in behavioral style B, followed by styles A, D, and C. Teachers felt the highest need to be *strategically oriented* as opposed to being *spontaneous* in behavioral style B, followed by styles A, D, and C. Teachers perceived the highest *superiority orientation* as opposed to *equality orientation* in behavioral style B, followed by styles A, D, and C. Supervisors were seen by teachers to be highest on *certainty orientation* as opposed to *provisionalism* in behavioral style B, followed by styles A, D, and C. The highest degree of *empathy* as opposed to *neutrality* was perceived by teachers to exist in behavioral style C, followed by styles A, D, and B. Teachers felt that their interaction with supervisors was most characterized by *evaluation* of behavior as opposed to *description* of behavior in behavioral style B, followed by styles A, C, and D.

These results yielded a consistent pattern that made sense in terms of the relationship between behavioral styles and particular characteristics of interaction between supervisors and teachers. Note, for example, how clearly style B (high direct, low indirect) is associated with defensively oriented interaction. Teachers who described their supervisor's behavior as predominantly high direct, low indirect also said that they saw the communicative climate as focusing on control, strategy, superiority, certainty, and evaluation. There was a reversal, when it came to the question of developing an empathic relationship, that reinforced these findings. Most empathy seemed to develop under style C (low direct, high indirect), and least was associated with B. Style A (high direct, high indirect) tended to follow B rather closely with regard to how defensive teachers felt toward their supervisor, and style D (low on both direct and indirect behavior) was closely associated with supportiveness and with C throughout the findings.

In sum, then, the teachers were most defensive when the predominant behavior of the supervisor was direct and the next most defensive when a heavy emphasis on directness was coupled with a good bit of indirectness. They said that their communications with the supervisor were most supportive when he behaved primarily in an indirect way and also when he appeared to be doing little, if anything! This last point, curious though it may be, becomes important in the matter of the productivity of supervision as teachers see it, which we ascertained by a simple, direct question. They were asked to rate productivity on a scale, the poles of which were: "Supervision is a very productive use of time and energy" and "Supervision is useless—a waste of time and energy." The results indicated that the order of productivity, from highest to lowest, corresponded to behavioral styles C, A, D, and B. The mean productivity scores of C and A were very close, while there was a sharp break between A and D and between D and B. Teachers seemed to be saying that, when their supervisor behaves in a manner that is either primarily indirect or both indirect and direct, their interactions with him are productive. When he does very little or behaves predominantly in a direct way, however, their interactions with him are quite unproductive.

Our prior knowledge of the effects of teachers' behavioral styles on behavior in the classroom (Flanders, 1960) led us to suspect that interactional problem-solving situations that were characterized by an indirect mode would be seen as more fulfilling than those that were mostly direct. Thus, our unspoken expectations that style C would result in communicative freedom and high productivity while style B would reflect defensiveness and low productivity were met. We were not nearly as sure about A and D. The data told us that, even though a heavy emphasis on both direct and indirect behavior combined seemed to effect a somewhat defensive atmosphere, it also resulted in high productivity. Yet, when the supervisor is seen as passive, even though the communications are supportive and free, there is little productivity; there may be a lot of unfettered talk, but not much seems to happen. It appears that teachers still, however, see more productivity coming from a relatively passive supervisor than from an overwhelmingly direct one. What the dynamics of that reaction are remain to be cleared up. It may be a sort of halo effect spilling over from communicative freedom to productivity.

The last question in this study was whether there might be a discrepancy between the behavioral style in which teachers perceived their supervisor to be engaged and how they wished he would behave. The least discrepancy was found in behavioral style C, followed by A, D, and B, the same order that we found for productivity. The big gap between mean scores came between A and D, and it was the largest difference in all our findings. Teachers were saying that supervisors following styles C and A were behaving in ways that apparently met the teachers' expectations and aspirations. Styles D and B, in contrary fashion, evoked a large amount of dissonance between what the teachers saw happening and what they would have liked to have observed. We found it interesting that D and B are such different styles, and yet teachers found the discrepancy in both similar. Our interpretation of this is related to the findings on productivity. Styles D and B were both rated low on productivity. It seems reasonable, then, to suggest that the critical issue in discrepancy is the perceived productivity of supervision rather than whether or not the behavioral style happens to generate communicative freedom. Simply to be concerned with open communication without paying attention to work and productivity seems to solve few problems and to create new ones. It may be pushing it a bit, but not too far, we think, to suggest that love is not enough. Other things have to happen, as well, or the love affair (communicative freedom) goes on the rocks.

Before going on to the second study of supervisor-teacher behavior that is part of this chapter, a few final comments are in order. As we have gone back over the results, we've been struck by a couple of points. First, though the research design was not sophisticated, the findings lent substance to our intuitions about a productive, helping relationship. We had listened to teachers talk about their supervision. Our casual observations had raised questions about the efficacy of what seemed to transpire between many supervisors and teachers, and our findings lent credence to the questions and criticisms we had. Obviously, all was not well, but some good things did happen. Second, the consistency of the findings suggests that we are not dealing with random bits of behavior but with a potentially systematic way of putting the supervisory house in order. This is not to suggest a slew of lockstep methodological training programs. There is no use in compounding a felony. The idea is that we can probably induce change into the system if we wish; the social technology is available if we want to use it.

DO SUPERVISORS SEE THE SAME THINGS AS TEACHERS?

Our next questions were: When supervisors think about their interaction with teachers, are their perceptions of behavior and productivity congruent with those held by teachers? And, if they are incongruent, where do the differences lie? Previous studies indicated that, when a person shifts his organizational role, he sees the work problems in a different light, and his attitudes become affected as well. One of the clearest examples of this has been reported by Lieberman (1956). Lieberman administered a survey to first-line industrial production workers that dealt with their attitudes about management and the union. During the following year, a number of these workers were promoted to foreman and a number of others were elected to position of union steward. The survey was administered to those who had changed positions and to a matched control group of workers who had remained on the production line. Those men who became foremen experienced a change in attitude that was more favorable to management. The attitudes of those who were elected union stewards became more favorable to the union. Those workers who continued on the production line experienced no change in attitudes. Thus, one's organizational position affects one's attitudes. Extending this point a bit, one might say that, as a person moves from one position to another within an organization, his reference group changes. Reference groups being a primary source of a person's attitudinal set, a person is likely to adopt attitudes that are congruent with the new reference group and so pay his admission into the group. Not to do so would leave him on the periphery of the group and would be an indication that he is not committed to his new role and function.

Another related interpretation of the way attitude shifts seem to go along with organizational position change has to do with job function and demands. Lower-level organizational positions are typically accompanied by rather narrowly defined work functions and territorial responsibilities. As a person gets promoted through the hierarchy, jobs come to be defined more widely and territorial responsibility gets enlarged. The higher one goes, the chances of having to interact with a broader scope of different organizational positions increases, and one gets much more information than one would in a lower position. Of necessity, the individual comes to see problems from a broader perspective and his attitudes about these problems are quite apt to undergo changes that would not occur if his informational world had remained circumscribed.

This second study was intended to test whether the shifts of attitude that Lieberman has observed in industry occurred also among educational supervisors. The design of the test was simple. A sample population of forty-five public school supervisors who had direct responsibilities for the improvement of instruction were asked to respond to the same instruments as the teachers had except that the items were worded so as to have the supervisors rate their own behavior as they saw it. The supervisors' data were compared with that of the teachers with the following statistically significant results:

1. Supervisors see themselves engaging in less direct behavior than the teachers perceive and in more indirect behavior. In effect, the supervisors were saying that they characterize their behavioral style as pretty much low direct, high indirect, while the teachers' perceptions are that supervisors tend to behave in a fashion that is more high direct, low indirect.

2. With regard to the question concerning the extent to which teachers learn about themselves as teachers and as people as a result of supervision, supervisors saw much more of this type of learning going on than did teachers. In other words, supervisors saw themselves as being relatively effective in helping a teacher gain insight into himself, but teachers did not share this view.

3. On the comparison of items that were concerned with Gibb's (1961) dimensions of communicative freedom, statistically significant results occurred twice. Teachers perceived supervisors as having both a much more dominant superiority and neutrality orientation than supervisors, as a group, thought they conveyed. There were no differences in regard to the issues of control, certainty, evaluation, or strategy orientations.

4. On the matter of the productivity of supervision, as was expected, supervisors saw the time they spent with teachers as clearly being more productive than did teachers, who rated their supervisory interaction as pretty much of a so-so affair.

In an analysis of the data that we had not originally planned, the inquiry was extended into supervisory productivity with this question: Would there be differences in supervisors' perceptions of the efficacy of their work with teachers that might be related to the predominant behavioral style in which they saw themselves engaging? We compared two groups of supervisors: the first, those who rated the productivity of their work on a comparable level with the mean rating of the teachers; the second, those who rated their productivity at least one scale point higher than the teachers' mean. (We were interested, as well, in those supervisors who scored well below the teachers' mean on productivity, but only two did so, a group not large enough to analyze.)

There were no differences between the groups in the amount of emphasis they saw themselves putting on direct behavior, but there were significant differences between the two groups in the amount of emphasis each saw itself putting on indirect behavior. The group that saw itself being more productive than the other also characterized its behavior as more indirect. This is not to suggest that they *were* more indirect, but only to say that that is the way they saw it.

The study of supervisors then, has provided us with some interesting findings. There is support for the notion that differences in organizational position affect a person's views and feelings. Supervisors tend to see things differently from teachers. We have little doubt that, as teachers become supervisors, their perceptions and attitudes about supervision change. Their organizational viewpoint is different, and they develop a personal stake in the operation. Thus, they are led by the nature of organizational life to take a more positive view of their work and its results than that held by teachers or objective observers. That this set of circumstances exists is, by itself, rather less a matter of concern than is some of its potential. The issue seems to center around problems of communication between supervisors and teachers, each group tending to see the results of supervision in different ways. By itself, this difference is a barrier that could be overcome if supervisor and teacher were skillful enough and motivated to talk about their differences in perception. But such appears not to be the case. It seems that very little of the talk between supervisors and teachers is concerned with a joint analysis of their work or of the state of their relationships. In fact, such discussion is assiduously avoided by most of them.

This is not hard to understand. Aside from the generally constrained tone of interaction between teachers and supervisors, the organizational norms of the school setting and the difficulty of measuring results discourage a joint analysis of productivity. Since the efficacy of supervision is taken for granted by the system, why talk about it, particularly when the results might be threatening to both parties?

Another reason for the lack of discussion of the results of

supervision—not to be deduced from our research—is that the teachers tend to feel that the whole process of supervision in the schools is a ritual, one of those processes in which the organization engages in order to lend legitimacy to the credential system and so to be tolerated but not taken too seriously. All of us have confronted similar situations. We put up with them because the energy required to change things simply would be more than the change merits. Rituals are, after all, just rituals.

Our findings on communicative freedom indicated that the two dimensions on which significant differences developed were those of superiority and neutrality orientations. Teachers saw their supervisors being more concerned with superiority than equality and less concerned with being empathic than supervisors saw themselves. The communicative orientations of control, certainty, evaluation, and strategy afforded no discrepancies. Evidently teachers see supervisors as not treating them as much as collegial equals as they would like to be treated and as not really understanding them and their problems as much as they might. The issues of equality and empathy may be critical for free communication between and among people. Though we have no data to support this notion, intuitively we feel it is plausible. Perhaps the best thing to do at this point is simply to make note of the finding and its possible meaning rather than to push beyond reasonable possibilities. The reader can examine his own communicative relationships with people to see if our interpretation makes sense.

Having grouped the supervisors' data according to their perceptions of their productivity, we compared the two groups by the way they described their behavioral styles. The "more productive" group saw themselves engaging in more indirect behavior than the "less productive" group but there were no differences on direct behavior. It seems obvious that we are dealing with a behavioral phenomenon that has clear implications for productivity in interpersonal problem solving. This point becomes stronger when we recall that teachers who felt their supervision was productive also described their supervisor's behavior as being mostly indirect—as do supervisors who feel they are the more productive. Something, then, is occurring in situations that are characterized by high indirectness. What this something may be will be discussed in the next chapter.

7 Behavior, Interpersonal Relations, and Morale

It will be recalled that neither of the studies discussed in the previous chapter was designed to test hypotheses. We asked some questions and, on the basis of the answers, we tried to develop a framework for looking at supervisory behavior. The findings of the studies and, thus, the answers to our questions seemed consistent. It would be less than honest not to say that the findings did confirm some of our preconceptions about perceptions of behavioral styles and some selected process and outcome variables. In addition, our notions about differences that might develop in perceptions of supervisory interaction, depending upon whether one were supervising or being supervised, were upheld.

More important than the specific answers, at least for our future work, was that we were able to develop the framework we had been lacking. We no longer had to wonder whether teachers could discriminate among their supervisors' behaviors. They could. And we no longer had to wonder if the behavioral styles teachers described had any systematic relationship with what went on between a supervisor and a teacher. They did. And, even though our samples were not large, the resulting patterns were consistent enough for us to be confident of them. Thus, in the future we could test directional hypotheses rather than ask open-ended questions or pose null hypotheses. We wanted to test our hunches about the relationships between teachers' perceptions of supervisors' behavioral styles and descriptions of the interpersonal relations between them and their supervisors. We were also interested in behavioral styles and the teachers' morale.

PERCEPTIONS OF BEHAVIOR AND RELATIONSHIPS

In testing some ideas about the relationship between the way teachers describe the behavioral styles of supervisors and the character of the interpersonal relations between supervisors and teachers, we wanted to add to our knowledge of interaction between supervisor and teacher and we wanted to see if the productivity of supervision would be affected by the amount of energy devoted to relationships between teachers and their supervisors. Benne and Sheats (1948) on early concepts of task and maintenance behavior and, among others, Fleishmann and Harris (1962) and Blake and Mounton (1964) on group and supervisory behavior have consistently made the point that productive interpersonal or group work is characterized by a balance between the energy devoted to the task itself and that devoted to the development of healthy relationships among the people working on the task. When this balance is out of kilter—when too much energy is expended on either the task or the relationships—the productivity of the system starts to break down. The system will not necessarily suffer if it is out of balance over the short run. Indeed, it appears that people can tolerate and be productive in almost any human condition for relatively brief periods of time. It does seem clear, however, that the long-term goals of any social system are achieved only if a satisfying balance, no matter how idiosyncratic, is struck. Theoretically and practically, this idea of balance should hold for supervisors and teachers as well as for any other system.

The particular interpersonal relations variables we chose came from an idea of the process dimensions of the helping relationship put forward by Rogers, Rablen, and Walker (1958) and developed and tested by Barrett-Lennard (1962). Both the original idea and the tests were done in the context of psychotherapy, but the concept has since been expanded to other situations where the interpersonal relationships to be found in a process will affect the outcome. The concept suggests four essential factors by which a helpful interpersonal relationship may be analyzed and judged: the amount of *regard*, as a person, that one person sees himself receiving from another; the amount of *empathy* that characterizes the helper's behavior; the amount of *unconditionality of regard* that one person sees himself receiving from another; and the amount of *congruence* that characterizes the behavior of the helper. Regard refers to the general tendency of one person to communicate to another that he holds him to be of worth simply because he is another human being and, as such, is of value. Empathy refers to the extent that one person is conscious of what another is thinking or feeling and is able to communicate his understanding, uncolored by evaluation, to the other. Unconditionality of regard refers to the ability of one person to communicate to another that, "My regard for you as a person is constant regardless of whether you behave in ways of which I disapprove." Congruence refers to whether the behavior of one person comes across to the other as matching the feelings that the first person has. "Can I trust this person not to try and mask any feelings he has so that I don't have to try and figure out any hidden meanings in his behavior?"

Barrett-Lennard (1962) constructed the Relationship Inventory, a sixty-four-item questionnaire designed to measure interpersonal relationship factors. The findings of his research, in which he used the inventory to measure the quality of interpersonal relations in psychotherapy, indicated that clients who judged their therapy to be most successful also rated their interpersonal relationships with their therapists higher than clients who judged their therapy to be less successful. For us, the problem was the nature of the relationship between the supervisors' behavioral style and the interpersonal factors germane to a productive helping relationship.

Our major hypothesis was that different descriptions of the behavioral styles of their supervisors by teachers would produce different perceptions of the state of their interpersonal relations. There followed two hypotheses:

1. That more positive interpersonal relations would be perceived by teachers who described their supervisor's behavior as style A (high direct, high indirect) than by those who perceived styles B (high direct, low direct) or D (low direct, low indirect).
2. That more positive interpersonal relations would be perceived by teachers who described their supervisor's behavior as style C (low direct, high indirect) than by those who perceived styles B (high direct, low indirect) or D (low direct, low indirect).

Recalling how A and C were grouped together on the question of productivity of supervision, as were B and D, we proposed two null hypotheses:

3. That there would be no difference in the quality of interpersonal relations perceived between conditions of supervisory inter-action that were either high direct, high indirect, or low direct, high indirect.

4. That there would be no difference in the quality of interpersonal relations perceived between conditions of supervisory inter-action that were either high direct, low indirect or low direct, low indirect.

(For practical purposes these two null hypotheses taken together are really directional.)

Finally, in the interest of getting a larger sample and because separating the behavioral styles into distinct groups yields a rela-tively small sample, a last hypothesis was made:

5. That the mean direct score would be lower and the mean in-direct score would be higher in the top quartile of interpersonal relations measures than in the bottom quartile.

The procedures and design of the study were the same as those used in our first inquiry. The sample population of 210 teachers was asked to respond to both the instrument that described their per-ceptions of their supervisor's behavior and to the Relationship In-ventory. Because the actual numerical scores, in this case, seem to convey some impact, the results will first be presented in tabular form and then discussed. The reader should know that the range of possible scores on the Relationship Inventory runs from $+64$ to -64.

Table 7.1 provides the findings by which the first four hypotheses can be tested. With one exception—Unconditionality of Regard— it can be seen that hypothesis 1 received strong support, that is, we predicted that the interpersonal relations existing under A would be significantly different and higher than under either B or D. Hypothe-sis 2, which made a similar prediction but focused on style C as the independent variable, was supported, as well. The support was stronger because, as reference to the table shows, there was a sig-nificant difference on the Unconditionality of Regard dimension for C, whereas A showed no differences. Hypotheses 3 and 4 also received substantial support. We had predicted that no differences in the quality of interpersonal relations would be found between styles A and C or B and D. With two exceptions, this prediction was upheld. In the case of Regard, a significant difference did occur

TABLE 7.1   Mean Relationship Inventory Dimension Score for Various Behavioral Styles

Dimension	Mean Scores Ranked by Style			
Regard	A 37.86	C 36.80 ←2→	D 10.07 ←2→	B 5.27
Empathy	A 24.60	C 22.73 ←2→	D −6.00	B −18.67
Unconditionality of Regard	C 13.60 ←2→	A 8.33	B 1.47	D −3.46
Congruence	A 32.40	C 27.26 ←2→	B −2.13	D −10.73

Note: Tests for significance were either the Significant Gap or Straggler test (Tukey, 1949); ←2→ indicates a significant gap or a straggler; $p < .05$.
Source: A. Blumberg, "Supervisor Behavior and Interpersonal Relations," *Educational Administration Quarterly*, 4 (no. 2, Spring 1968): 39.

between B and D, with D being more positive. On the dimension of Unconditionality of Regard, a significant difference can be observed between A and C, with C yielding a more positive score. For hypothesis 5, in confirmation of our prediction, we found that the mean *direct* scores accompanying the top quartile of interpersonal relations scores were significantly different from and *lower* than those of the bottom quartile, and that the mean *indirect* scores accompanying the top quartile of interpersonal relations scores were significantly different from and *higher* than those of the bottom quartile.

The results of this study supported both of the specific hypotheses we had generated about supervisors' behavioral styles and interpersonal relations and about the broader concepts of the effects of behavior that had led us to engage in this research.

A number of points are worthy of further discussion. The effects of the mix of behavioral styles have come into ever-clearer focus. Different things that happen to a relationship seem to be a function of how a supervisor comes across to a teacher. The quality of interpersonal relations seems to be higher when the supervisor is seen to be behaving in a way that is rather more indirect and rather less direct than when the opposite condition obtains. It seems as though, if we hold the degree of indirectness constant, the amount of perceived direct behavior tends to make some interesting differences. For example, note the case of Unconditionality of Regard in the table. We had predicted that no differences would occur between A and C. One did occur, however, and it was the only case where A and C changed places as far as the mean score was concerned. This suggests that, as direct behavior receives more emphasis, Unconditionality of Regard is apt to go down. Styles D and B are somewhat similar on the Regard dimension. We had predicted no differences for these two styles, but one did develop. Though both scores are comparatively low, it appears that the high directness associated with B yields lower perceived Regard than the relative passivity that describes D.

To summarize, generally *positive* evaluations by teachers of the quality of their supervisory interpersonal relations appear to develop when a teacher perceives his supervisor's behavior as consisting of a heavy emphasis on both telling, suggesting, and criticizing, and on reflecting, asking for information, opinions, and so forth (high direct, high indirect), or when a teacher perceives his supervisor as putting little emphasis on telling and much on reflecting and asking (low direct, high direct).

Generally *less positive* or even *negative* evaluation by teachers of the quality of their supervisory interpersonal relationships appear to develop when a teacher perceives his supervisor as predominantly telling and not doing much reflecting or asking (high direct, low indirect), or when a teacher sees his supervisor's behavior as relatively passive (low direct, low indirect).

Finally, and perhaps more important, the results suggest some possible clues about the style of supervisory behavior that might tend to put into effect Likert's Principle of Supportive Relationships, which holds that

the leadership and other processes of the organization must be such as to ensure a maximum probability that in all interactions and all relationships within the organization each member will, in the light of his background, values, and expectations, view the experience as supportive and one which builds and maintains his sense of personal worth and importance (1961, p. 103).

A certain amount of motivation to work productively is achieved by supplying economic need satisfaction. Once these needs are relatively well met, however, they take on the character of hygienic, relationship-maintaining factors (Herzberg, 1967), rather than serving as a source of motivation. It is at this point that the Principle of Supportive Relationships starts to take over, building on and supplementing whatever motivation to work arises when economic needs are relatively satiated.

Though Likert has been concerned mostly with industry, he has treated organizational relationships and behavior in a generic fashion. There would seem to be no particular reason why his ideas would not apply to education. The Relationship Inventory can be seen as a way, perhaps, to put the Principle of Supportive Relationships into reliable operational and researchable terms. The four dimensions of the Inventory—Regard, Empathy, Unconditionality of Regard, and Congruence—might illustrate Likert's belief that "each member [should] view the experience as supportive and one which builds and maintains his sense of personal worth and importance" (1961, p. 103). The use of the Inventory to measure teachers' perceptions of supervisors' behavioral styles appears to be a valid way in which to get some clues about the manner in which supervisors affect the supportiveness of their relationships with teachers. The essential problem in the practical use of this or any other research or training tool in the schools is to get supervisors to want to use it.

For our fourth study, to see whether or not our ideas about supervisors' behavioral styles held up when the dependent variable was the teachers' morale, we used the same population that we had used for the research on interpersonal relations and added an incomplete sentence test to measure teachers' morale (Suehr, 1962). The test consists of forty stems for incomplete sentences that the respondents are asked to finish. The stems range widely in content, dealing with children, administration, the community, the school board, personnel policies, and the like. Scoring of the form is based on a content analysis of the completed sentences and is concerned with the degree of positiveness or negativeness of the reactions. A five-point scoring system is used, running from highly positive (denoting high morale) to highly negative (denoting low morale). Suehr found that his interscorer reliability was high and provided a good assessment of teachers' morale.

We followed Suehr's method of scoring the incomplete sentences by content and related them to supervisors' behavioral patterns by an analysis of variance. Differences in morale scores were, indeed, related to teachers' different perceptions of supervisors' behavior, and the differences could not be accounted for by chance. Most interesting for us, the source of variation was the relative indirectness, not the directness, of the supervisor's behavior. That is, differences in morale scores seemed to be mostly a function of the amount of emphasis that teachers saw their supervisor putting on indirect behavior. This result was reinforced by the mean morale scores by behavioral styles. The order will be familiar. The highest morale score occurred under style C, next came A, followed by B and D. Thus, as directness is added, from C to A, and indirectness subtracted, from A to B, morale goes down. The lowest morale score occurs in style D. It is almost as though teachers were saying, "He doesn't even care enough about me to criticize me."

This study also yielded something else of interest—separate from the substance of the study itself. The three previous studies all used bipolar scales. This one was radically different in using a content analysis. Still, the expected difference held up, lending, from our point of view, more credence both to the concepts with which we were dealing and our methods of measurement. Clearly, we were not dealing with a now-you-see-it-now-you-don't phenomenon, and the consistency of our findings led us to model building. It is not enough simply to accept the findings as interesting and potentially productive. As with any other research, it is necessary to relate the findings to existing theory or to attempt to build something that is new. One must find out why the results are as they are; that is the fun of research.

To determine the reasons, we first engage in model building by relating the connotations of specific direct and indirect behavior to social and emotional components of problem solving and morale. Then we deal with the psychological implications of the various behavioral patterns.

PROBLEM SOLVING AND MORALE

The concept of morale is nebulous. Definitions of it—a general level of satisfaction with self in the job—vary depending on the orientation of the definer and, we suspect, the work and organization under consideration. For example, the components of morale will certainly differ for assembly-line workers, top executives, door-to-door salesmen, teachers, or youngsters in school. Supervision is intended to improve instruction by solving the teacher's problems. Given this, the next step is logical. In gestalt terms, if the process of problem solving is the "ground" of supervision, its "figure" is the nature of the interaction that takes place in the process, and this interaction should be related to morale.

It makes sense to look at the behavior of supervisors that has been used to identify behavioral styles and, through induction, infer from that behavior what might be communicated to the teacher.

The *direct* categories in the instrument we called Teacher Perceptions of Supervisory Behavior were expressed thus:

1. Gives his opinions about current teaching practice.
2. Suggests that you do things in specific way or tells you specifically what to do.
3. Criticizes your teaching behavior.

If what is communicated to a teacher by a supervisor when his behavior, aside from what he actually says, is predominantly direct, we postulated a concern for controlling the behavior of the teacher, a concern for excluding the teacher from problem solving (a noncollaborative approach), and a concern for evaluating the teacher.

The categories of *indirect* behavior we expressed thus:

1. Accepts and clarifies questions about your teaching problems.
2. Asks you uncritical questions about your teaching behavior (that is, why you did what you did).
3. Praises your teaching.
4. Asks for your opinions about how to overcome your teaching problems.
5. Discusses your feelings about the productiveness, ease of communication, threat, etc. in your relationship with him as a supervisor.

When a supervisor is predominantly indirect, we postulate that he conveys a concern for the teacher as a person (personal consideration) and a concern for collaborative problem solving (engagement).

Control refers to the extent of a supervisor's need to control both the teacher's classroom behavior and the supervisory setting. *Engagement* refers to the degree to which a supervisor, by his behavior, conveys that he wishes to involve the teacher in collaborative problem solving. *Personal consideration* suggests how much the supervisor communicates that he is concerned with the teacher, not only as a vehicle for getting work done but also as a unique person with goals and feelings that play an important part in his work. *Exclusion*, the other side of the engagement coin, refers to the extent to which the supervisor seems to conceive of problem solving in supervision as his province and no concern of the teacher. *Evaluation* refers to the degree to which the supervisor suggests to the teacher that the most important purpose of supervision is the evaluation of the teacher as a worthy professional.

Table 7.2 illustrates some reasonable potential relationships between supervisors' behavioral styles and the concerns they communicate. The model suggests that the supervisor's words are less important than what he conveys by his behavior. For example, it is not necessary for one person to tell another how much he wishes to control him; his behavior speaks for itself and communicates quite adequately.

This model enables us to make a more systematic interpretation of the results of this study by providing some operational notions about the components of morale, and relating these notions, in a

TABLE 7.2   Relationships between Supervisors' Behavioral Styles and Their Concerns

Concern for:	HD-HI (A)	HD-LI (B)	LD-HI (C)	LD-LI (D)
Control	High	High	Low	Low
Engagement (problem solving by collaboration)	High	Low	High	Low
Personal consideration	High	Low	High	Low
Exclusion (problem solving without collaboration)	High	High	Low	Low
Evaluation	High	High	Low	Low

Source: A. Blumberg and W. Weber, "Teacher Morale as a Function of Perceived Supervisor Behavioral Style," *Journal of Educational Research*, 62 (no. 3, November 1968): 112.

reasonable fashion, to the supervisory styles that have been previously defined.

In considering morale, we assumed, first of all, that basic needs for economic and physical security had been met. A high state of morale is unlikely in work, no matter what the job or interpersonal relationships are, if a person is hard pressed financially or deeply concerned about his health and safety. We assumed morale to be high when a relatively competent person has reasonable freedom of action, has a sense of being involved in problem solving with others who are part of his work, is dealt with as a person, and is relatively free from external evaluation.

It will be recalled that the results of our study indicated that high to low morale scores were related to perceptions of supervisors' behavioral styles in the following order: low direct, high indirect (C); high direct, high indirect (A); high direct, low indirect (B); and low direct, low indirect (D).

Style C	Low direct, high indirect	In this behavioral style, the model indicates that the supervisor communicates to the teacher his relatively high concern with engagement, personal consideration, and a relatively low concern with control, evaluation, and exclusion. Apparently, then, the teacher sees himself as being freed from inhibitions on his action and from external evaluation. His energies can be devoted to the job, and he perceives that his own feelings and needs will be considered in his relationships with his supervisor. One would predict, then, that a high state of morale would exist under these conditions.
Style A	High direct, high indirect	Here the situation changes. Concerns with control, exclusion, and evaluation, low in the previous condition, now tend to be high. Thus, though there is strong emphasis on the two concerns that should lead to high morale, there is also emphasis on three that would theoretically temper the overall effect. On the basis of this model, then, one

would look for high morale but not as high as in the first case. The results of this study are in line with this notion.

Style B	High direct, low indirect	This time, according to the model, two social and emotional factors, engagement and personal consideration, which seem to produce a high morale, appear to be lacking. We are led to conceive of this situation as one in which morale would tend to be low, and, indeed, the data indicate that this was the case.
Style D	Low direct, low indirect	The model suggests that this behavioral style is marked by little concern for all five major social and emotional areas. This style would seem to communicate to the teacher that the supervisor does not even care enough about the teacher to control and censure him—a classic condition of laissez-faire. Our prediction that morale would be low was confirmed by the data.

The various pieces of the model-building kit seem to fit together. We are reminded of what happens when youngsters build model airplanes out of a lot of apparently unrelated pieces of balsa wood. In behavior as in airplanes, the end product looks so good, and so much work has gone into it that there is, at times, a reluctance to see whether or not the model will fly. But, if we are to go beyond words and into action, it must be tested and criticized so that we can understand where it needs buttressing and where it is solid as it stands.

There has been a clear consistency in the patterns of the results and from this consistency we have deduced what we think are critical dimensions of a person's productive relationship with an organization and what seem to be some of the implicit assumptions of both direct and indirect behavior. Our list of critical dimensions is not intended to be definitive or all-inclusive. Nor is it based on any simple theoretical formulation. It represents a mixture of personal experience, ideas gleaned from the experience of others, and the thoughts of our colleagues. A person is likely to feel fulfilled as a person and in his relationships with his organization when:

— He feels a communicative openness, when it is all right for him to share his concerns about himself with his supervisor, to disagree, to feed back to his supervisor any reactions he may have about their relationship, and so forth.

— He feels a sense of his own professional competence by way of helpful feedback from his supervisor and colleagues. This feedback, though it may be critical, is given in a supportive manner, inducing growth and confidence.

— He feels that his relationships with his supervisor and co-workers give him a *sense of colleagueship*, a collaborating share in the enterprise.

— He senses that his supervisor and his colleagues value his *worth as a person*; when he is not merely a cog, no matter how skillful or important, in a larger machine.

— He senses that the organization, primarily through the behavior of his supervisor, is concerned with his *personal and professional growth*, with providing the climate and opportunities for the individual to mature, to reach whatever potential his skills and predispositions permit.

— He feels a sense of *personal independence and freedom*; when he can make decisions affecting his work on his own or with the help of his supervisor or colleagues. The decision to seek help is not seen as a confession of inadequacy.

— He feels a sense of *support for risk-taking* and a concomitant sense that the failure of a new venture is not taken as a sign of immaturity and incompetence.

For an organization to fulfill the demands implicit in those dimensions is surely a big order. It is certainly presumptuous of us to assert that the behavioral style of the supervisor is the most essential factor in their fulfillment. Yet, particularly when the supervisor is the principal or department head, we have a feeling that his behavior is crucial. Our notion may be tested, if casually, by going from school to school; talking to teachers to ascertain where they see themselves in relation to the school, their degree of commitment to their tasks, and their excitement about what they are doing; and watching the supervisors in action. It is a revealing experience.

The second part of our task was to examine the assumptions of the behavioral styles. We examined, first, direct and indirect behavior as pure categories of behavior (which they rarely are) and then the mixture of behavioral styles. The way in which one person approaches another symbolizes his personal theory about people — how they learn, what excites them, how their needs are fulfilled, and so forth. Our approach to students, for example, tells them more about us, about our values and our theory about people *in the prevailing situation*, than any words we could speak. We emphasize "situation" to suggest that our theories about people are multifaceted in nature and vary depending upon our perception of the situation, its demands, and the role we play in it. Thus, one supervisor, when confronted by an insecure new teacher, may see the situation as needing rigid control. His theory is that in such situations people need to be told what to do so they can survive. A different supervisor, viewing the same situation, may decide to do nothing but offer a sympathetic ear. His theory is that the teacher will find his own best survival strategy, but that he needs someone with whom to talk and share his concerns.

A supervisor using predominantly *direct* behavior might well be assuming that:

— The control of a situation is based on the authority of one's position in an organizational hierarchy.
— People in higher organizational positions have more expertise.
— People in lower organizational positions can best be evaluated by those who are higher.
— The most important external rewards of a job come to a person primarily from a person who holds a higher position.
— Empathic listening to the teacher is not a necessary dimension of helping.
— People learn best by being told what to do by someone in a higher organizational position.
— Work is rational; there is little place in supervision for discussion of feelings or interpersonal relationships.
— Collaborative problem solving between supervisor and teacher is not a critical concern in supervision.
— Teaching as a skill can generally be separated into the right and wrong ways of doing things.

The assumptions about people that appear to accompany a supervisor's heavy loading on *indirect* behavior are that:

— Control of the situation depends on the demands of the problem. The problem determines the direction that events take.

—Expertise is a function of knowledge and experience, not necessarily of organizational position.

—The product of a teacher's work is the best evaluative tool to use in measuring his performance.

—The important rewards of teaching are intrinsic to the job, but they need to be supplemented by external rewards.

—People learn best by being confronted with a situation and, with help, finding their own solution.

—It is important for teachers to feel that they have been listened to and understood.

—Work is both rational and emotional; discussion of feelings and interpersonal relations may be as important as discussion about the job.

—Collaborative problem solving between supervisor and teacher is an important concern of supervision.

—Teaching is a complex process, and what works well for one person may not for another, so that most of what goes on in a classroom needs to be viewed experimentally.

Though the two sets of assumptions read pretty much as polar opposites, it is necessary to reinforce the idea that they are merely the dominant tendencies and not unequivocal statements of fact. Life is much too complex for us to stake out positions with impermeable boundaries. Thus, the assumptions we have made about direct or indirect behavior in supervisors are assumptions about what we see as the central themes that tend to get communicated by that behavior in a fashion that does not necessarily exclude other themes.

The relationships between the assumptions underlying direct and indirect behavior and the conditions necessary for fulfilling, productive relationships between the individual and the organization seem clear, though they are not simple. The potential for fulfilling, productive relationships between individuals and the organization requires a social system that is open (Katz and Kahn, 1966) and collaborative. The system should also be concerned about knowledge and competence, regardless of organizational position, accept provisionalism and experimentation, and foster the intrinsic rewards of a job and the norms that sanction the expression of interpersonal concerns, as well as those of the problem at hand. A supervisor's emphasis on direct behavior (style B) tends to generate forces that do not support an open collaborative social system. A supervisor's emphasis on indirect behavior (style C) would generate forces that do support fulfilling, productive relationships between individuals and the organization. Supervision that emphasizes both direct and indirect behavior (style A) would be generally supportive, but would generate some counterforces, in particular the communicative freedom that develops under this style is not as great as that promoted by styles C or D. The social system created under style D supervision, even though there is a lot of communicative freedom, would not be fulfilling or productive for an individual, primarily because of the low level of productivity, interpersonal relations, and morale that seems to accompany this style, which appears to communicate a directionless, uninterested, uncaring attitude on the part of the supervisor that contributes little, if anything, to the teacher.

It is always interesting, and intellectually honest, to argue the other side. The primary arguments that can be directed against our generalizations are that they contain obvious and questionable value loadings, that the data upon which the conclusions were based were perceptual and did not come from direct observation, that the study samples were too small, that the phenomena being dealt with are too complex to admit of such straightforward interpretations, and that no consideration has been given to individual differences. There is some substance to each of these arguments. They are, on the one hand, acknowledged limitations of our work, and, on the other, they present challenging opportunities for further research. Nevertheless, our studies and interpretations represent an important brick in the wall of our understanding about behavioral styles and their effect on both individuals and organizations.

8 The Teacher's Perspective on Motivation

Although we are still concerned with the behavioral nature of supervisors' transactions with teachers, the focus now shifts to a discussion of some of the types of things that happen in these transactions that seem to make teachers feel good or bad about their work with their supervisor. We adopted the notions and methodology from Herzberg and his colleagues (1959), who studied motivation in industry. The scope and depth of our studies are more limited than those of Herzberg, but the results seem to justify more intensive research and training in this aspect of education.

THEORETICAL BACKGROUND

The isolation of those factors that motivate a person to do a more efficient and productive job has been the focus of much research. This concern has probably derived from the natural curiosity of scientists, the urgent needs of managers in a competitive society for the highest quality produced in the most efficient manner, or the tremendous increase in automation, which has prevented many people from gaining much intrinsic satisfaction from their work. In any event, the literature of organization and management is now replete with such terms as organizational culture, management philosophy, financial incentives, the achievement motive, competence motive, and so forth. Though the problem has not been solved, all of these concepts and the research they have engendered have widened the boundaries of our knowledge about man and his work and enabled managers and administrators to deal more adequately with motivational problems on the job. (Very little effort, however, seems to have been expended on motivation in professional education. Perhaps, for love of children, teachers are presumed to be highly motivated to work well—a dubious point of view at best.)

Herzberg and his associates, studying the motivations of engineers and accountants in industry, interviewed more than two hundred subjects and asked them to recall particular times in their job when something very favorable had happened and when something very unfavorable had happened. They were also asked to estimate the duration of the effects of the events. The researchers were then able to conceptualize the difference between *motivational* factors and *hygienic* factors, and to elaborate a theory of motivation centered on need that is based on Maslow's pyramidal or hierarchical notions about individual needs (1954).

Motivational and Hygienic Factors

Two factors, motivational and hygienic, emerged from Herzberg's research. Motivational factors are those favorable things happening in the course of work that spur people on to higher achievement. Related to specific facets of job performance, they include achievement, recognition, responsibility, growth, advancement, and other aspects of the individual's self-actualization on the job, and they pull the individual toward an ever-widening grasp and mastery of his environment.

Hygienic factors, when present in favorable measure in the work situation, provide a base from which motivating events could take over. By themselves, they contain little potential for motivation, but, when they are absent, the individual becomes dissatisfied— hence, the term "hygienic." These background factors, including pay, benefits, and the behavior of supervisors, are part of the organizational context, and they provide the relative richness of soil that affects the growth and productivity of the individual. They are not the seeds.

The concepts of motivational and hygienic factors in work led to further thought about a theory of need-centered motivation. The notion is that man's behavior is always directed by need. Some needs are more basic than others, and their satisfaction is necessary before a person can attempt to satisfy higher needs. A need that is satiated will no longer serve as a motivator when a person is offered more of the same.

Hygienic factors can be seen as representing more basic needs than motivational factors, which are associated with a higher level of human functioning and related to personal growth. Motivational factors are powerful because they are concerned with attaining mastery over one's environment, a need that is relatively insatiable. This leads to the development of Maslow's notion (1965) of the importance of understanding the nature of the things people complain about in their work. It is not necessarily true, for example, that, unless people have something to complain about, they will not be happy. It is more important to consider what their gripes are about than the mere fact that they are griping. (See Maslow's delightful chapter on low grumbles, high grumbles, and metagrumbles in *Eupsychian Management* [1965].) If the complaints or grumbles are related to hygienic factors, one assumes the situation to be unhappy. If they are concerned with unsatisfied motivational factors, one might consider it to be a sign of a dynamic, growing work group and organization.

Our application of the content and methodology of Herzberg's work to supervision in education took the following form. We asked 130 practicing teachers who were enrolled in graduate courses to respond, in writing, to two statements:

Please think of a time when, in your relationship with your supervisor (principal, department head, or another title), something very favorable and positive happened that made you feel good about your teaching and your relationship with your supervisor.

Please think of a time when, in your relationship with your supervisor, something very unfavorable and negative happened that made you feel bad about your teaching and your relationship with your supervisor.

They were also asked to note the quality of their supervision on a nine-point scale, the poles of which were: "A great deal of help; I couldn't ask for it to be better," and, "No help at all; just about useless."

Results

The content of the responses to the statement was analyzed and then categorized according to the needs that were being satisfied or frustrated either by the substance of a supervisor's behavior or the connotative value of the behavior itself. The results of this analysis are found in Tables 8.1 and 8.2.

The data in Table 8.1 suggest a strong similarity to the results of Herzberg's research, even though the job is different and we were dealing only with supervision. Herzberg considered the entire job. The first four factors, which account for 80 percent of the category responses, are motivating factors. They deal with recognition, but with different facets of recognition. Factor 1 typically referred to the teacher's having been praised by the supervisor for an achievement in a particular class. Factor 2, though it obviously has overtones of praise, was related to a teacher's being told that he had the makings of a fine teacher and to continue working in a particular direction; his potential for advancement and recognition has been noticed. Factor 3, in most cases, had to do with a teacher's being appointed to a special committee or study group (frequently

TABLE 8.1   Favorable Factors in Supervision—Needs That Are Filled

Factor	Percentage
1. Need for teaching achievements to be recognized	41
2. Need to have personal and professional potential recognized	17
3. Need for status and public recognition	13
4. Need for sincere appraisal and help	9
5. Need for interpersonal warmth	6
6. Need for organizational support	3
7. Need for freedom	3
8. Need for security	3
9. Need for organizational influence	2
10. Need for openness and trust	1
11. Need not to be perceived as anonymous	1
12. Need for collaboration	1
Total	100

TABLE 8.2   Unfavorable Factors in Supervision—Needs That Are Not Filled

Factor	Percentage
1. Need to avoid punishment	34
2. Need for fair play	26
3. Need for trust	12
4. Need for support in decision about students or parents	10
5. Need for consideration	8
6. Need to be appreciated	4
7. Need for help	3
8. Need to be treated like an adult	2
9. Need for involvement in decision making	1
Total	100

by passing old hands) or being asked to make a presentation about a creative technique to a group of peers—public status and recognition. Factor 4 is classified as a job-oriented motivator, somewhat contrary to Herzberg's idea that the technical quality of supervision was a hygienic factor as far as the total job is concerned. The difference, in this case, is that the job is that of supervision.

The remaining seven factors are, in Herzberg's terms, hygienically oriented. They don't seem to play an important part in the teacher's attitude toward supervision as do the others. Concerned with the organizational and interpersonal climate of the supervisory setting, they are part of the environment and not the job.

Table 8.2 deals with teachers' needs that appear to be unsatisfied. When these factors appear in supervisory relations, they indicate the teacher's perception that the psychological contract (Levinson, 1962) the school implicitly signed with him when he accepted the job is not being observed by the supervisor. The teacher has certain expectations about his supervisory relationships that do not match his perceptions of what has occurred.

An example will provide clarification. It is generally agreed that people have a need to avoid punishment. This need would be a "clause" in one's psychological contract with a work organization. Yet 34 percent of the teahcers in our sample said that this need was not met in their work with their supervisor. Quite the opposite, some of them felt very much punished.

The data presented in Table 8.2 appear, once more, to parallel Herzberg's findings. His study showed that positive job attitudes tended to be associated largely with the substantive aspects of work itself, while the hygienic factors played a relatively minor role. Conversely, negative job attitudes developed under conditions related more to hygienic factors—when the conditions were not satisfactory. The only job-related factors that came to light in the analysis are seen in Factors 5 and 7, the need to be appreciated and to deal with what the teacher sees as important teaching problems. They play a minor part in the unfavorable attitudes toward supervision. The rest are environmentally oriented, the environment being the interpersonal state between the teacher and the supervisor.

The emphasis on the relative importance of the unfavorable factors is heavily skewed. Factors 1, 2, and 3, for example, account for about two-thirds of the total. Factor 1, in general, referred to the teachers' need to avoid what they saw to be hostile interpersonal criticism: "My supervisor found out that I had done very well on the National Teacher Exam, and then she said that she didn't see why my discipline wasn't better since I was so smart." Perhaps such a comment reflects the antagonism fostered by intergenerational conflict—old-timers against newcomers.

Factor 2, the need for fair play, typically referred to situations where supervisors made decisions about or criticized a teacher on what the teacher saw as inadequate information. The result was that the teacher saw himself being treated unfairly. For example, one teacher said that he was criticized by his supervisor for poor spelling when the words he had written on the board had been purposely misspelled. The supervisor had never bothered to check.

Factor 3 suggests the teacher's need to be able to count on the supervisor's doing what he says he will do. When he does not, the teacher feels betrayed and develops the negative feelings most of us do in betrayal. Factor 4 is concerned with situations in which a teacher's decision about a student or parent is reversed by the supervisor. The issue seems to be partly jurisdictional and partly substantive: Does the teacher have both the prerogative and the expertise necessary to make the correct decision? A number of teachers thought they had both, but their supervisor did not. Need for consideration, Factor 5, means the teacher's desire to be treated as a person and not merely as a small cog in a larger machine. It is the teacher's asking for a teacher-centered view of school organization and not an administration-centered view.

Tables 8.3 and 8.4 illustrate the results of teachers' rating the quality of the supervision. High ratings were those in the upper third of the scale; low ratings, those in the lower third. A percentage comparison was then made concerning the favorable and unfavorable factors noted by the highs and lows. Twenty-six teachers rated their supervision high; forty-eight, low.

In Table 8.3 we found some interesting differences between teachers who rated the quality of their supervision high and those who rated it low. Our discussion will be limited to the first four factors since these, meeting our expectations, provided the bulk of responses. Almost half of the lows, compared with about one-third of the highs, noted Factor 1 as a favorable element in their supervision, a response that is interesting and important because this factor essentially means that, "My supervisor *praises* my teaching."

TABLE 8.3   Favorable Factors Mentioned by Teachers in Rating the Quality of Their Supervision

	Percentage	
Factor	High	Low
1. Need for teaching achievements to be recognized	31	47
2. Need to have personal and professional potential recognized	10	21
3. Need for status and public recognition	15	9
4. Need for sincere appraisal and help	19	5
5. Need for interpersonal warmth	8	7
6. Need for organizational support	5	0
7. Need for freedom	5	0
8. Need for security	3	2
9. Need for organizational influence	0	7
10. Need for openness and trust	0	2
11. Need not to be perceived as anonymous	2	0
12. Need for collaboration	2	0
Total	100	100

Evidently, then, personal praise is not seen as being as important an ingredient of favorable supervisory relationships as one might think. If it were, the highs and lows might be expected to change places. This point is reinforced by the results related to Factor 2, which is really another form of personal praise. Twice as many lows mentioned Factor 2 as did highs. This finding is all the more interesting for it seems to lend some empirical support to the notion that the use of praise as praise, while it may create a short-term glow of good feeling, may also place demands on an individual with which he is uncomfortable. If it is part of a supervisor's style to give a lot of praise, he may also be making the teacher dependent on him, the praise becoming a reward doled out when the teacher does things of which the supervisor approves. We are not suggesting that supervisors should not praise teachers. We are suggesting that the supervisor's reliance on praise as a motivator may not achieve what he wants and may, indeed, be counterproductive.

There are differences, though not quite so sharp, between the highs and lows on Factor 3. It can be argued that, when needs for status and public recognition are met, a form of praise is being meted out. Here, the praise is open. It is no longer a matter between supervisor and teacher. It becomes an item of public record. Apparently, such public praise is ego enhancing for the teacher because of the value of peer recognition, of collegial acknowledgment of competence.

The different reactions on Factor 4 are very clear. The highs seem to be saying, "I need and receive a good bit of sincere appraisal and help. It makes me feel good about my supervision." If the lows are similar kinds of people as the highs, and there is no reason to suspect otherwise, they are saying, "The relative lack of sincere appraisal and help influences me to devalue the worth of my supervision." Teachers are like other people in their need to know where they stand and to receive help to improve. Apparently, these conditions exist more frequently in productive than in unproductive supervision.

In Table 8.4 it becomes apparent that a different set of circumstances exists from those that developed when the highs and lows were asked to mention the favorable factors of supervision. When the teachers responded to the question, they were saying, "Here are needs that I have—they are not being met in my relationships with

TABLE 8.4   Unfavorable Factors Mentioned by Teachers in Rating
the Quality of Their Supervision

		Percentage	
Factor		High	Low
1. Need to avoid punishment		33	30
2. Need for fair play		25	23
3. Need for trust		0	11
4. Need for support		4	11
5. Need for consideration		4	4
6. Need to be appreciated		4	4
7. Need not to deal with trivia		0	6
8. Need to be treated like an adult		0	2
9. No comment		30	9
	Total	100	100

my supervisor." Another difference between the two sets of data is
that the favorable and unfavorable factors of the highs and lows deal
with distinctly different substances. Both highs and lows indicated
that most of their favorable reactions had to do with the motivating
factors; most of the unfavorable reactions, with hygienic factors.
This finding seems to support Herzberg's ideas. When teachers think
about the unfavorable aspects of their supervision, they tend to concentrate on the hygienic aspects of the relationship rather than on
the motivators; the unfavorable aspects have a distinct flavor of
maintenance, while the favorable tend to be task oriented.

The specific findings in Table 8.4 reveal some interesting similarities in, and contrasts between, the highs and the lows. For example, both groups give nearly equal weight to the needs to avoid
punishment and for fair play. Regardless of whether or not a teacher
felt the quality of the supervision was high or low, these two factors
played a major role in unfavorable reactions, accounting for over 50
percent of the total comments. People tend to remember vividly
when they have been punished or treated in a manner that, from
their point of view, is unjust.

Similarities in the other results, especially in Factors 3, 4, and 7,
tend to disappear. We can see that 11 percent of the lows indicated
as unfavorable factors that their needs for a trustful and a supportive

relationship were not being met by their supervisor. The correspond-
ing figures for the highs were zero and 4 percent. The needs for
trust and support—perhaps, the disregarding of these needs—seem
to have a relatively important effect on teacher's ratings of the
quality of supervision. Again, recall the maintenance character of
these factors, which reinforces a major premise about the necessity
of relationship-building behavior as a foundation for productive
work.

Factor 7, the need not to deal with trivia, plays some role (6
percent of the responses) in the lows' evaluation of their supervision,
but it is not mentioned at all by the highs. Comments from supervisors about whether or not the window shades are drawn evenly
or the teacher's desk is neat only make supervision a laughing matter
in the eyes of the teachers. "If that's all he has to say to me, why does
he bother to visit my classroom?" Help is needed, but it must be
substantive help with teaching and not mere silliness.

Finally, Table 8.4 indicates that 30 percent of the high evaluators
had no unfavorable things to say about their supervision, while
only 9 percent of the lows gave no response. The highs seem to be
saying simply that their supervision is good, period. In the "No
comment" response of the lows, we feel that, though they have no
specific unfavorable comments to make, there is just a general feeling of poor supervision. One reasonable, though unsupported,
speculation is that the "No comment" of the lows may be a result of
a supervisor's behavioral style that is low direct, low indirect—where
nothing seems to happen but it's hard to put your finger on what
isn't happening. You are simply left with little to which to react.

One way of thinking about the points raised in this chapter is
that they suggest types of behavior that teachers would prefer supervisors engage in "more of" or "less of." In another study mentioned
earlier (Blumberg, Loehr, and Goldstein, 1978), the "more of"-
"less of" problem was approached directly. Two checklists, derived
from teacher responses to open-ended questions, were developed.
The first contained items whose focus was on the behaviors that
teachers wished their supervisors would engage in more often than
they do. It contained two major categories: classroom focus and
supervisor behavior and attitudes. The second checklist, concerned
with behaviors teachers wished supervisors would engage in less
often, was a one-category list that contained supervisor behaviors
that teachers felt were distasteful. It was a sort of cease and desist order.

A second group of 150 teachers responded to the checklists. I report here the top three rankings in each list as these seem to give an adequate flavor of what the teachers involved had on their minds as they thought about how their supervisor behaves with them.

Relative to "more of," it is interesting to note that the teachers completely ignored the classroom curriculum and activities in their top rankings. They focused on supervisor behavior and wished their supervisor would offer constructive criticism of their teaching behavior, let them know how they were doing, and be more open and flexible. What they seemed to be saying to their supervisor was, "I would find our relationship more satisfying and I would also do a better job if you could really learn to be level with me." Why supervisors do not engage in these behaviors more often is a question I cannot answer. My hunch, though, is that the answer is probably found in other circumstances discussed earlier, that is, supervisor selection and training. The system, as it certifies and selects supervisors, seems to pay little heed to the demands of the complex interpersonal situations supervisors must confront daily. It simply assumes that the structure is sound and that good people will do good things.

The rankings of the do "less of" checklist seem to confirm all of this. The top three were: to be less self-centered, to be less rigid, and to treat me less like a child and more like an adult. In other words, consonant with the data reported in Tables 8.2 and 8.4, these teachers seemed to be saying, "Don't, by your behavior, make our relationship a punishing one for me." And perhaps that is enough said.

9   As Supervisors See Their Job

To deal with those aspects of interaction between supervisors and teachers that give a lift to supervisors and those that seem to have a negative impact, we repeated the study we had made of teachers. The primary difference was that the supervisors were asked to use themselves as the reference point for favorable and unfavorable reactions. There was also a conceptual difference. With the teachers we were interested in seeing whether or not Herzberg's notions of motivators and satisfiers would hold up in supervision. The teachers, we hypothesized, being the receivers of the supervisors' attempts at influence, should respond with some motivational consequences. In studying supervisors, we were interested, not in the receiver of influence, but in the person who influences—or tries to.

The findings tend to state the obvious. After all, if you ask a person whose job it is to influence others about his favorable job experiences, he is likely to think of those times when he has been a successful influence, while his unfavorable job experiences are likely to have occurred when his attempts to influence were unsuccessful. The obvious is frequently taken for granted, however, and some valuable potential insight is neglected. Like the husbands and wives who claim that their partners take them for granted, saying that "As far as you're concerned I have become a fixture; you have forgotten my special needs as a person," we take for granted the influencing character of the supervisor's role, and forget what enables the supervisor to do what he has been employed for. The

103

results can affect the kinds of people a school district appoints as supervisors and the organizational support system in which supervisors work.

In Table 9.1, we report the reactions of fifty supervisors asked to recall something favorable that had occurred in their work with teachers. As we had predicted, the findings contained no big surprises. Most favorable experiences in supervisory life seem to come when supervisors are able to get teachers to try different ways of doing things or when they are able to change the way that teachers think or feel about the job of teaching. The ramifications are clear, particularly when there is positive feedback from the teacher.

Factor 2, a supervisor's need to be seen as a source of help to teachers, would seem to flow from both the successful induction of influence and from Factor 3, his being effective as a group problem-solving consultant. It is an interesting situation. Factors 1 and 3 are clearly task oriented and the result of direct action. Factor 2 seems to be a result of Factors 1 and 3, that is, as supervisors are able to work effectively with teachers, a natural side effect is that their job becomes more consultative than supervisory, less a matter of intruding on teachers with all of the organizational baggage of supervision and more a matter of accepting invitations.

When such a shift in relationships occurs between supervisors and teachers, we can infer that a number of interacting variables are producing the supervisor's satisfaction. First, merely being asked to

TABLE 9.1   Favorable Factors Mentioned by Supervisors—Needs
                 That Are Fulfilled

Factor	Percentage
1. Need to influence methods or attitudes	43
2. Need to be seen as a source of help	29
3. Need to be seen as a productive, group problem-solving consultant	15
4. Need for open communication	9
5. Need to influence the organization	4
Total	100

help ("Will you visit my class?" "Can you help our study group?") has an ego-building effect. It communicates to the supervisor that he is seen as a person with valuable resources. It is a form of praise and, coming as it does from people who do not usually ask for help, it is all the more worthwhile. His feelings are like those of a student who gets an A from a professor who has the reputation of giving very few A's.

Second, the long-term effect of a supervisor's being asked for help, particularly by several teachers, is that that aspect of his role is legitimized in the school. No longer is the supervisor the central office spy or the intruder. He has a home base for his role and, given the relative ambiguity of the role, such a home base is important for his mental health. Research by Kahn and his colleagues (1964) seems clearly to indicate that organizational positions and roles that overlap several organizational functions and relationships are potentially much more ambiguous than clearly limited positions. Role ambiguity tends to lead to tension and stress in the incumbent—the degree of tension and stress felt by a person on a job being taken as an indicator of the person's mental health on the job. Supervisors have boundary-line roles, even when they happen to be school principals. One would suspect then, that the more that teachers seek out help from a supervisor—thus legitimizing his role—the greater the likelihood that the tension-inducing aspects of his boundary-line position would be dissipated. It is unlikely that supervisors consciously articulate these circumstances to themselves, but it seems reasonable that the role-legitimizing part of being asked for help is important in inducing satisfaction in a supervisor's work.

Third, the necessity for a supervisor to justify his role is potentially disturbing. Almost any supervisor would be hard pressed to produce any substantial data to indicate a direct link between what he does and the enhanced learning of the students. Like the boundary-line functions and relationships, this will potentially produce tension. Supervisors, with few direct measures to determine their success in their job, must wonder, from time to time, whether it is all worthwhile—and perhaps be disturbed because they cannot produce a satisfactory answer.

If no direct measures of productivity are available to a supervisor, the next best would be indirect or inferential measures. These are precisely what teachers' requests for help are. In addition to satisfying his ego and legitimizing his role, teachers' requests for assistance assure the supervisor that he must be doing something right. He not only feels good about himself, but he also has some measure of the value of his position in the larger system.

The last two factors noted in Table 9.1—need for open communication and need to influence the organization—apparently play a relatively minor role in the satisfaction that supervisors derive from working with teachers. Supervisors' need for open communication with teachers comes close to what Herzberg sees as a hygienic factor in work relationships, which, as we shall see shortly, are more conspicuous when they are not satisfied than when they are. The minor satisfaction that seems to come to supervisors from being able to influence the school organization is of interest less because of its substance than because of what it may tell us about supervision. Though some people might wish it otherwise, the main thrust of supervision is on the individual teacher and not on the school as an organization, thereby creating a problem with which schools have been loath to deal. Productive, exciting, and self-renewing schools will not be established by attention to the behavior and values of individual teachers if the behavior and values of schools as human organizations are ignored. Teachers and supervisors come and go; the organization continues. Perhaps there should be some shift in the emphasis of the supervisor's role from a one-to-one relationship with the teacher to a position of organizational or group consultant, a point that will become central in a later chapter.

Table 9.2 presents some parallels, and differences, when it is compared with Table 9.1. The percentage (42) of supervisors who indicate that their unfavorable experiences with teachers were related to the rejection of influence was almost identical with the percentage (43) of supervisors who mentioned the acceptance of influence as a favorable factor. Both Factors 2 and 4 deal with communications between supervisors and teachers. The difference between the two, as they are stated, is that the need not to be seen as a threat is a self-oriented problem of organizational role, while the inability to develop open communication probably represents the behavioral wrestling with that threat. We infer that, for some supervisors, the perception of being seen as a threat by a teacher is enough to create an unfavorable situation. For others, apparently, this perception may not be a problem (or they may not be aware of the threat implicit in their role), but their inability to deal openly with teachers is. It is not important whether the threat comes before the communications as the cart before the horse. Between them, these factors account for almost 30 percent of the unfavorable items mentioned by supervisors.

Factor 3, feeling helpless, is not simply the converse of "being seen as a source of help" that was mentioned as a favorable event in a supervisor's life. The supervisor seems to be saying, "I tried the best I could but things just didn't seem to pan out." Experiences of failure are experiences of failure. No emotionally healthy person enjoys them, and supervisors are no different. What is important is the reason for the failure. It is possible that many supervisors' failure to help and many cases where their influence was rejected have begun as failures of communication that resulted from feeling threatened by teachers.

If this line of reasoning makes sense, we have some empirical data to reinforce our earlier contentions about the effect of the organizational culture of schools on supervision and the way a supervisor enacts his role. A system that guarantees frequent failure for supervisors is, as some contemporary writers suggest, much like the system that guarantees failure for many students. The problem is not pleasant and we are under no illusions that it will be confronted except, perhaps, in a very few cases. But it is better that

TABLE 9.2   Unfavorable Factors Mentioned by Supervisors

Factor	Percentage
1. Need not to have influence rejected (methods or influence)	42
2. Need not to be seen as a threat	18
3. Need not to feel helpless	15
4. Need not to have closed communication	11
5. Need not to lose self-control	8
6. Need not to lose control of the situation	6
Total	100

such circumstances be common knowledge, rather than hidden away except for occasional use (very occasional, we suspect) in courses in supervision or chats over coffee.

The last two unfavorable factors in Table 9.2, losing control of oneself and losing control of a situation, were cited in a relatively small number of cases. Supervisors seemed to be describing times when they became so upset with a teacher that they simply lost their tempers, and then they had all sorts of guilt feelings about it. It is a different experience of failure. Professional people are not supposed to lose their temper, and those who do so have, in a sense, failed as professionals. Likewise, skilled professionals are not supposed to lose control of a situation. It is failure again, though it is probably more acceptable to lose control of a situation than of yourself. The former can be forgiven and forgotten, but memories of a display of temper can linger on and, not infrequently, become part of the organization's folklore to the relish of competitive colleagues.

Tables 9.1 and 9.2, then, broadly reinforce each other. What seem to give supervisors the most favorable reactions to their job are conditions in which they can be influential, receive positive feedback on their attempts to influence, and have their role legitimized in a school. Unfavorable reactions most often occur when influence is rejected or communications with teachers become disrupted or defensive.

We found it interesting that, while not totally missing from the list of favorable conditions, the communications issue plays a minor role there, but has a major impact on the unfavorable conditions. This finding would seem to lend support to Herzberg's classification of the communicative climate as a hygienic factor. A healthy communications system seems to become important when it is absent rather than when it is present. If in-service or organizational training programs aim, as so many of them do, at "communications" in the abstract, their long-run effect on the school and supervisory relations is apt to be relatively minimal. If training in open communications is part and parcel of school and supervisory processes, however, the potential for integrating an open communications climate into the school organization will probably be enhanced.

Two other questions were of interest in this study. First, to what degree do supervisors see themselves as being productive and helpful to teachers? Second, at whose door would supervisors lay the blame for obstacles they saw in the way of their being more productive and helpful?

We tried to answer the first question by asking the supervisors to respond to the identical scale the teachers used when they rated the quality of their supervision. It was a nine-point scale, the poles of which were "A great deal of help" and "No help at all." The results were interesting, expected, and in sharp contrast to teachers' responses. The mean rating of the productivity of supervision by supervisors was significantly different from, and higher than, the mean rating of the teachers: 6.2 and 4.1, respectively. The variance in the supervisors' ratings was very small, while that of teachers was large: the supervisors' scores clustered closely around the mean. They all felt so much the same about the question that it was impossible to distinguish any useful high and low groups. The variance of the teachers' ratings was large, and we had no difficulty in developing high and low groups.

It is possible that the supervisors in our sample had an objectively realistic picture of their effectiveness as supervisors and that the results of their efforts *were* productive. However, another interpretation of this high mean productivity, together with the small variance, makes more sense to us. People generally tend to look at themselves and their work in a positive manner. Most of us can scarcely afford to do otherwise. It would be the rare teacher or college professor, for example, who would continuously judge the results of his work as unproductive. A study of college professors conducted many years ago indicated that, by and large, each individual professor considered himself to be the best of all possible teachers, and there was no known way to convince him to the contrary. (I came across this study over twenty years ago when I was just starting graduate study. The specific reference has long been lost but, because I wanted to be a professor, the findings made an impression on me. I believe the research was conducted by the American Association of University Professors.) So, though unquestionably some of our supervisors had an adequate picture of their work, we interpreted the data as suggesting that the mean productivity score is high because supervisors need to have it high. This would be especially true in-light of our earlier comments about the vagueness of the supervisory role and the difficulty in

getting valid data on productivity. Security has to come from some-
where, and "through the eye of the beholder" is as good a source
as any.

   Data for the last question we asked (What was blocking higher
supervisory productivity and helpfulness?) came through an analysis
of the content of an open-ended question. The forty-eight responses
are shown in Table 9.3. Though the total sample is small, a pattern
seems clear. Half of the supervisors point at the situation for being
responsible for their problems, most of them citing a lack of time:
there are too many responsibilities and too many teachers for one
person to handle. Supervisors see their primary job as working with
teachers, but they are sidetracked by many routine matters that
take time and energy away from where they really want to be. There
is undoubtedly much truth in this perception, particularly if the
supervisor in question has administrative responsibilities. And yet,
the possibility does exist that some supervisors blame the situation
as a means of rationalizing their feelings of unproductiveness or
inadequacy. All of us have experienced failure. Rather than look at
our own fallibility for the answer to our problem, we place the blame
on one or more organizational constraints. It is easier and less
threatening to our sense of competence. In addition, because of the
anonymity of the system, we can gain sympathy from our colleagues
and provide ourselves with a handy "fall guy."

   Nearly one-third of the supervisors indicated that there was
something about teachers and their attitudes that blocked their
productivity. In the huge majority of cases, the specifics of the
situation were connected to the tenure system. Supervisors said

TABLE 9.3   Supervisors' Perception of the Source of Blocks to
                 Their Productivity

Source	Number
Situation	24
Teachers	14
Self	10
Total	48

that they had difficulty just getting to talk to teachers who were tenured. In some cases, the supervisors were not even able (or so they felt) to gain physical access to tenured teachers, let alone establish any sort of helping relationship with them. We mentioned the tenure problem before, and we think that there is probably a large amount of credibility in the supervisors' reactions. We deal later with the problem in depth. Suffice it to say, at this time, that, in the name of academic freedom and security, we seem to have created something of an untouchable monster, and we are stuck with it.

Finally, about one-fifth of our supervisors located the source of their problems in themselves, most typically in their feelings that their communications skills were inadequate and that they were incapable of reaching teachers, not because the teachers were unreceptive, but because they themselves could not find the key that would unlock the relationship. In a number of cases, the specifics of the situation were related to their feeling threatened in the supervisory role. The respondents said, in effect, "When I sense that I am having difficulty with a teacher because I am perceived as a threat, I become helpless. I feel inadequate."

Though no claim is made for the exhaustiveness of our research, it seems clear that the data do provide a view of supervision through the eyes of the two most important beholders of that world. The view is somewhat cloudy. It suggests that we know things that we are not acting on and, in a congruent fashion, that the people involved let the system carry itself, but no one knows where. While this is not a pleasant prospect, it is still better that this particular world become known, rather than remain hidden.

10 Analyzing Supervisor-Teacher Interaction

Accurate descriptions of any interactive phenomena that are based solely on perceptual data are, by definition, incomplete. Thus, with our studies of teachers' and supervisors' perceptions of supervision, the questions remain: How do supervisors and teachers actually behave toward one another? And, will an objective view of interaction between supervisors and teachers lend credence to some of the inferences we have made?

A great deal of attention has been paid by educators in recent years to understanding the interaction between teachers and pupils in the classroom. The notion behind this concern is that, by studying interaction between teachers and pupils, it will be possible to gain a better understanding of classroom life and enable teachers to do a better job.

For whatever reason—perhaps because of the "taken for granted," somewhat ephemeral place of supervision within the school system— there has been relatively little interest in, or energy expended on, trying systematically to understand the interactive world of the supervisor and teacher. We know of only three category systems, besides ours, that deal with the problem (Weller, 1971). The behavioral category system described here is based on the Flanders model (1960) for analyzing classroom interaction.* Conceptually,

---

* The reader may find this chapter quite detailed and a bit out of context with the preceding chapters. I include it for two reasons. First, an understanding of the category system is a necessary prelude to understanding and interpreting the data presented in Chapter 11. Second, consultation with colleagues and students (who are supervisors) indicated that a detailed description of the system is useful for it enables a supervisor to get a systematic view of his behavior and can thus provide a basis for change.

there are no problems in making the transfer from the classroom to the supervisory scene. Any situation in which people are interacting face to face is amenable to behavioral analysis by categories appropriate to it. Once the goals of the projected interaction are stated, it should be possible to deduce the kinds of information needed to understand it better.

A SYSTEM FOR ANALYZING SUPERVISOR-TEACHER INTERACTION*

The superordinate goal of supervisory relationships is the improvement of education. This suggests that supervisor-teacher interaction is a social system that exists in order to create change in the teacher's ability to deal with the problems of teaching more adequately. An implication of this idea is that help is given by the supervisor (the authority figure and expert) and is utilized by the teacher. Taking this one step further, an assumption can be made that the goals of supervision will be best met under conditions where, other things being equal, there is a high degree of communicative freedom existing between the parties involved.

An interaction system that is concerned with the supervisor and teacher, then, should offer its users, minimally, information about:

1. How change efforts are made (i.e., how help is offered);
2. The relative supportiveness or defensiveness of communication.

It should also be able to reflect:

1. How the supervisor's behavior affects the teacher;
2. How the supervisor reacts to the behavior of the teacher.

The supervisor-teacher interaction system that is presented in this [chapter] has fifteen categories. Of these fifteen, ten are concerned with the behavior of the supervisor; four with that of the teacher; and one indicates silence or confusion. It may seem that too much consideration is being given to the supervisor's behavior. Such is not the case. The reason for including a sharper delineation of the behavior of the supervisor is that, hierarchically, he is the person in the social system who has more influence and control. It is his behavior, not that of the teacher, and the manner in which

* I am grateful to the copyright holders for permission to reprint my contribution, "A System for Analyzing Supervision-Teacher Interaction," in *Mirrors for Behavior, VIII,* edited by Anita Simon and E. Gil Boyer (Philadelphia: Research for Better Schools, Inc., 1970), pp. 34.1-1 to 34.1-15.

he reacts to the teacher that [are] primarily responsible for setting the emotional tone and communicative atmosphere of the situation. Therefore, it makes sense to try and learn more about his behavior in this setting than it does to get more detailed about the teacher. The corollary of this is seen in the Flanders system where, out of ten categories, seven are devoted to the teacher and only two to the pupils. (One is concerned with silence.)

Supervisor Behavior

Category 1. *Support-inducing communications behavior.* This category includes all statements on the part of the supervisor, with the exception of praise, the effect of which is to help build a "healthy" climate between him and the teacher. Behavior that releases tension is in this category, as is that which conveys an acceptance of feelings. Encouragement is categorized here.

Category 2. *Praise.* This is behavior on the part of the supervisor that connotes primarily the value judgment of "good" in connection with a teacher's idea, plan of action, past behavior, feelings, etc.

Category 3. *Accepts or uses teacher's ideas.* Included here are statements that clarify, build on, or develop ideas or suggestions by a teacher.

Category 4. *Asks for information.* This is behavior by the supervisor that is aimed at asking for clarification or orientation about a problem or situation under consideration. It is factually oriented and is not concerned with opinions or ways of doing things.

Category 5. *Giving information.* This is the opposite of Category 4. It involves the supervisor giving objective information to the teacher, orienting, summarizing, etc.

Category 6. *Asks for opinions.* This category is meant to describe supervisor behavior, the aim of which is to ask the teacher to analyze or evaluate something that has occurred, is occurring, or may occur in the classroom or in the interaction taking place.

Category 7. *Asks for suggestions.* In this category are statements by the supervisor that ask the teacher to think about ways of doing things or ways in which things might have been done differently. It has an action orientation, past, present, or future. Category 7 also refers to asking for ways in which the supervisor and teacher might work together.

Category 8. *Gives opinions.* This category is the opposite of Category 6. It has the same substantive meaning with the exception that the supervisor is "giving" not "asking."

Category 9. *Gives suggestions.* In a like manner as Category 8, this one has the opposite meaning as 7. The difference is in the "giving" instead of "asking."

Category 10. *Criticism.* This category includes all negative value judgments about the teacher, his behavior in the classroom, any behavior on the part of the supervisor that can be interpreted as defensive, aggressive, or tension producing.

Teacher Behavior

Category 11. *Asks for information, opinions, or suggestions.* This is task-oriented behavior on the part of the teacher. It is the teacher-counterpart of Categories 4, 6, and 7.

Category 12. *Gives information, opinions, or suggestions.* This category, similar to Category 11, is the teacher-counterpart to Categories 5, 8, and 9.

Category 13. *Positive social-emotional behavior.* This behavior is described in the same way as that in Category 1. It is not task oriented and helps build the supervisory relationship. Encouragement would probably not be found as constituting very much in the way of a teacher's repertoire in this category. Statements that convey agreement by choice are part of this category, but those that indicate compliance in the face of supervisor power are not.

Category 14. *Negative social-emotional behavior.* Any behavior on the part of the teacher that tends to disrupt the supervisory relationship, produce tension, or convey defensiveness on his part is part of this category. Compliance in the face of supervisory power is defined as defensiveness, as is rationalization.

Category 15. *Silence or confusion.* This category is used when there is silence or both supervisor and teacher are talking at the same time so that it becomes impossible to categorize behavior specifically. An exception would be when there is silence after a behavior on the part of either supervisor or teacher that seems to have the effect of producing defensiveness (either Category 10 or 14, depending [upon the person] at whom the original behavior was aimed).

Readers who are familiar with the work of Flanders (1960) or that of Bales (1951) will recognize that this system combines some ideas from each. Two primary reasons influenced the decision to make this combination. First, Flanders does not provide all the kinds of information that are necessary to get into the supervisory situation. Yet, he does specify certain categories that are not made discreet by Bales, and his method of recording and interpretation is seen as more usable for present purposes than is Bales's. On the other hand, the Bales system focuses more on problem-solving processes and behavior than does Flanders', and problem solving is seen as the essence of supervision. So, the combination was made.

Procedures for Using the System

Recording. This system has been designed to help supervisors get some insights into their behavior and its effects in the course of their interaction with teachers. Unlike the use of the Flanders system in the classroom, however, it is not expected that an observer will record the interaction. Therefore, a tape recorder is a necessary adjunct to the scheme of things.

After the supervisory interview is completed, the supervisor replays the tape by himself (or, if he feels free enough, he might want to have the teacher listen with him). He tallies the interaction in the following manner: every three seconds he records, in column form, the category number of the verbal behavior that is occurring at the moment. (Obviously this implies learning the system and committing the categories, though not their complete definitions, to memory, so that "thinking in numbers" becomes automatic.) If, at first, he finds that three seconds is too short an interval for him to keep up with, he can spread his tallies to four or five seconds and then, as he becomes more familiar with the system, increase the tempo. He will probably want to stop the tape recorder from time to time to make sure that he is tallying correctly. This need will occur particularly at moments of rapid-fire interaction. The supervisor may also want to make occasional marginal notes concerning the content themes that are being discussed.

The question of reliability of observations is one of continuing concern. The issue is whether or not, when two people are tallying the same interaction, they hear the same things. It is possible to train people to be highly reliable in their recording, but a good bit of practice is needed. Here are some ground rules that are helpful to follow:

1. View each act as a response to the last act of the other person or as an anticipation of the next act of the other. The point is that we are dealing with sequentially related behavior and not that which occurs in isolation. Operationally, this means that interaction is recorded from the point of view of the recipient of the behavior, not the giver. This is so because we are interested in recording the *effects* of behavior, not the intentions of the person behaving.

2. Difficulty is apt to arise in differentiating behavior in the following categories: 1 and 2, 6 and 7, 8, 9, and 10, and 13 and 14. (In the latter three categories problems arise when the person who is recording is not sure whether or not the teacher's behavior is agreement on a positive level or compliance.) In such cases the ground rule is, after replaying the sequence to understand the context, choose the lower-numbered category of those that are in question. In other words, if it is in doubt whether a behavior is a 6 or a 7, choose 6.

3. If more than one category occurs during the three-second interval, then all categories used in that interval are recorded; conversely, record each change in category. If no change occurs in three seconds, repeat the previous category number.

4. The use of "Ohh-h" or "Hm" by itself is taken to be encouragement and is in category 1. When "Uh-huh" is followed by a rephrasing or use of the teacher's idea, it is in Category 3.

5. Start and end the tallying with a "15"—silence. This is done for two reasons. First, it is assumed that the conference begins and ends in silence. Second, by including the "15," it is possible to ensure that the total number of tallies in the rows and columns of the matrix will balance.

Transferring the Tallies to a Matrix. This system, similar to Flanders', makes use of a matrix onto which pairs of tallies are transferred in order to analyze and interpret the interaction in a meaningful way. The only difference between the mechanics of the two systems is that this one makes use of a 15 x 15 cell matrix whereas the Flanders matrix is 10 x 10. Otherwise, the procedure is exactly the same. It involves considering the tallies in pairs, because this indicates the sequence of behavior, and finding the appropriate cell in the matrix to insert the tally. This is done by thinking of the first number in a pair as the "row" number and the second as the "column" number. The appropriate cell is that where the row and the column meet.

In order to clarify this procedure, a brief part of a supervisory interview will be repeated below, tallied, and then put on a matrix. The situation involves a principal in conference with a third-grade teacher a day after having observed a reading lesson. The conference begins:

Principal: "I'd like to discuss with you, briefly, the two reading groups I observed yesterday."

A 5 is recorded, giving of orientation.

Teacher: "Uh-huh."

A 13 is recorded. Teacher agrees with orientation.

Principal: "The first group was your top group. Is that right?"

Record a 5 and a 4.

Teacher: "That's right."

Record a 12.

Principal: "And there were seven children there, but altogether you have how many?"

Record a 5 and a 4.

Teacher: "Nine."

Record a 12.

Principal: "Nine?"

Record a 3.

Teacher: "Uh-huh."

Record a 12.

Principal: "I know the time wasn't good—2:15 . . . . It's not a real good time to visit."

Record two 1's.

Teacher: "Well, we were running a little late and . . . uh . . . we had just completed reading a story and with the questions along . . . page by page, and, uh, the summation was where you came in."

Record four 12's.

Principal: "I thought the session was good because . . . ."

Record a 2 and an 8.

From this bit of interaction, the following sequence of numbers— each indicating a behavioral category—is tallied:

$$\binom{5}{13}$$
$$\binom{5}{4}$$
$$\binom{12}{5}$$
$$\binom{4}{12}$$
$$\binom{3}{12}$$
$$\binom{1}{1}$$
$$\binom{12}{12}$$
$$\binom{12}{12}$$
$$\binom{2}{8}$$

Linking the pairs of tallies together, as has been done in the above example, is an operation that is undertaken after all the tallies have been made and, as has been noted, this linkage is performed in order to denote the sequence of interaction and to enable tallies to be put on the matrix [see Figure 10.1]. In order to help the reader understand how this is done, it will be helpful to refer to the matrix . . . as the process is explained. Note that the first pair of tallies in the interaction sequence is 5-13. The appropriate cell for this pair is found by going across row 5 until it intersects column 13. A "hash" mark is put in this cell, which means that there has been one behavioral sequence of the nature of 5-13. The next pair is 13-5. The same procedure is used to record this on the matrix, and a mark is found in the row 13, column 5 cell. The complete sequence of interaction is thus recorded in Figure 10.1.

Analysis and Interpretation of the Supervisor-Teacher Interaction Matrix

It is possible to derive both quantitative and qualitative information from the matrix. The first step in analysis is a quantitative one. That is, it may be of interest, for example, to find out how much of the time of the interaction is taken up by the supervisor and how much

FIGURE 10.1 Supervisor-Teacher Interaction Matrix

	1	2	3	4	5	6	7	8	9	10	11	12	13	14	15	T
1	/											/				
2								/								
3												/				
4												//				
5				//									/			
6																
7																
8																
9																
10																
11																
12	/	/	/		/							///				
13				/												
14																
15																
T																
%																

by the teacher. Further, it would be valuable for the supervisor to know how much of his time is spent in one kind of behavior as compared to another.

In order to obtain these data, the following steps are taken:

1. Add all the tallies in the rows and columns and put the total in the "T" cell at the end of each row or column. Then, sum the "T" rows and columns. These sums should be the same and give a figure which is the grand total of all the tallies in the matrix.

2. Using the grand total, it is then possible to figure the percentage of time the supervisor has used by dividing the total number of supervisor tallies by the grand total. Obviously, it is also possible to find out, on a percentage basis, how much of his time he spends

on specific behaviors by simply dividing the total for the behavior in question by the total number of supervisor tallies.

For example, supposing the supervisor wants to know the amount of emphasis that he places on trying directly to influence the teacher without criticism (Categories 8 and 9) relative to the emphasis he puts on trying to get the teacher to come up with his own answer to a problem (Categories 6 and 7). He divides the sum of columns 8 and 9 into the sum of columns 6 and 7. This would give him a ratio similar to Flanders's I/D ratio. If the ratio was 1, it would be an indication that he expends about equal effort in both areas. If it was .5, the suggestion would be that he spends about twice as much time trying to tell the teacher what to do or think as he does trying to ask the teacher for his ideas about the problem under discussion. Contrariwise, if the ratio is 2, the interpretation would be the opposite. In a similar manner, ratios may be obtained for other categories or groups of them.

In addition to the kind of information just mentioned, a wealth of other types of data may be gotten by examining particular cells or groups of cells in the matrix. Analysis of this type will provide some insights into how the supervisor uses his behavior by shifting from one category to another, how the teacher reacts to various kinds of supervisor behavior, and what kinds of supervisor behavior are elicited by teacher responses.

Reference to Figure 10.2 will be helpful at this point. It will be noted that the blank matrix is divided into different areas. An explanation of these areas follows: Areas A, B, C, D, E, and F are called "steady state" areas of behavior. A heavy concentration in any of these indicates that the supervisor is making extended use of a particular kind of behavior. Such concentrations might be expressed as interactive "concerns" and can be interpreted as follows:

A heavy loading in:	*Indicates a "concern" for:*
A	Building and maintaining interpersonal relationships
B	Utilization of the teacher's ideas
C	Working on the informational data level [that is, concerned with nonevaluative information]
D	Working on the opinion data level [that is, concerned with evaluative information]
E	Methodology and/or control
F	Controlling the teacher's behavior

FIGURE 10.2   Matrix for Interaction between Supervisor and
                     Teacher Showing Steady State Cells

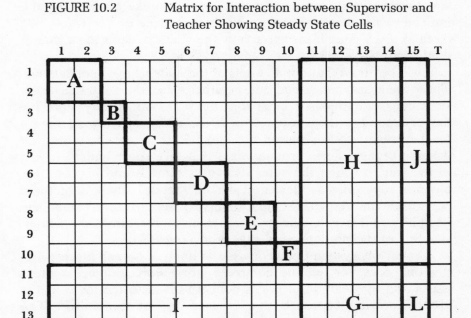

Area G shows the amount of extended teacher talk that occurs in the conference. A concentration here would show that the teacher takes a good bit of the time with his questions, answers, agreements, or disagreements.

Tallies in Area H give information about how the teacher reacts to the supervisor's behavior. And, on the other side of the coin, Area I produces data concerning the manner in which the supervisor reacts to the teacher. For example, a tally in the 9-13 cell indicates that the teacher reacts to the supervisor's suggestion in a positive way; one in the 9-14 cell suggests a negative reaction. Similarly, a tally in the 12-2 cell says that the supervisor reacts with praise to the teacher's idea, opinion, etc., while a tally in the 12-10 cell means that the supervisor reacts critically.

Area J indicates the nature of supervisor behavior which tends to produce silence or confusion, and Area K shows the way the supervisor reacts to silence or confusion. In a like manner, Area L indicates what teacher behavior produces silence or confusion, and Area M gives some ideas about how the teacher reacts to silence or confusion.

It will be noted that not all areas of the matrix have been labeled. These are areas that extend out, in either direction, from the steady state cells of supervisor behavior. They are not steady state behaviors; nor are they interactive in the sense of showing how a teacher reacts to supervisor behavior. Rather, the patterns that develop in these areas produce data that give some understanding of the way in which the supervisor uses himself and his total behavioral repertoire as measured by this system. Analysis of these parts of the matrix would help a supervisor see, to some extent, the flexibility of his behavior and would also give him some understanding of the predominant ways he makes use of self.

As with any system that is devised to analyze human interaction, this one does not tell the complete story. For example, content issues are not dealt with; nor is concern given to the logic of the problem-solving approach that is used by the supervisor. The notion—pure and simple—is to try and produce reliable data that will help supervisors and teachers understand the behavioral implications of their interaction better.

11   The Realities of Interaction

This chapter takes the abstractness of the previous one and brings it down to earth. That is, our concern was to use the category system to inquire into and describe what might be called the objective reality of supervisor-teacher interaction — or as close as we could come to it. Our discussion and interpretations are based on four assumptions:

1. When a supervisor and teacher interact, they are both participants in a temporary social system intended to improve the teacher's teaching ability.
2. Their interaction consists in the supervisor's giving help and the teacher's receiving and using this help.
3. The supervisory process works best when both parties consider it to be collaborative problem solving.
4. A collaborative situation develops best when the parties have a high degree of communicative freedom.

Implicit in these assumptions is a model of supervision at variance with traditional concepts of relationships between authorities and subordinates that have, apparently, been transferred intact from scientific management to education. These traditional concepts suggest that the superior (supervisor), by virtue of certain — but vaguely defined — innate qualities and training, knows best how the

The bulk of this chapter is adapted, by permission, from A. Blumberg and P. Cusick, "Supervisor-Teacher Interaction: An Analysis of Verbal Behavior," *Education*, 91 (November 1969): 126-134.

job should be done. The worker (teacher) has simply to follow the suggestions and directions of the supervisor and a better job (teaching) will result. This point of view would be compatible, more or less, with Theory X (McGregor, 1960). The concept upon which we base *our* assumptions would be more closely aligned to McGregor's Theory Y, which suggests, in part, that more effective work will result as the people involved, including those at different hierarchical levels, conceive of themselves as collaborators in a common problem-solving effort.

The collaborative concept of supervision takes on added importance when consideration is given to the work technology of teaching, which may be typed as single-unit or small-batch technology (Woodward, 1958). This is the type of work in which a person or a small group of people have the major responsibility for planning, operating, and evaluating what is done. Certainly this describes most teaching. A critical implication of this idea for educational supervision is that the supervisor is confronted with the problem of influencing a situation in which he has a minimal amount of power to control the manner in which his attempts at influence are implemented. For example, he cannot be in the classroom all the time to see that the teacher is doing what has been suggested or directed. So, for a supervisor to be effective, he would have to work with a teacher in such a manner that the teacher sees him as a source of help and is willing to test the results of their work together in the classroom. Obviously, we are dealing with a complex set of relationships which, in our judgment, have been grossly oversimplified in education.

PROCEDURES

For the study we analyzed tape recordings of fifty conferences between supervisors and teachers. Our subjects were graduate students who were either teachers or supervisors. As can be imagined, these kinds of data are not easily collected. Supervisors seem reluctant to have their conferences recorded, and teachers seem to be reluctant to ask. Because of this, we did not have a random sample. The recordings were analyzed by the interaction system discussed in the previous chapter. Each conference was tallied onto a separate matrix and a composite made from these formed the basis of our findings.

RESULTS

Figure 11.1 is the composite matrix of the fifty conferences. Because we did not have a random sample, the words "supervisors" and "teachers" will apply only to those who were part of the study. Reference to the model matrix (Figure 10.2) will help in the interpretation of this figure.

The total interaction time indicated on the composite matrix is 11 hours and 18 minutes, the average for each conference being 13.5 minutes, the range being between 2 and 39 minutes. Supervisors were talking 45 percent of the time; teachers, 53 percent. The remaining 2 percent of the time was spent in silence or a state of confusion.

Supervisors gave information slightly more than five times as often as they asked for it—a ratio of .18 (column 4 divided by column 5). Supervisors tended to be more direct than indirect by about one-third—a ratio of .65 (columns 1, 2, 3, 4, 6, and 7 divided by columns 5, 8, 9, and 10).

While talking, supervisors spent 10 percent of the time in positive and 5 percent of the time in negative social-emotional behavior. In interacting with teachers, supervisors spent approximately twice as much time inducing positive as negative emotionality—a ratio of 1.9 (columns 1 and 2 divided by column 10).

The ratio of telling to asking, in what might be conceived of as problem-solving behavior was 2.8 (columns 4, 6, and 7 divided by columns 5, 8, and 9); in task-oriented behavior, supervisors appeared to be weighted about 4:1 in favor of telling. Supervisors asked opinions of the teachers about one and a half times more often than they gave opinions—a ratio of 1.58 (column 6 divided by column 8). Approximately seven times as much time was spent by the supervisor in telling the teacher what to do as was devoted to asking the teacher for his ideas or suggestions for action—a ratio of 15 (column 7 divided by column 9).

The loadings in the steady state areas of the matrix were:

Area A— 50 percent
Area B— 10 percent
Area C— 63 percent
Area D— 38 percent
Area E— 63 percent
Area F— 72 percent

FIGURE 11.1

Composite Matrix of Fifty Conferences Between Supervisors and Teachers

	1	2	3	4	5	6	7	8	9	10	11	12	13	14	15	T
1	15	8	0	5	27	2	0	0	0	0	2	33	21	3	6	122
2	2	273	1	11	70	13	0	7	3	9	1	45	35	1	4	475
3	2	13	67	22	77	10	1	10	7	3	2	436	10	26	12	698
4	0	3	0	153	36	6	0	0	1	0	6	277	4	28	13	527
5	8	94	7	113	1892	81	10	36	37	38	20	463	116	11	39	2965
6	2	2	0	6	40	162	0	3	2	1	8	159	13	12	15	425
7	0	0	0	0	5	1	16	1	0	0	1	21	1	0	0	46
8	0	3	0	2	37	9	2	151	10	6	1	32	5	2	2	262
9	1	3	0	4	35	3	0	1	194	1	0	42	10	4	4	302
10	1	2	0	7	19	2	0	1	3	225	2	19	2	24	5	312
11	3	1	5	0	32	3	1	0	0	1	20	10	1	2	3	82
12	38	54	572	163	530	101	15	43	37	10	14	4752	12	26	57	6424
13	20	14	13	4	93	8	0	4	5	0	2	49	24	1	19	256
14	4	2	32	31	10	15	1	2	2	17	2	26	0	299	15	458
15	26	3	1	6	62	9	0	3	1	1	1	60	2	20	27	222
T	122	475	698	527	2965	425	46	262	302	312	82	6424	256	459	221	13577
%	1	3	5	4	22	3	.04	2	2	2	.06	48	2	3	2	

Source: A. Blumberg and P. Cusick, "Supervisor-Teacher Interaction: An Analysis of Verbal Behavior," *Education*, 91 (October 1970): 132.

These loadings mean that, of the time a supervisor spent on positive social-emotional behavior, one-half was of an extended nature, which means he evinced the behavior for more than just a brief moment (Area A); of the time spent on reflecting on and clarifying teachers' ideas, 10 percent was of an extended nature (Area B); on giving or asking for information, almost two-thirds was of an extended nature (Area C); on asking for opinions or suggestions, about one-third was of an extended nature, and most of that was spent in asking for opinions, not making suggestions (Area D); on giving opinions or suggestions, almost two-thirds was of an extended nature (Area E); on exhibiting negative social-emotional behavior, mostly criticism, almost three-quarters was of an extended nature (Area F).

Less than 1 percent of the supervisor's time (the total of column 7) was spent in asking the teacher for actual suggestions. This was the behavior supervisors used least. The behavior teachers used least was that of asking supervisors any kind of question at all. This category occurred slightly more than 1 percent of the time (the total of column 11).

A more detailed analysis of the matrix indicated that the supervisors' behavior that evoked the most negative reaction was that of asking for information (cell 4-14). The next most negative reaction came from that of reflecting or clarifying ideas (cell 3-14). It appears that supervisors tend not to deal with a teacher's negative feelings in a manner that helps clarify those feelings. Cell 14-1 indicates that the supervisors accepted or clarified negative social-emotional behavior in the teachers less than 3 percent of the time.

SOME SUBJECTIVE REFLECTIONS

The category system focuses only on behavior, not content. The behavior of supervisors and teachers cannot be fully understood unless one is aware of what they are interacting about. An analysis of the content of the tapes yielded a number of impressions. A teacher's legitimate complaints or gripes tended not to be dealt with directly by the supervisor, who, more often than not, tended to agree that the complaint was indeed legitimate. In no case, when a supervisor gave some advice or admonition to a teacher, did the teacher ask, "Why?" Almost all the discussion was about maintenance procedures: schedules, correcting papers, lining youngsters up, being in the classroom when the pupils arrive, and so forth. When teachers became defensive, the supervisor declined to deal with the defensiveness. Key words or phrases such as "discipline," "homework," "good response," "behavioral problem," or "poor home conditions" seemed to serve as discussion. Untested common assumptions about the meaning of such words enabled the participants to close conferences without ever discussing the issues. Supervisors seemed to ask pat questions; teachers responded with pat answers. One felt that supervisors and teachers were all playing roles, for rarely did they appear to be people.

The data give rise to a number of questions about the nature of interaction between supervisors and teachers, about supervisors' styles of solving problems, about the productivity of supervision, and about the assumptions that underlie it. Interaction between supervisors and teachers seems to be pretty much a matter of instruction, with the supervisor spending most of his time giving information. He also expends a fair amount of energy inducing a positive social-emotional climate, albeit through the use of praise. the effectiveness of which has been questioned (Herzberg, 1967). One might ask, "Positive social-emotional climate for what?" It appears that action following the interaction of supervisors and teachers is minimal. Only 2.5 percent of the supervisor's behavior, for example, is devoted to action (total of columns 7 and 9).

But perhaps more important is that supervisors apparently seldom ask teachers for ideas about action or problem solving, with the result that teachers are not engaged by the supervisor in trying to solve problems they face in the classroom. The interaction does not appear to be collaborative. The lack of collaboration is reinforced when one considers the teachers' behavior. Much as the supervisor does not ask the teacher questions, so the teacher rarely asks a question of the supervisor—perhaps because people do not ask questions of those whom they perceive to be unhelpful. This damning interpretation is supported by the studies described earlier. When teachers consider their supervision to be productive, the particular behavioral styles of the supervisors are different from the data indicated in the matrix (Blumberg and Amidon, 1965), in that the supervisor appears to engage the teacher in solving the problem and communicates some real sense of understanding the teacher.

An interesting clue to the supervisor's understanding of the teacher is provided by Area B on the matrix, the steady state cell related to Category 3, the acceptance and clarifying of the teacher's ideas. Of the total time supervisors spend in this behavior, it appears that they use only 10 percent in an extended manner, which suggests that 90 percent of the time they are giving short responses, such as "I see" or "Uh-huh," and only a small part of the time do they really attempt to clarify with something like, "What you're saying is . . .," or "As it comes across to me, the problem is . . . ." This may seem a minor matter; actually, it is not. One must differentiate between the all-purpose "I understand" and the response that helps both parties clarify the ideas that have been expressed.

We mentioned that the behavior of the supervisor evoking the most negative reaction (both absolutely and proportionately) was that of asking for information (cell 4-14). Why do teachers tend to react to requests for information in a defensive manner? The most obvious answer is that, even though the supervisor may intend his question to be just that—a search for information—fairly often the teacher will see it in a different light, for example, as an attempt by the supervisor to "box him in," even though no such thing was intended. One wonders if supervisory confrontation is oriented toward collaborative helping, negative evaluation, domination by a superior, or another direction. Certainly, our data raise the question.

We have also noted how supervisors deal with negative social and emotional behavior in the teacher. We found little evidence of a "therapeutic" response—3 percent (cell 14-1). By contrast, negativism in the teacher met negativism in the supervisor 13 percent of the time (cell 14-10)—an attitude of "fighting fire with fire." The other responses (except for somewhat mysterious praise in cell 14-2) are rationally oriented, which suggests that perhaps the supervisor does not realize that the behavior is negative, he prefers not to deal with it as such, he is unskilled and uncomfortable in dealing with it, or he deals with it by trying to reason with the teacher.

We must be cautious about making generalizations from this study. Only fifty conferences were analyzed, and the behavior varied from case to case. But the images of both process and content that developed seem to reinforce many of the inferences we drew from our research on the perceptions and cross-perceptions that supervisors and teachers have of their own and one another's behavior.

We are led to question the ultimate productivity of interaction between supervisors and teachers. Neither party apparently wants these interactions, and both parties would like to disengage as soon as possible. This statement does go beyond the data, but the feeling, corroborated by other research, persists. This is not to say that supervisors and teachers are incapable of changing their patterns of interaction. There is, however, a possibility that supervisors' insights into, and skills to deal with, interpersonal relations are inadequate for a helping relationship. It is also possible that, if available at all, the training provided for supervisors by school systems is inadequate or that supervisors are selected without regard to the behavioral demands of the job. More than likely, it is a combination of all three.

Many supervisors and professors who teach courses in supervision will not like what they have just read. It is not easy to confront negative feedback about one's efforts. Do not despair. The methodology of this study—the systematic observation, recording and analysis of behavior—carries with it the seeds of a model for training and feedback that could help change supervisors' behavior. For such training, school systems would have to be committed, as few of them are—probably because they can see no necessity for it—to make the change. This lack of commitment, too, could change.

12 A Data Base for Supervisors

A long-prevalent view of American society, relative to changing and improving our way of life, might be entitled "the mousetrap concept." The point is simple. If someone can build a better mouse-trap, as efficient and economical as the one that has been used for years, it will make the old one obsolete, which means that it will not be used. This view is extremely rationalistic and mechanistic. It assumes that, when people have access to resources they did not have previously and if these resources help them do things better, those resources will be used. This is, after all, the reasonable thing to do.

It is the "mousetrap" view of the world that seems to have had the most impact in applied science and technology. New ideas and ways of doing things are constantly being substituted for older ones. But when attempts are made to transfer it to the arena of human affairs, the concept tends to fail rather badly. Witness the countless educational innovations that have been developed over the past twenty years or so—the new math, for example. And witness their fate (Sarason, 1971). Witness, further, the testimony of many, perhaps most, supervisors that their curriculum and teaching expertise are rarely used to the full. The rationalistic and mechanistic assumptions implicit in the mousetrap concept simply do not hold water as they attempt to work with teachers. Other factors, distinctly human ones, are at work affecting the extent to which a supervisor's resources are used.

It seems to me that primary among these other factors is his

concept of his job and the understandings about human relationships that flow from that concept, and not, for example, whether he
happens to be an expert on the teaching of science. From the idea
that the supervisor's concept of his job is critical to how fully his
resources are used by teachers, stem the following hypotheses. The
supervisor's resources will best be used by the teacher to the extent
that the supervisor understands that his job involves a creative mix
of interpersonal and task orientations that will be different for each
teacher with whom he interacts; that interpersonal factors probably
take precedence over task factors, at least at the initial point of
entry into the teacher's system; that in trying to help the teacher he
is really dealing with two sets of relationships—the first that between the supervisor and the teacher and the second that between
the teacher and the students; and that technology and techniques,
though important, are less important in the relationship than the
foregoing elements. Relative to the focus of this chapter, these
hypotheses suggest that the supervisor needs information about
himself, about the teacher, about the teacher's behavior in the classroom, and about the students' behavior.

INFORMATION ABOUT HIMSELF

There are several types of information about the supervisor,
himself, that bear on his ability to establish a working relationship
with a teacher and to help him, including information about his
interpersonal needs, the manner in which he reacts to the behavior
of others, his ability to recognize when he is in conflict and how he
handles conflict, and his own levels of competence. These categories
of information focus on the two main functions that need to be
performed in any situation in which problems are to be solved.
These functions are generally conceived to be those of group
building and maintenance and performance of the task (Benne and
Sheats, 1948). The first three information categories noted obviously
are concerned with group building and maintenance, and the fourth
category, with the task. The theoretical position is that, if productive
group or interpersonal problem solving involves enacting both
types of behavior when appropriate, the supervisor needs information about himself that may affect his ability to enact these behaviors.

The Supervisor's Interpersonal Needs

A rather thorough theoretical and empirical formulation of interpersonal needs was developed by Schutz (1958). His research indicated that, in our relationships with other people, we all need varying degrees of affection, control, and inclusion. Schutz suggests that these needs exist in an "expressed" and a "wanted" form. I have a certain level of need to express affection and warmth toward other people, and I also have a particular need to receive affection and warmth from others. The same holds true for control and inclusion.

For the supervisor, an active awareness of the level of his interpersonal needs is not simply an academic exercise or a matter of intellectual curiosity. To the contrary, these needs affect both the ways in which one wishes to behave toward others and the kinds of behavior one feels most comfortable in receiving from others. For the supervisor, they affect his desire and ability to help a teacher. By way of example, I happen to know that I have relatively high needs both to express affection toward others and to receive it from them, by sharing my feelings of warmth and receiving the same. My need to control others is quite low, and the need to be controlled or directed by others is very low. My need to include others and be included by them is moderate. This configuration of interpersonal needs clearly affects both my desire and ability to work with people, most specifically, in my case, doctoral students working on dissertations—a very clear case of supervision. I think I do my best job with those students with whom I can share my feelings of warmth if I have them, with those students who do not depend on me greatly for detailed direction and control and who do not need to control me, and with those students who are willing to work with me and who seek to involve me in their work. My problems center mostly on the control dimension. I become irritated and less helpful to a student when he demands more direction than I am comfortable giving him. I am aware that some students have chosen not to work with me because we were relatively incompatible, and others have chosen to work with me on the basis of our compatibility. All this is not to say that the needs I have are good and the needs of those with whom I am incompatible are bad. It is simply a fact of life and an important one.

There are differences between the supervisor's work with a

teacher and my work with doctoral students. I can refuse to deal with a student, but a supervisor would have great difficulty refusing to help a particular teacher. The supervisor must, therefore, be aware of his needs so that he can recognize the kinds of interpersonal situations with teachers that will give him trouble. It would be impossible to make the teacher's needs compatible with his, so he should be aware of his interpersonal needs so as to be able to deal with himself in relating to a teacher who is potentially or actually incompatible. Instead of feeling vaguely uncomfortable for a reason he cannot pinpoint, he should be able to locate the reason. He does not have to develop smoke screens for his feelings and behavior, but can deal with them directly. He does not, for example, need to feel angry because "that teacher resists my help" when the real issue may be that his high need to control is incompatible with the teacher's need not to be controlled. The more insight a supervisor has into his own need to give and receive, the better able he becomes to deal with whatever basic problem he may have with a teacher rather than with its symptoms.

Data on his interpersonal needs are easier to come by than one might suspect. One rather casual, but perhaps quite adequate, way to collect such information is by introspection and self-analysis. "Honestly, now," asks the supervisor of himself, "in working with a teacher, do I feel most comfortable when I am directing things or when I let the teacher take control of the situation?" "Does it typically make me feel good when my boss spells out my job functions specifically or when he leaves things very loose?" "Does it make me feel tense to think about becoming close to someone, and how do I feel about the prospect of others becoming close to me?" "How important is it for me to have others work with me on projects I initiate, and how important is it to me that others include me in work they are doing?" Such questions might not be very sophisticated, but they will be adequate, particularly if the supervisor is able to share his thoughts with another person who knows him well.

Another way for a supervisor to collect data about his interpersonal needs requires a bit of outside help, but it is quick. He can take an interpersonal needs inventory. The inventory I have in mind is Fundamental Interpersonal Relations Orientation—Behavior (FIRO—B) (Schutz, 1958), which requires only about ten minutes to complete and score, but should be discussed afterward with whoever administers it.

A third way to get information about one's interpersonal needs is to take part in a sensitivity training or encounter group. This is time consuming but potentially enriching. It can help a supervisor learn not only about his needs, but also about his behavior and its effects on others.

Reactions

A supervisor would also do well to learn about his reactions to the behavior of other people—specifically, what, in other people, influences him to want to move toward another, to collaborate with and help him; or to move away from another, to avoid working with him; or to move against another, to fight him. (The concepts of moving toward, away from, and against other people are taken from Horney, *Our Inner Conflicts* [1945].) Again, I use myself as an example, although the reader might learn much from making his own list.

I move toward people when:
They are willing to argue with me.
They share feelings with me.
They are excited about and pursue their ideas, even if I disagree with them.
They are willing to experiment with new ideas.
They deal with me more as a person and less as a professor.
They are able to see absurdity and and to laugh at some parts of of life.
They are willing to work with me.
They can take ideas and "run with them."
They can laugh at themselves and their mistakes.
They initiate projects that involve me as a participant.

I move away from people or fight them when:
They beat around the bush or do not level with me.
They deal only on a rational level and refuse to work on emotional issues.
They become highly dependent on me.
They place my status as a professor in the way of our dealing with each other as two people.
They do not laugh.
Their behavior says "teach me," but they are not willing to teach *me*.
They do not commit themselves to a project in which they say they are interested.
They are not willing to take risks with new ideas.
They let me overpower them.
They take life so seriously that it is hard for me to laugh when I am with them.

On looking back over what I have written (and I did not consciously set out to develop two lists of ten items) I notice some clear relationships between my interpersonal needs and these reactions, expecially reactions influenced by my needs for control and affection. I found it interesting that, while I am pleased when someone involves me in what he is doing, I am not necessarily displeased when he does not.

I also notice, although I did not plan it this way, many opposites in the two lists. In a sense, then, I set up a number of polar experiences to which, spontaneously, I react positively or negatively. Because the reactions are spontaneous, it seems that they represent a good part of my interpersonal value system. I value intellectual disagreement, emotional honesty, risk taking, and fun. I value relationships in which I can be myself and in which others can be what they are. I do not value situations in which I am forced to be the professor by the other person, when I feel too powerful, when there is emotional dishonesty, and when people are closed or secretive.

The point of that digression into my own value system is to show the sort of awareness of oneself that is fairly easily attained and can serve as a self-monitoring device. The concept of self-monitoring is critically important, if for no other reason than to answer the question, "Who supervises and helps the supervisor?" The most typical response is, "No one." The supervisor must somehow help himself. (Self-monitoring is rather a lonely, if necessary, process. A supervisor could get outside help by asking the teacher also to assess what is going on interpersonally between the two of them.) On his own, the supervisor can develop self-monitoring skills. He might start by becoming acutely aware of the behavior of others—in this case, teachers—that affects him in an emotionally satisfying or dissatisfying way. Without this awareness, he can feel happy or unhappy about what is going on between him and a teacher, but be unable to deal specifically with the situation, either by reinforcing productive or changing unproductive behavior.

Conflict Situations

A supervisor also needs to recognize when he is in conflict with a teacher and to be aware of how he handles conflict situations. One might be tempted to say that the problem of being able to recognize a conflict situation is really no problem at all. How else would one describe a shouting match between a supervisor and a teacher? However, more subtle kinds of conflicts arise in the course of supervision. By subtle, I mean conflicts in which the surface issues are substantive but the side effects are emotional (Guetzkow and Gyr, 1954). For example, a supervisor might easily recognize that he is in conflict with a teacher over the goals of teaching American history, but be unaware that the teacher is really engaging him in a battle for power. A supervisor would certainly know that he is having difficulty getting a teacher to experiment with different ways of relating to youngsters in a classroom, yet be unaware that the conflict stems from the teacher's distrust of the supervisor's competence, or, perhaps, from his own distrust of the teacher's competence.

My point is that, even if one is aware of the emotional conflict, one tends to ignore it as much as possible and focus on matters of substance. It is much easier to interact about different goals than over matters involving trust, even though the conflict over goals may not be resolved until the matters involving trust are confronted. If a supervisor ignores or denies the existence of emotional issues between himself and the teacher, his efforts can only be ritualistic. By remaining unaware of them or pushing them out of his consciousness, he deprives himself of the data he needs in order to work productively with a teacher. The most likely effects are that the teacher ostensibly complies with the supervisor and then does what he wants when the supervisor is not around, or that there is an agreement to disagree and each leaves the situation convinced that he is right and that, if only the other were brighter or more aware of reality, he would see it. The prospects for future productive work together are not good. Too much unfinished emotional business remains.

Having recognized that he is in a situation of conflict, a supervisor will find it useful to be aware of his own reactions to it. People in conflict tend to react by fighting, taking flight, pairing (developing more intimate relationships with the other), or by confronting the other with their own feelings about what is happening. (The ideas of fight, flight, and pairing come from Bion, "Experiences in Groups: III" [1949].) If I become aware of a conflict between me and another person, I can choose to fight, I can try to overpower him or use subtler means to win. I may decide to take flight, to avoid the problem, at least overtly, by ignoring what is happening perhaps by changing the subject or simply leaving the field. I may react to the stress I am feeling by attempting to get psychologically closer and more intimate with the other (a form of flight, it seems to me). Or, I may choose to confront the other person with my perceptions of what is happening between us and my feelings about it.

Whether it is best to fight, take flight, pair, or confront depends on the situation. What is critically important is the choice. Consciously or unconsciously, I choose my strategy, and my choice is partly based upon the data I have about myself. I can provide myself with these data by trying to answer a number of questions. For example, is fighting fun for me or is it painful? What are the costs to me and the other if I choose to fight? What do I gain from avoiding conflict? Are the gains worth it if I lose self-esteem by fleeing from the situation? Am I comfortable getting close to others, or is the tension I feel in intimate relationships something I do not care to deal with? Do I have the skills to engage in a productive confrontation, or am I apt to botch it up?

These are not easy questions for a supervisor to answer. But if he can try, honestly, he may develop at least the beginnings of an information bank that he can draw on to make intelligent decisions about himself in conflict situations. Without such knowledge, the chances are good that, when he and a teacher are in conflict, his behavior will tend to be stereotyped. One result will be that little heed will be paid to the consequences, either on the level of productivity or of interpersonal relationships.

Competence

A supervisor also needs to know his own competency. Perhaps knowing what he is not good at is more important. Being a supervisor can be self-seducing. The pressures to be helpful and to be seen as helpful are large and, combined with the ambiguities and conflicts of the supervisor's role, can make a supervisor think he should be and can be all things to all teachers—like some professors who, for whatever reason, feel that they can and should be helpful to any student who comes along, no matter what the problem.

To illustrate, I feel that, as a professor or a consultant, I need to be keenly aware of my incompetence. I am less concerned about my competencies, which can take care of themselves. But from time to time, if I am not careful, I find myself venturing into areas where I have no right to be because I lack either the knowledge or the skill to deal with the problem. The results of these ventures are not productive, for me or for the person with whom I am working, and it would have been much more helpful for me to have been aware of what I cannot do and to have been honest about it.

It is not written anywhere that a supervisor must know everything. It is more helpful to be able to say "I don't know how to do that" than to try and bluff one's way through. The bluff is usually seen for what it is anyway, if not at the moment then when the results develop, and, apart from making the teacher distrust the supervisor, will give him the reputation that all teachers should be cautious when dealing with him.

There are several ways of gathering data about our incompetency. A person can simply be aware of and sufficiently interested in himself to acknowledge what he can and cannot do. Most of us decline to bluff ourselves. The crunch comes when we have to disclose our lack of skill to someone who may be depending on the help that a particular skill can supply.

To find out how one's abilities are seen by others, one can simply ask. A supervisor might just ask a teacher to point out where he thinks the supervisor is really competent and where he thinks he is less than skillful—or where he thinks the supervisor is kidding himself about what he can do. To be productive, such an interchange needs considerable trust and open communication, or the engagement will turn into another game in which the teacher tries to avoid being trapped.

If the straightforward question is too personal, the supervisor can incorporate it into a concrete problem, in a collaborative manner. The teacher and the supervisor might discuss a problem the teacher is having and plan to deal with it. The teacher puts the plan into action; the supervisor observes what occurs. Afterward, the two of them discuss not only what happened but also what the supervisor could have done to be more helpful and where, perhaps, he failed altogether. This discussion, too, will need considerable trust and openness, without which the problem becomes the teacher's ("You didn't follow my advice correctly") and not the supervisor's ("What was there about my advice or the way we worked together that affected the outcome?").

INFORMATION ABOUT THE TEACHER

What the supervisor needs to know about the teacher parallels, in many ways, what he needs to know about himself. The teacher's interpersonal needs—the behavior that pleases or displeases him, his methods of dealing with conflict, and his competence or lack of it—are as important to a productive helping relationship as those of the supervisor. It is important for a supervisor to be aware of the extent of a teacher's need to control a situation or his need to receive much or little direction, to know what in the behavior of others enables the teacher to respond affirmatively or negatively, and so on.

If the supervisor has and is able to use these data, he has the basis for a satisfactory work relationship. If not, things tend to become mechanistic, and conflicts remain unmanaged. Unfinished business accumulates and the relationships become burdened. I am reminded here of my daughter when she was sixteen. It took me a while to learn, but now I know that, whenever my "Parent" (Harris, 1969) emerged in our discussions, whenever I moralized or called on the wisdom of my years, she was apt to get angry with me and not use whatever resources I may have had to help her solve a problem. Though I knew this to be true, there were times when the words just slipped out of my mouth. Fortunately for me, she was honest enough to let me know what I had done, and, after my initial defensiveness, I could usually deal with myself and with her. My daughter had provided me with data about herself that was important to our relationship. It paid me to use it.

In like manner, a teacher continually provides the supervisor with data about himself that is important to their ability to work together. The information is made available by the teacher's behavior. But the supervisor needs to be alert and skillful enough to gather it. For example, if a supervisor notes that a teacher seems to resist implementing all his suggestions, he may feel that the teacher is saying, "Don't smother me with your experience. Work with me to help me develop my own solutions." The supervisor, as he collects data about the teacher, must learn to listen, not only to words of the teacher but also to the music.

A second reason that the supervisor needs the kind of data on teachers about which we have been talking is that, much as the teacher's needs and behavioral preferences interact with the supervisor's and affect their work together, so do they affect the teacher's behavior in the classroom. The social systems of interaction between a supervisor and teacher and between a teacher and his class are related. The behavior, problems, and conflicts that arise in either of these systems are likely to mirror those evident in the other (Mueller and Kell, 1972). The symptoms may be different, but, for example, if power becomes an issue between supervisor and teacher, the issue is likely to pervade the classroom. Or, if a teacher usually deals with conflict in supervision by avoiding it, he will probably do likewise or, perhaps, fight it to compensate in the classroom. As a supervisor becomes more aware of the teacher as a person, he becomes better able to help develop a productive work relationship with him *and* to help him diagnose classroom problems.

Behavior in the Classroom

When the supervisor is in the classroom, either on his own initiative or by the teacher's request, what should he pay attention to as he observes what is going on? If he has been asked by the teacher to observe his method of teaching science, he should do just that. But, although a supervisor ought to be able to help a teacher with methods, method is less important than behavior in interpersonal or group relationships. For example, regardless of how well a teacher knows the mechanics of teaching reading, it does little good if he punishes his pupils in the process. While not denying the input of the students, I suggest that the social and psychological culture of the classroom has its roots in the behavior of the control person, that is, the teacher. To give a teacher information about the very complex setting that he influences so largely, the supervisor should find out:

—How much of the time the teacher talks.
—Of the time the teacher talks, how much of it is devoted to lecture, how much to asking questions?
—Whether the teacher's questions are broad and probing, or can usually be answered briefly.
—How the teacher deals with wrong answers. Does he help the student trace his thought processes, or does he simply say, "That's wrong," and go on to the next student?
—How the teacher reacts if things seem to get out of control. Does

he put the lid on or engage the class in an analysis of what happened?

—Whether the teacher is aware if some of the students seem not to be involved, and, if he is, what he does: ignores the situation, puts the students on the spot with a question, criticizes them, engages them privately or publicly in an analysis of their not being involved.

—If, when disagreements come up, the teacher appears to communicate that he is the final authority.

—Whether the teacher's behavior seems to devalue the worth of students or enhance their self-esteem.

—Whether the behavior of the teacher communicates a desire for interpersonal closeness or for distance.

—If the teacher deals with conflict by avoiding it, fighting it, or confronting it.

—Whether the teacher seems to be having fun, or whether he conveys that what he is doing is a chore.

—If the teacher listens to what students are saying, both to the words and to the music.

Undoubtedly, the reader can expand on this list. These items occurred to me in a brief span of time, which probably suggests the kinds of things that I am most apt to pay attention to in a classroom. (I think it is also true that many of these questions convey my value system about teachers' behavior, but, then, I do not pretend to view the behavior of supervisors or teachers in a way that is devoid of my values.) In any event, the issue is not whether these questions apply to every supervisor. What is important is that, as a supervisor and teacher start to come up with the answers, some pictures of the nature of the interpersonal and group relations of the classroom should emerge, and these pictures constitute an extremely important part of the supervisory data base.

The answers to some questions are matters of fact. It is possible and not difficult, for example, to get accurate estimates of how much time a teacher talks simply by using a stop watch. A supervisor trained in interaction analysis (Flanders, 1960) can obtain detailed information about the nature of the teacher's talking—how much is lecture, praise, questioning, and so forth. Answers to most of the questions, though, are not as readily categorized. The supervisor must be able to distinguish between collecting behavioral data and making inferences about the teacher's motivation or personality. Suppose the supervisor notices that, when disagreements develop in the classroom, even on issues that may be hazy, the teacher's word is usually final. There are several ways in which the supervisor might deal with his observation. He might say, "You seem to be a very dominating person" or "Why do you always insist on being right or having the last word?" Or, to push it to perhaps a ludicrous extreme, he might say, "I think we ought to talk about your early childhood authority relationships, because they are obviously affecting the way you deal with the kids." It is not hard to imagine a teacher's reaction to this use of observational data. He would probably be highly defensive, and the conference would escalate into a battle, overt or covert. Our supervisor, having noted some specific behavior in the teacher, that of always having the last word, has trapped himself by making unsupported inferences and personal remarks about unconscious defects of the teacher's character. Admittedly, I have exaggerated, but only to make the point. Not only is it important to collect specific information about the teacher's behavior, but it is also necessary to use it helpfully. The supervisor might do better to say, "I noticed that, when disagreements come up, they were ended by your making a statement that seemed to close off the discussion. I wonder if you were aware of that and how you feel about it?" There is no guarantee that the teacher would respond positively to receiving this information about himself but, at the least, it probably wouldn't paralyze him.

I am not suggesting that supervisors and teachers should not discuss each other's motivations and needs. Indeed, there are times when this is most appropriate. But if the two are to have a reciprocal helping relationship, any sort of playing at therapy, particularly judgmental therapy, needs to be avoided.

There is one more guidepost for the collection of behavioral data about a teacher's behavior in the classroom. The supervisor and the teacher need to agree beforehand on what the supervisor will be looking for as he observes the teacher, so that a common frame of reference is established for their work together. Teachers would probably appreciate being asked what kind of feedback they would like. In fact, the department head of a junior high school did just that and discovered that the teachers liked being involved in their own supervision.

STUDENTS' BEHAVIOR AND ATTITUDES

My discussions with supervisors indicate that only rarely do they take into account, in any systematic way, the students' behavior and attitudes. This seems incongruous, particularly if one holds that the classroom is a social system, largely controlled by the teacher, but one in which the students play an integral part. It is even more incongruous if one takes into account that the way students behave and the attitudes they hold in a classroom depend largely on the teacher and how he behaves. How else can we account for the fact that youngsters, particularly in the secondary schools where they have several teachers in any one day, are excited and motivated to learn in one class and completely uninterested in another? The subject matter may be the critical variable. A student may like social studies, but not biology. But then, how do we account for the students who, for example, like social studies, but not the class they are in, and, after changing teachers, have a wonderful experience? It is a matter not merely of good teachers and bad teachers. It is a more important issue concerned with providing an adequate data base for understanding student behavior.

A number of questions come to mind, the answers to which can provide a base for a supervisor's observations of students:
—Is there interaction between and among students, or only between the teacher and the students?
—Do the students question or comment, or do they speak only in response to the teacher's questions or demands?
—Do the students respond to classroom discussion as if they were having their teeth pulled, or does the discussion flow easily?
—Do some students seem involved while others are simply not there?
—Do students seem to use one another's comments as building blocks for ideas, or do they tend to devalue these comments? Put another way, do they react to one another cooperatively or competitively?
—Do the students take issue with the teacher's ideas, or do they appear to accept them even if they are doubtful?
—Do the students seem to be having fun?

There are, without question, a number of other aspects of the students' behavior in the classroom that a supervisor could choose to observe. As I review those that I have chosen, I see that they, too, reflect my values in the classroom. They all deal with the social and emotional climate of the classroom; they are what I am interested in, and, were I supervising a teacher, I would have to determine his interest in these items. A supervisor can ask the students to complete some of the pencil-and-paper instruments that tap students' perceptions and feelings about the classroom. Or, though it would be time consuming, he could interview groups of students about their perceptions of classroom activities and the teacher's style. If either of these two sources of information were to be used, the teacher would have to agree to them and work closely with the supervisor. It is extremely difficult to measure students' behavior unobtrusively, short of bugging the classroom, and this is not recommended. Most students are aware of the reasons for a supervisor's presence in the room. If they like the teacher, the almost palpable reassurance, "Don't worry Teach, we'll take care of you," will effectively prevent the supervisor from obtaining a valid picture of their normal behavior. The teacher, perhaps with the supervisor present, must somehow persuade the class that the supervisor is part of the woodwork there, but of no account.

Realizing that the supervisory attitudes and skills I advocate differ from those usually associated with the supervisor's role, I would not be surprised if many of my readers resisted their implications as being burdensome or even missing the mark by a wide margin. Perhaps so, but, whether one is teaching, supervising, or administering, the information one collects to improve one's job reflects one's opinions about what it takes to do the job well. If a supervisor concentrates on methods and the appropriate use of curriculum materials (or bulletin boards, or the height of window shades), his value system would seem to be mechanistic and fragmented. If he is concerned with the character of relationships among supervisors, teachers, and students, his value system would seem humanistic, an organic approach to education, which is the approach I consider essential.

13   Tenured Teachers and Supervisors: Mutual Avoidance

Perhaps the two most problematic situations that supervisors confront on a day-to-day basis involve working with, or trying to work with, tenured teachers and the role conflict supervisors sense between wanting to be of help and having to evaluate the same person. This chapter deals with supervision and the tenured teachers; the next, with the helping-evaluating conflict.

One seeks almost in vain for public discussion—in writing or debate—of supervisors' problems with the tenure system. With one exception that I know of (Mosher and Purpel, 1972), texts on supervision seem to ignore the situation utterly; there is simply no reference to it. Avoidance, or the ignoring of an issue, is a curious phenomenon for which I cannot account, but one thing seems clear. Although there are times in the lives of all of us when it is prudent to deal with problems by avoiding them, the chances of long-range solutions to these problems through an avoidance mechanism are pretty slim. This appears to be particularly true when, as is the case with the relationship of supervisors to tenured teachers, the problems are long term and deeply rooted in a system's normative structure. The question will at least be confronted here. I am under no illusions that this confrontation will have a major or even a minor impact on the system or that it will provide pat answers to problems that arise as supervisors contemplate their work with tenured teachers. Perhaps it will stimulate others to seek creative solutions of their own. The reader should also understand that I am not judging the tenure system. I accept that system as a given—a part of school life with which supervisors must live, no matter how difficult. Further, though from time to time we read of isolated community agitation against the system of tenure, a responsible tenure review process in the public schools (as well as in colleges and universities) seems improbable, particularly with the growing power of teachers' unions. We have what we have, the chances of changing it are not bright, and schools and teachers may have made themselves unwitting victims of their own system. It provides comfort and security for many and a lot of unhappiness for others.

Though tenure laws may differ somewhat from one state to another,

in general they provide permanent employment to a teacher after a probationary period (usually three years). Provisions are made for dismissal for reasons of incompetence or improper conduct, but dismissal for the former is rare and can involve costly and extended public hearings. Tenure laws protect the outstanding, mediocre and incompetent teachers alike, and represent one of the most frustrating barriers to the improvement of teaching. They exemplify the way a response to one set of problems—the protection of teachers from political manipulation—can create a further set of problems (Mosher and Purpel, 1972, pp. 24-25).

What the tenure system does, and this must have been unforeseen, is to establish a large body of people in the schools who, at *their* option, can set up relatively impermeable boundaries between themselves and most attempts the system may make to influence them. Sometimes these boundaries become physical (a teacher absents himself from a meeting or refuses a supervisor access to his classroom). Mostly, though, they are psychological. For example, teachers typically are required to attend in-service programs. Anybody who has conducted such programs and not been aware that some teachers are present but divorced from the proceedings has been somewhat out of touch with social reality. If one simply observes the behavior of these teachers, one could easily get the impression that they are dull, not to mention stupid and rude, and really care little for improving their own skills. It would be a mistake to make this assumption about all tenured teachers, though undoubtedly it would be true of some.

I think that a more likely reason for tenured teachers' resisting the influence of supervisors may be found in their early and unsatisfactory experiences with supervisors. Many teachers must have gone through the hoops, engaged in whatever ritualistic games of supervision were seen as necessary, found their supervisor unable to be helpful, and finally, having received tenure, said, "That is the end of that." It is not unlike the sense of relief a Ph.D. candidate feels when, having successfully defended his dissertation, he says, "Thank God I'll never have to do that again." The point is that, much as in any classroom, things are taught that are not part of the curriculum, so, in the course of the supervision of probationary teachers, things are taught that are not intended. A supervisor trying to help a young teacher may also be enabling the teacher to avoid receiving help, while at the same time giving the appearance of accepting it. Thus, by the time he receives tenure, he has learned how to render the best-intentioned supervisor helpless if he chooses. He knows the games that have to be played in order to give the image of seeking and receiving help while really rejecting it.

Another factor that affects a teacher's attitudes about supervision is something that may be outside the supervisor's hands. Change in schools frequently means that someone has sold the school administration a bill of packaged goods. The package, sometimes with the teachers' support and sometimes only with peripheral compliance, is loaded on top of already existing packages and structures and, being used halfheartedly, goes the way of previous packaged programs—into oblivion, with few people to mourn its passing. The supervisor, because he often becomes the agent of the package and is associated with both its introduction and its demise, finds his reputation tainted. He may not have initiated the whole scheme, but, as long as he was visible in its promotion, his relationships with teachers, whether tenured or probationary, have been compromised—merely for doing his job.

Tenure frees the teacher, potentially, from many organizational sanctions that might otherwise be used to get him to behave in certain ways. This may be desirable. (For a brief but thoughtful comment, see Kingman Brewster's "On Tenure" [1972]. Though he speaks of higher education, I think his ideas are applicable to the schools.) But there is another side of the coin. The tenure system also enables the teacher to insulate himself from people or forces he does not care to deal with, regardless of their potential value. Tenure creates a new set of work conditions for the teacher and demands of him an equally new set of decisions about his work and the relationships he wishes to develop and maintain. Tenured teachers tend to reject formal supervision, freeing themselves from relationships they may have found troublesome in the past. But freedom has its price, and they seem to have forsaken a source of help in the near or distant future. Whether these teachers take this cost into consideration is not known. If they do, however, clearly they consider the price small compared with the benefit of *not* working with people who are supposed to be able to help them do things better. A queer situation, without doubt.

The granting of tenure to a teacher is a public and explicit stamp of competence concerning that teacher's ability. It is also an implied expression of confidence that the individual involved will continue to grow and develop as a teacher, to become ever more skillful. What is even more important here is the fact that, when a teacher receives tenure, new work conditions are created for the teacher, and these new conditions automatically create new circumstances for the supervisor. For one thing, the bases of influence that a supervisor may be able to call on in supervising a teacher without tenure become severely circumscribed when attempting to relate to a teacher on tenure.

CONDITIONS OF RELATIONSHIP

By way of a conceptual detour, I should like to cite five conditions—interpersonal or organizational—through which one person may gain entry into the system of another in order to influence him (French and Raven, 1959). These conditions are called bases of social power.

Legitimate Power

A has legitimate power over B when the values held by B are such that he acknowledges the legitimacy of A's right to influence him. These values may be associated with conditions of formal organizational life, "He's my boss and therefore I acknowledge, within limits, his right to influence my behavior," or with elements outside an organization, "He is older than I am, and, within limits, I will accept his influence because of his age." No legitimate right to influence can exist unless the person being influenced sanctions that right. The right will always be limited. For example, my students in a classroom legitimize my right to influence them in a wide variety of ways. I call the class to order, dismiss it, get them to sit in groups, direct them in learning, and so forth. They follow my directions because of their attitudes about the classroom, "He is the professor, and we are the students. He has certain prerogatives that we acknowledge." But these prerogatives have limits, and, if I exceed them, my legitimate base of power would have no meaning. To be somewhat facetious, but to make the point, if I told my students that we would conduct a two-hour class with everyone standing up for the full period, I rather doubt they would follow that direction. They would simply refuse (I hope) to acknowledge my right to have them behave in that way.

Reward Power

This basis of social power is familiar. A will be able to influence B to the extent that A controls the rewards that B wants. The more control A has over B's most coveted rewards, the more influence he will have. If B considers the rewards unimportant, however, A's ability to influence diminishes. It does little good to say to a child, "If you do this, I will give you a candy bar" if the child does not particularly care for candy.

Coercive Power

Coercive power is the other side of the reward coin. Its dynamic base is the same because it involves the manipulation by A of those things that are important to B, in this case, those things that B wishes to avoid. Just as there are rewards that are not rewarding, so there are punishments that are not punishing. A punishment that my wife and I would invoke from time to time when our children were young was to send them to their separate rooms when they misbehaved, thus depriving them of each other's company. This was very effective until they, and later we, discovered that they rather enjoyed spending enforced and uninterrupted time by themselves. We had, thenceforth, to seek out punishment that our offspring really wanted to avoid.

Expert Power

Expert power resides in A when B perceives that A has knowledge superior to B's in an area that is important to him, and, therefore, wisdom dictates that he accept A's influence. Expert power becomes effective as a basis for exerting influence when B is seeking the help of A's knowledge or expertise. When a person knows he lacks information necessary to the successful completion of a task, he is much more apt to accept influence from another than when the would-be influencer decides that information is lacking. I thought I knew more about good study habits than my older daughter did when she was in school. I did not see her developing my model of good study habits, but she did not sense this lack. My attempts to influence her went for naught, and she has been a successful student, which ought to be some sort of lesson for me and for supervisors, too.

Referent Power

A basis for influence between two people exists when one feels an identification with another: when B identifies with A and thinks, feels, and behaves as A does, or when B wants to be like A and adopts A's ways of thinking, feeling, and behaving. The influence has little to do with the specific intent of the person with whom B identifies. An exception to this point would be the attitudes and behavior that parents may intentionally model for their children. Children, however, cannot choose their parents. A more appropriate example of the process, for our purposes, might be taken from graduate schools where students seem to seek in the professors potentially appropriate models for themselves and to assimilate the values and ways of thinking of their models. They do not become carbon copies, but there is a great deal of resemblance.

The various bases for influence put forward by French and Raven, fairly easily found in the relationships between teachers and supervisors, are markedly affected by the institution of tenure. When a teacher is tenured, there is a radical change in the relative potency of the supervisor's bases of influence. A supervisor's influence over a teacher who is not tenured may well be established on the basis of his expertise, but it is most certainly reinforced by legitimacy and his ability to reward or punish. The legitimacy arises from the conditions of appointment: a nontenured teacher must be supervised. A teacher might prefer not to be psychologically involved with a supervisor, but he must acknowledge the supervisor's prerogative to observe his teaching and to talk to him about it afterward, even though he may pay little attention to what was said.

The supervisor's power to reward and coerce certainly applies to the nontenured teacher, but tenure itself is a reward for accepting, or appearing to accept, a supervisor's influence. There are other rewards, and they may apply to tenured or nontenured teachers. Supervisors frequently control scarce resources, which they can make available to teachers. I know teachers who have pretended to accept a supervisor's influence precisely so that they could gain access to his "mother lode" of materials. Another reward that supervisors have at their disposal, from time to time, is the granting of funds to enable teachers to travel to conferences. Supervisors, being human, would probably hesitate to make such funds available to teachers who were, apparently, rejecting them.

Theoretically, the position of a nontenured teacher is such that referent power as a basis for influence might quite easily be established. A new nontenured teacher in a school is like the child in the family or the beginning doctoral student in the university. They all need to become socialized into the system, and the identification process is one way to meet this need. It would seem logical that a teacher chooses to identify with, and try to be like, his supervisor, but the supervisor might not present a satisfactory model. In many cases, the kind of model that evolves from a supervisor's behavior is not one with which teachers care to identify. The perception, "He is so far removed from the classroom that he doesn't know what's going on," states the case clearly. People who are "getting their hands dirty" tend not to adopt the values of those who are not. Even if the model is acceptable, the supervisor, who has a reputation for being simply an agent of higher powers, will find barriers against his ideas no matter how appropriate they are. The attitude is irrational, but by now the possibility of man's being motivated solely by rational considerations in the context of supervision should have been pretty well discarded by the reader.

As soon as a teacher receives tenure, his relationships with his supervisor, particularly those of influence, change. No longer is the legitimacy of the supervisor's right to observe a teacher in action acknowledged by the teacher. Even if it is not formally acknowledged, the situation is reversed: the supervisor recognizes the legitimacy of the teacher's refusing him entry into the classroom. He may not feel good about it, but he accepts it. The rewards a supervisor can give a teacher who is tenured may remain the same (access to resources and so forth), but they are probably less compelling. Most teachers, after a few years, are either wise enough to know how to get the resources they want from the system or creative enough to find their own. The most valuable reward to a teacher for accepting a supervisor's influence, the granting of tenure, has been completely removed, as Mosher and Purpel have implied.

In much the same way that tenure severely circumscribes the supervisor's ability to use rewards to influence teachers, it also limits the use of coercion. There is little that a supervisor, either by implication or action, can do to punish a tenured teacher, at least formally. There are exceptions, of course. I know one teacher who feels she must do what her principal wants her to, on the face of it, or be scheduled into teaching courses she does not want to teach. But, on the whole, as long as the tenured teacher does not upset things, he is relatively free from censure. He can scarcely be coerced into doing anything, at least with respect to his teaching, that he does not want to do. When a teacher receives tenure, the supervisor is left primarily with his expert and referent powers to influence. Referent power is a chancy thing, depending on the identification model the supervisor presents and the teacher's needs to be socialized into the system. The need for socialization becomes minimal because not only does tenure confirm a teacher's competence, but it also says, in effect, "You fit. We have socialized you." What it boils down to is that work relationships, if there are to be any, between supervisors and tenured teachers, depend on the teacher's seeing the supervisor as a source of valuable expertise and wanting to use that expertise. An expert base of influence is valid only when someone wants that expertness, and not otherwise.

If a supervisor concentrates on influencing tenured teachers to want to use his expertness, he needs to decide whether it is worth the effort. The costs in time and emotional energy in trying to gain entry into a tenured teacher's system are likely to be sizable. Success, no matter how skillful the supervisor, is not guaranteed, and, even if he is successful, the return may not warrant the investment. If he chooses not to try, he will in all likelihood not be penalized. School systems tend to have minimal, if any, expectations about the supervision of teachers on tenure, so there can be few sanctions imposed on a supervisor for simply refraining. Caution, or simple avoidance, may be the supervisor's best strategy. The only problem he might have to deal with is his own frustration, but that can be swept under the rug in the rush of daily events.

Should the supervisor venture into the land of tenure, he has the choice of several strategies, depending on how he perceives and diagnoses the problem. He may conceive of his difficulties solely on the interpersonal level, for his relationships may be satisfactory except with one or two tenured teachers whose teaching leaves something to be desired but who have been impervious to the supervisor's attempts to do anything. A situation like this calls for a confrontation between the parties, but not a confrontation about the poor job that the teacher is doing, for that would not get to the root of the trouble, which is the inability of the supervisor and teacher to communicate and work together. Any attempt to deal with the teacher's competence would probably shut the door forever. The issue needs to be resolved on the interpersonal level, and the confrontation ought to deal with the supervisor's problems and feelings about not being able to communicate with the teacher. To illustrate the differences between confrontation on the level of the teacher's competence and on the level of interpersonal communications, the following two examples are offered. It might be interesting for the reader to picture himself a tenured teacher on the receiving end of each statement from our hypothetical supervisor and to react to the statement as he thinks the teacher might.

Confrontation about the teacher's competence:

Supervisor: Mr. X, I've been wanting to talk with you about the things that you are doing in class. I've a feeling that there are lot of new ideas about which you may not be aware, that could help you do a better job.

Mr. X: (The reader supplies his own reaction, keeping in mind the general attitudes of tenured teachers and the way they tend to perceive supervisors.)

Confrontation about interpersonal communications:

Supervisor: Mr. X, there's something I've been wanting to talk to you about. It has to do with our relationship. I sense a difficulty in our communicating with each other. It's almost like ships passing in the night, as though we had decided to avoid each other. This bothers me because I think if we could talk about education and kids, we could learn something from each other.

Mr. X: (The reader supplies his own reaction.)

There is no way of predicting precisely what would happen in either of these instances. In the first one, the supervisor's concern was a highly rational and evaluative focus on the teacher's competence. Mr. X would be most likely to react defensively, and the confrontation would end in a stalemate. In the second, the supervisor has focused on the communications problem and his own feelings about it. The teacher may react defensively here as well, but it is possible that Mr. X, even though there are some evaluative overtones in the comment, would appreciate the supervisor's attempts to reach him. Whichever confrontation the supervisor chooses, there is risk, and he will have to take this risk into consideration when deciding whether to deal with the teacher or just let matters stay as they are.

If problems of communication and working with tenured teachers in a school involve more than one or two teachers, the situation is not just interpersonal, and different strategies and tactics are required. The remedy must fit the problem and not the other way round. If a supervisor decides that every human problem he faces must be dealt with as an interpersonal confrontation, it seems likely that, regardless of his skill with that technique, his effectiveness will be short lived.

There is a wide variety of ways in which a supervisor might intervene in an effort to work with reluctant tenured teachers throughout a school. Two examples will be described, but one must remember that the root problem is to change the attitudes of the teachers toward supervision. The supervisor must regard himself as somebody who is able to change the organization, and not merely as somebody who has new and potentially productive ideas about curriculum and teaching methods.

The first example, a rather gentle, scarcely risky intervention, was described to me by an instructional specialist in a city school district. The specialist, who was a highly skilled teacher, was assigned to a particular elementary school to see if he could move it out of its very comfortable rut. Most of the teachers, but not all, had been at the school for a number of years. They were comfortable, if relatively ineffectual. The specialist knew he could expect no help from the principal, who had been removed from one principalship by parental pressure and had then spent a year in the central office doing, one suspects, not much of anything. His concept of the role of the principal seemed confined to maintaining peace and quiet. The specialist decided that a frontal attack on the problem of establishing a relationship with the old-timers would be foolhardy, particularly in the light of the ineptness of the principal who, above all, wanted no disruption. There were a few younger teachers in the school who were interested in developing new and better ways to teach. (The gulf between old and young is unfortunate. There are many older teachers who are "young," and vice versa. But, in general, the longer one has been teaching, the more convinced one becomes that he is right and the more one resists change from an outsider.) The specialist convened a group of those teachers who were interested in examining new ways to approach the teaching of reading. No pressure was brought to bear on anyone to attend. The group continued to meet for a time. The teachers who met regularly started to test some new ideas and found them satisfactory. When I last talked to the instructional specialist, he indicated that some small diffusion effect seemed to be taking place. Some of the older tenured teachers were starting to take an interest in what was going on, and there seemed to be a possibility of establishing direct links with them. Particularly because of the principal's values, such a strategy may have been the only one possible. But low-risk ventures in education, much as in economics, tend to reap relatively minor results. Such was the case here. Some inroads into the tenure system were made, but it is questionable (and the specialist acknowledges this) whether any basic attitudes or relationships have changed. Nonetheless, the instructional specialist did do something; he did not simply ignore the situation. If he can stay in the school long enough, he may really be able to reach the tenured teachers.

The second example of an organizational intervention is one that attacks the problem directly. Though I have never seen it used for the specific problem under discussion here, I have been involved in its use in industry and, in two cases, in the relationships between a principal and his faculty. The confrontation consists in a meeting of the entire faculty, administrative staff, and supervisor. The problem to be discussed, with no hedging allowed, is the nature of the relationships that the supervisor sees between himself and the faculty and that the faculty members see between themselves and the supervisor. The specific exercise may be labeled *cross-image sharing* (Golembiewski and Blumberg, 1967; Blansfield, Blake, and Mouton, 1964). Teachers are formed into groups to describe in writing, in as many ways as they can, the nature of their relationships with the supervisor, the nature of the supervisor's relationship with them, and the way they *think* the supervisor perceives their relationship with him. The supervisor does the same thing from his perspective. When everyone has finished developing his cross-images, the information is shared and discussed publicly.

A number of previously buried and avoided problems tend to become unearthed and talked about. Both perceptual congruencies and conflicts about role relationships become legitimate objects of inquiry and discourse. Many people, as a result of this experience, seem to feel freer in their communications with one another because much of what they previously could not talk about has been sanctioned as legitimate. It is important to remember that this is not a name-calling exercise; nor is it sensitivity training. It is simply one way of dealing with role relationships in work. It needs to be understood that, if such a project is successful, it is only a wedge into the system of the tenured teachers. Potentially it may open up communications channels that have not been previously used, but, by itself, the sharing of cross-images does not solve any problems, although it may make it possible for people to approach and test new ways of dealing with one another because they are able to talk on levels that had been blocked off earlier. The chances of engaging a school staff in this kind of exercise would seem to be minimal without the support of a principal prepared to take risks, and this is a relatively risky means of intervention, in that it is concerned with human relationships and emotions and not, by way of example, on how to teach the new math. Though the return may be high, the outcome might also be an outstanding failure with long-term, unfortunate consequences for both principal and supervisor. The potential costs and benefits have to be weighed. At the heart of the issue is the importance that the supervisor and principal attach, for the sake of the schools, to the changing of established relationships between supervisor and tenured teachers, in spite of the risks involved.

Little has been said about legal remedies for the ills of the tenure system. One hears occasionally of a proposal that would grant tenure for a specified period of time after which the appointment would be reviewed. It seems to me that the chances of laws such as this being passed are minimal, given the political power base of teachers' associations. Even if a law of renewable tenure were enacted, I believe it would prove to have little effect on the situation. The conscience of some schoolmen and lawmakers might be salved ("We have done all that we can do."), but that would be the end of it. The unintended problems created by the tenure system are interpersonal or organizational and will be resolved as they are confronted on those levels and not by legal patchwork.

14 Helping and Evaluating: Role Conflict

Inevitably, as we talk about the helping focus of supervision in classes or workshops, the same questions come up: "Yes, but how about evaluation of the teacher? How can a supervisor be expected to develop an open, supportive, and trusting interpersonal climate when he is also expected to evaluate the teacher?" These are good questions because there are points of severe conflict between the two functions. For instance, a supervisor, in his helping role, might say to a new teacher: "What I would like to do is to establish the kind of relationship with you that will enable the two of us to communicate openly and freely with each other. I want to feel that I can tell you how I see you behaving in the classroom so that you won't feel threatened by what I say. And I would like you to be free to ask for help in your work and also to tell me what I am doing or how I am behaving that is unhelpful as well as helpful to you." And then, in his evaluating role, he might add: "And, incidentally, I will be evaluating you as to your fitness as a teacher in our system."

This duality of role is not peculiar to schools. It is pretty much a fact of life in all organizations where the holders of various hierarchical positions are responsible, not only for the growth and development of others, but also for the evaluation of their performance. The feeling I get, as I talk to people in education and in industry, is that the issue is largely ignored. What seems to happen, in most cases, is that supervisors talk about the problem among themselves and then shrug their shoulders; the game will be played.

163

Teachers also talk about the problem and play their own, often elaborate, game. It is another supervisory problem that typically gets dealt with by being avoided.

Problems that are acknowledged by both parties but never discussed remain unresolved by collaboration. They become sources of tension between and among people and stand effectively in the way of productive interpersonal understanding and work. The best example I know of outside the field of education—but with direct implications for it—takes place in the sales department of the pharmaceutical industry. The sales manager is usually responsible for about ten salesmen with whom he spends two or three days every six weeks or so visiting physicians in an effort to help the salesmen do a better job of selling. The salesman knows that he is being evaluated on his performance in the physician's office, and he also knows what kind of sales behavior his manager likes. For a while, he complies with the manager's wishes, even if they differ from his own, because he knows that, for another six weeks, he can approach the physicians as he pleases. In effect, the salesman is evaluated on his ability and desire to comply and not on his effectiveness as a salesman. The curious part of all this is that both managers and salesmen know this; both are parties to the game and seem content to live with it, perhaps feeling that it is a relatively small cost to pay in order to maintain the image of productive work together.

A similar situation arises in educational supervision when the conflict between evaluation and assistance arises. Overtly, the supervisor is helping, but the teacher is aware that the evaluation of his performance really depends on his adopting, within limits, the supervisor's way of doing things.

When confronted with a problem in human relationships, I find it helpful to frame the problem in some conceptual setting, to provide conceptual handles, so that what I observe I can deal with intellectually as well as behaviorally. I need to make rational sense of the interactive world of which I am a part so that I have some rational guide to action. For the problems in helping and evaluating, the most appropriate conceptual avenue is one that seeks to describe and explain the different types of role conflict. Kahn and his colleagues (1964, pp. 11-34), in their analysis of role dynamics, provide a framework. Their model for understanding role behavior and role conflict involves the relationships that exist between a *focal person*—

the supervisor, in our case—and members of his *role set*, that is, other people in the organizational setting—teachers, administrators, other supervisors. (It is quite possible for some members of one's role set to be outside the organization. Our analysis, however, does not require this consideration.) These other people are called *role senders* in that, as they perform their jobs and relate to the focal person by one means or another and to a greater or lesser extent, they try to influence his behavior by giving him information, expressing expectations of him, and so forth. The focal person is a member of his own role set inasmuch as he has his own expectations and perceptions of himself in his role. This means that every attempt to influence a focal person that is made by a member of his role set is weighed against the messages that the focal person sends himself about his own behavior on the job.

In the enacting of any role, a certain sequence of events occurs. The *role sender* has expectations for the focal person's role, has perceptions of the focal person's behavior, and evaluates the focal person's behavior in terms of his expectations and perceptions. Having evaluated the focal person's behavior, the role sender reinforces it (perhaps by praise, perhaps by ignoring it) or tries to change it, subtly or otherwise, or does nothing about it even if his evaluation is unfavorable. The *focal person*, on the other hand, receives the attempts to influence (or notes the absence of them) and evaluates them in terms of his own expectations and perceptions of himself. Based on his evaluation, the focal person complies with the attempt to influence, resists it, or copes with it indirectly. Whatever the focal person's particular behavior, it is fed back into the role sender's system of expectations and perceptions, and the process begins again.

This formulation of role behavior, though somewhat abstract, provides a useful way to examine a supervisor's functioning in a school. Further, it lays the groundwork for a typology of role conflicts that bears directly on the supervisor's dilemma in being both an evaluator and a helper. Kahn and his colleagues (1964) help us again by suggesting several types of conflicts that derive from their role behavior model.

Intrasender conflict. A member of the focal person's role set sends him two conflicting messages about the same situation. A principal may tell a central office supervisor that he wants him to maintain an open, helping relationship with a teacher and, at the same time, that he would like the supervisor to hold to high standards of evaluation. A teacher may make it quite clear to a supervisor that he really wants him to "tell it like it is," while nonverbally telling him that, if he really does, the teacher may have difficulty dealing with it. A teacher may indicate that he wants to work with the supervisor as a colleague, but communicate in their work together that he is uncomfortable and really needs evaluation and direction.

Intersender conflict. The focal person receives conflicting attempts to influence him from two different members of his role set. The supervisor is told by a principal to hold to high evaluative standards with new teachers and is told by other supervisors not to bother with what the principal says. A supervisor's own supervisor tells him to conduct an in-service meeting in a school in which the teachers have previously communicated to him in a variety of subtle ways that they consider such meetings a waste of time.

Person-role conflict. A member or several members of the focal person's role set communicate expectations of his role that are incongruent with the values that he attaches to his own behavior in that role. I know of a supervisor specifically employed because he had the reputation of being very skillful in helping young teachers gain security and competence in short order. After he had been on the job a short time and seemed to be succeeding, his central office superior told him that he hoped the supervisor would keep tabs on "the troops" and function as a sort of central office CIA agent. A second example might be found if the principal's needs to have his teachers evaluated conflicted with the philosophy of the supervisor who rejects external evaluation and prefers, instead, to have the teacher be his own internal evaluator.

The relevance of this brief discussion of role behavior and role conflict is that, if we are able to describe a problem in conceptual terms, we gain a perspective that would not otherwise be available. In this instance, it is a perspective on the conflicts that a supervisor has between evaluating and helping, but it could apply to any other situation a supervisor confronts. Each of us uses a variety of styles or mechanisms to cope with a situation of conflict. The style we invoke at a particular time depends on our perception of the conflict. For, if we diagnose the problem incorrectly or simply treat it impulsively, we are likely to deal ineffectively with the situation or to make matters worse. It makes a difference for the supervisor's behavior, then, if he diagnoses a conflict, for example, as *intra-sender*, where the principal is sending him conflicting messages; as *intersender*, where the principal is sending him one message and the teacher another; or as *person-role*, where the way a teacher or principal may want him to behave is at odds with his own value system. (The supervisor can be involved in the three types of conflict at the same time.)

The particular strategy a supervisor will choose to deal with the conflict he has diagnosed will depend on such things as his skill, his need for power, friendship, and security, and his willingness to take risks. Regardless of what he does specifically, however, unless he makes an adequate diagnosis of his situation, his solutions are likely to be hit or miss. The issue is the ability to make some intellectual sense out of what is going on and not the ability to speak a particular jargon. I find it helpful to analyze human problems in conceptual terms that are familiar to me. I think it unimportant whether the reader uses my concepts or others that he finds more useful.

CONFLICT AND THE TEACHER

The supervisor's conflicts in his role as evaluator and helper stem largely from the organization's demands for that role. But teachers are part of the situation, and their problems, also organizationally oriented, arise from a different set of circumstances. The teacher's dilemma is that his need for help on the job conflicts with his need to be seen as competent, for which he must be evaluated favorably. These needs do not, rationally, necessarily conflict, but they clearly are seen as irreconcilable. Talks with teachers in many cases reveal that, "As long as I maintain the image of competence and confidence in myself and don't fight with my supervisor, I will receive a positive evaluation. If I convey my needs for help and feelings of not knowing what to do, it is likely that I will be seen as a weak and marginal teacher."

There does seem to be an element in school life that dissuades teachers from asking for help, an element that perhaps developed out of some misguided concept of professionalism. A professional is a professional is a professional and is, therefore, competent to do the job without seeking outside help. To seek help is to confess incompetence and is, thus, unprofessional. The point may be too baldly stated, but the attitude is there. Another possible reason for the teachers' reluctance to ask for help is that teaching is idiosyncratic and each teacher develops a personal stake in his way of teaching. My style as a teacher, for example, is very much a reflection of myself, my value system, my notions about what I think it is important for students to learn and how they should learn it. If I admit that what I am doing is open to question, I raise a whole host of issues about myself that might not be overly pleasant. The best strategy is not to make the admission. The only people who might question my style are students, and I can deal with them. Again, the point may be too baldly stated, but I think the reasoning holds and the norm exists, regardless of its genesis.

Back now to our teacher and his problem: Should he ask for help or not; admit to problems and weaknesses or maintain the image of competence and strength? It seems abundantly clear to me that forces, both organizational and personal, will persuade the teacher to project the image of competence and shy away from actively seeking help. All this is not to say that teachers, old ones or new ones, never seek help from their supervisor or other teachers, but that, when they do, they are likely to use methods both subtle and face saving. And any indication of helplessness, especially in a probationary teacher, is absolutely the wrong strategy if one wishes to stay in the system.

There are many teachers and even some schools that do not fit the pattern I have just described. I can only applaud teachers who are open about their problems of teaching and who actively seek help regardless of its source. I am delighted when I visit the rare school in which the teachers are actively engaged with one another and their supervisor in seeking the answers to problems that confront them in the classroom—a situation that is most likely to occur in inner-city schools where many of the teachers are young and have some sense of mission. But I think the generalization that evaluation is a threat wins out.

CAN THE SITUATION CHANGE?

A former student of mine, a bright and skilled school psychologist who became a school administrator, frequently made a telling point in his discussions with me: "I am tired of hearing you professors sit back and criticize the schools. There are a lot of good people out there who are trying their darndest to do a good job. And all that you do is carp at them." Touché. It is comfortable to be able to point out the failings of others while offering no useful alternatives, and sometimes it serves the productive purpose of shaking the system. Many social critics today earn a handsome living doing just that. But I think that social criticism is less important than the provision of alternatives. Not that alternatives will eliminate conflict, but they might enable us to solve the problems better.

On the question of the conflicting functions of evaluating and helping, it is necessary to make two major assumptions. The first is that the system is not going to change radically. With a few exceptions here and there, school systems will continue to be organized the way they are and the various office holders in the system (principals, supervisors, teachers, and so forth) will continue to operate as they do today. The second assumption is that the primary role conflict in which the supervisor becomes engaged, particularly with new teachers, is of the intrasender variety, that is, he receives mixed messages from the teacher about his needs for help, growth and development, and constructive evaluation. Under these assumptions, the interaction between supervisor and teacher will be circumscribed by the supervisor's external evaluative role and his having to confront teachers who have mixed feelings about it. "I want to be evaluated so I can grow, but I want the evaluation to be positive and minimally important as far as our relationship is concerned." The most productive strategy for the supervisor in this situation would seem to be to confront it head on and avoid any sort of game playing. It would certainly be dishonest for a supervisor to say to a teacher, "I'm really here to help you, and, although I must also evaluate you, don't pay any attention to that." Teachers are not dumb. What is more, the process by which they are socialized into a school setting begins almost as soon as they are employed, if not before. They know the name of the game that is being played, and, if they are not adept at learning all of the defensive maneuvers necessary to protect themselves, they probably will not survive long in the system anyhow. Knowing the name of the game, however, does not preclude its being played. Sometimes games are necessary, harmless, and provide a certain amount of comic relief to the players, each chuckling to himself about how he outwitted his adversary.

But the issue is more than one of survival. It is a question of creating an interpersonal climate between supervisor and teacher in which a productive balance is reached between the demands for freedom and creativity and for control and evaluation. When both parties can talk about the bind they are in, the possibility exists that the conflict can be managed to the satisfaction of both. As long as the overtly obvious constraints of the situation remain beneath the surface, acknowledged individually but not mutually, the conflict will be avoided unproductively, so that one, ostensibly, wins and the other, therefore, loses.

Confronting the Conflict

The supervisor has the responsibility to initiate the confrontation. He is organizationally in control of the interaction between himself and the teacher, so he might as well acknowledge it and take the risks that are implicit in a position of control. Just how he raises the issue is a matter of personal style but, essentially, a productive confrontation involves two major elements. First, the problem has to be defined and accepted by both teacher and supervisor. Because most supervisors are in fact charged with what appear to be two conflicting responsibilities (evaluation and helping) there is not much sense in trying to make light of it or to ignore the circumstances as if they did not exist. The second element, determining whose problem it is, is of a different nature. The problem needs to be owned personally by both the supervisor and the teacher because both of them are involved. The supervisor must deal with his feeling about having to perform the dual function; the teacher, with his feelings about functioning in the conflict. A supervisor might initiate the confrontation by saying, "Look, Mr. Smith, we know that my job involves both evaluating you and trying to help you. How do you feel about it?" Or, "Look, Mr. Smith, we know that my job involves both evaluating you and trying to help you. As I go about this, you may feel yourself in a bind. Let's talk about it." Or, "Look, Mr. Smith, we know that my job involves evaluating you and trying to help you. Both of us are part of the conflict, and I'd like to know how you feel about it." Or, "Look, Mr. Smith, we know that my job involves both evaluating you and trying to help you. I always experience some conflict about this, and I think you will, too. But let's talk about it so we can try to clear away any feelings we might have. Let me start. . . ."

Words on paper, particularly when they are hypothetical, rarely capture the flavor of a human situation. These approaches are not intended to put words in the supervisor's mouth, but to indicate a range of possibilities. I prefer the last suggestion because, in effect, the supervisor is saying that they both really are involved in the problem and that he wants to be open with the teacher about his own feelings. Thus, the supervisor takes the initiative and legitimizes the discussion. The conflict becomes shared and not simply something with which the teacher has to deal.

Is there a way out of the dilemma that results from the supervisor's dual function of evaluating and helping? The answer is probably no, short of a drastic restructuring of whatever system currently passes for evaluation of teachers' performance. Interestingly, there appear to be some moves in the direction of such restructuring. One example is the program developed by the School Management Institute (Armstrong, 1972) and used in some school districts.

The school district develops the initial parameters of the evaluation program. Teachers, supervisors, and administrators are involved in the development, so that the decision becomes as collaborative as possible. Targets for individual jobs are set, within the guidelines of the overall plan, by the teacher and the supervisor. This is a critical point in the process. The teacher takes the initiative by proposing objectives or targets for himself. The supervisor decides whether the targets are realistic for the teacher and congruent with the goals of the school and district. The issue is not strict compliance but acknowledgment of a tolerable range of agreement. The third step in the process consists in deciding what data are necessary to evaluate performance, collecting them, and deciding when the data should be available to the teacher. Frequently, it seems, feedback on performance is delayed by the supervisor and, when the teacher finally gets it, his point of reference is lost, thus depriving him of the opportunity to improve. Suffice it to say that data about a teacher's performance should be made available to the teacher as soon as possible. At the end of a specified time, the supervisor makes an evaluation of the teacher's performance based on the data collected. In some situations this evaluation is made by groups or committees. In this process, the teacher is a subordinate, though Armstrong does not preclude the possibility of self-evaluation as a step in the process. The supervisor and teacher hold an evaluation conference to decide how well job targets are being met and what can be done to improve the job. After the conference, the supervisor and teacher plan follow-up activities that may be designed for both the personal and professional growth of the teacher. And the cycle begins again.

The initial step involved overall organizational goals and objectives, thus placing the relationships between supervisor and teacher in a larger context. Both the teacher and his supervisor need to guide their behavior not only by their own idiosyncratic objectives but also by the extent to which these objectives mesh with those of the larger organization. As soon as this is understood and accepted, both the supervisor and teacher can develop a wider perspective about their relationships with each other. Then, as the teacher initiates job goals and the supervisor reacts to them, there emerges a set of conditions to which the teacher agrees to be bound: "Within the range we have agreed on, it makes sense for me to be evaluated on the following criteria." This is a reasonable point of view, for people tend to be willing to be evaluated along lines they have had a hand in establishing, but will resist, if they can, being evaluated by criteria established by others. When the teacher has developed goals for himself, the supervisor becomes freer to offer help because the help is directed toward the fulfillment of these goals.

Even when the goals have been established, the scheme will not work unless both supervisor and teacher agree on the nature of the data to be collected, when and how they will be collected, and how they will be used. Without such agreement, the system will degenerate to the question of how well the teacher has socialized himself to the supervisor's style, which means that the important issues will not be whether objectives are met, but whether, for example, the teacher is enthusiastic enough to suit the supervisor.

The fourth step in the process, the actual evaluation of the teacher's performance, depends on the locus of evaluation. According to the School Management Institute program, the evaluation is made by the supervisor. The locus of evaluation, then, is external. The possibility of the teacher's evaluating himself, an internal locus, is suggested, but in passing. From what otherwise seems to have the makings of an ideal supervisory world, this external locus may be a detractor. When the teacher becomes his own evaluator, the supervisor will no longer be an evaluator and can concentrate on helping. Teachers would commit themselves to be bound by their evaluations and, ultimately, might be expected to make their own decisions about their competence and whether they ought to remain in teaching. Quite possibly, this development would be too much to expect of the system as it now exists; the hierarchy may need to retain its evaluative function. But it remains that, as long as the supervisor carries the evaluative baggage with him, he will be weighed down when it comes to offering help.

The supervisor's helping role also flaws the program at the point of the evaluation conference: does the supervisor have the skills to hold a conference that is focused, simultaneously, on evaluation and helping? We noted earlier that these skills are not widely held by supervisors, not because they are incapable of attaining them but because they have had little training. The mere altering of educational structure or technology, which seems to be the focal point of change efforts, is not enough. The human side of the enterprise (McGregor, 1960) needs consideration, for, without it, the best of programs tends to run aground on the shoals of indifference or resistance.

The final step in the performance evaluation process, that of planning follow-up activities, makes sense both for the supervisor as a helper and the teacher as a person. Here links can be made with an as yet unforeseen future. The success of any follow-up plan depends on how productive the teacher perceives the whole process to be. The teacher's perceptions, in turn, depend on his relationship with his supervisor. If the relationship has been helpful and has satisfied his needs, one might predict productive follow-up activities. If the relationship has broken down at any point along the way, the follow-up is apt to be pointless.

It would seem that a performance evaluation program for teachers (supervisors, administrators, and others) such as the one described offers a productive alternative for dealing with the conflict between evaluator and helper that is inherent in the supervisor's role. Its major intent is not to resolve that conflict, but, if the program is to achieve its purpose, supervisors and teachers must understand the problems they will confront together. The program requires a systemwide attitudinal and behavioral reorientation toward instruction and relationships between supervisors and teachers, a shift away from what might be called socialization toward a concern with results. The supervisor, instead of trying to make the teacher's style a model of his own, concentrates on helping the teacher achieve his objectives regardless of style, within limits. If the supervisor and the teacher are concentrating on the results of the teacher's work with the students, the question of whether or not his methodology or teaching style suits the tastes of the supervisor fades into the background, and the supervisor and teacher can relate to each other as adults who share a common concern, who respect each other's skills, and who can communicate openly with each other in a mutually helpful way. Without such a reorientation, the chances are good that the evaluation program will become mechanistic, maintaining an image of rational concern and problem solving aimed at results, but not changing things in any way that particularly matters.

Here is another example, much more modest in scope than the one just discussed, of an effort to deal with the helping-evaluating role conflict experienced by supervisors. It stems from a situation in which I am currently engaged, working with a junior high school faculty in an effort to upgrade the quality of instruction in a school which, by all reports, is functioning quite well. The project is still in process, and the results are not yet clear. But it is worth recounting to this point since it highlights the role conflict problem to which this chapter has been devoted.

The request for consultative help came to me from the department chairpeople who have direct responsibility for working with, helping, and evaluating teachers. Their initial request was for assistance in developing a teaching observation instrument that would enable them to observe and talk with their teachers in a way that would enable the teachers to benefit from the observations. The instrument was to be based on a statement about school goals and teaching philosophy that had been developed several years ago but never implemented in any systematically meaningful way.

My first meeting with the group that requested assistance was exciting. They were obviously serious and enthusiastic about their task. I listened and, after a while, raised two questions: Do the teachers buy into the schoolwide statement? Is the observation instrument to be used for helping teachers or evaluating them? The response to the first question was one of doubt. Since the statement had been developed, teachers had come and gone in the school, and it was questionable whether what had been written some time ago had any real meaning for the faculty today, at least so far as providing a rallying point for them. The response to the second question was not so ambiguous. It was characterized by a few embarrassed grins, nonverbal shuffling, and the verbal comment of "helping, but . . . ."

It seemed clear that, if the concern with enhancing the quality of instruction in the school was to become more than an academic exercise, the questions I had raised had to be dealt with directly. Merely to develop an observation instrument without working on the two issues would be a waste of time. Further, what needed to be understood was that the whole process of development would be relatively long term, perhaps as much as a year. A simple in-service session would not do. The group agreed, and initial time was made available during a teachers' workshop day so that the faculty as a whole could start to confront the issue.

Confront things they did, and on the levels of both questions! The faculty first developed statements about effective teaching *in that school*. The original group met and reacted to the statements with the rest of the faculty sitting around them, listening, and interjecting their own comments from time to time. It is this latter point that is important, for it was the faculty that raised the question, "Are you doing this to help us improve or to evaluate us?" Back again we were to the starting point, but not quite. The point is that the issue had been raised publicly for the first time. Thus, congruent with the theme that has been suggested several times in these chapters, if the problem is to be resolved satisfactorily it will be by dealing with it in an open fashion and not by avoiding it.

I mentioned above that this project is still in process. It is, indeed, an unfinished symphony at this writing. But the people involved have not shied away from troublesome questions. Subsequent meetings have been held, and more are scheduled. Much work has been done, and more remains to be done. If the project is to be successful, three major things will eventually have to happen. First, some consensus, leaving room for irregularities, will have to be reached concerning criteria for effective teaching. Second, considerable energy will have to be expended on role negotiations between the teachers and chairpeople. Third, both groups will have to learn how to give and receive help in the context of teaching and supervision. This is a large order, and whether or not it will be filled is still an open question. As I have noted, however, the situation has changed from one in which problems were previously dealt with in a covert manner to one where they be spoken of openly—no mean feat. Perhaps supervisor-teacher relationships will change in that school, after all.

15   Balancing Things Out: Reciprocity

This chapter deals with the reciprocal nature of relationships between supervisors and teachers. On another level, this chapter is a plea to supervisors to understand the dynamic qualities of interpersonal reciprocity—an understanding that can guide more productive work with teachers. In considering reciprocity, I shall be discussing the notion of the psychological contract (Levinson *et al.*, 1972; Levinson, 1968) and the various integrating mechanisms through which organizations attempt to fuse the goals of individuals with the organization's objectives (Barrett, 1970).

The idea of a psychological contract between an individual and an organization seems to have been originated by Levinson (1962), a clinical psychologist who became interested in problems of mental health in work situations.

My colleagues and I observed transference phenomena and people's efforts to fulfill various psychological needs in their relationship with a company. It was apparent that, in large measure, the relationship arose out of and constituted efforts to fulfill expectations (only part of which were conscious) of both parties, person and organization. This process of fulfilling mutual expectations and satisfying mutual needs in the relationship between a man and his work organization was conceptualized as a process of *reciprocation*. Reciprocation is a process of carrying out a psychological contract between person and company or any other institution where one works. It is a complementary process in which the individual and the organization seem to become a part of each other [Levinson, 1968, p. 39].

177

Levinson seems to be saying that an individual going to work for an organization carries with him a set of expectations or needs, many of which may be subconscious. He hopes that his work environment— the job itself and his relationships with superiors and co-workers— will help fulfill these needs and expectations. By the same token, the organization has expectations of the individual both in the job, which tend to be explicit, and in the relationships he will develop and maintain with others, which tend to be subtle and frequently part of the organization's informal structure. A school's expectations of a second-grade teacher may be quite clear and in writing as far as the curriculum and his pupils' achievement is concerned but, as far as behavior is concerned (whether the teacher is expected to be assertive, passive, dependent, warm, or distant with other teachers or the principal), the expectations are rarely expressed formally although they do exist and are frequently powerful. So it is in any work organization: the individual wants to make the organization satisfy his needs, and the organization wants the individual to satisfy its needs and help achieve its goals. (Bakke [1953], in an earlier conceptualization, refers to this process as one of fusion.) This is the psychological contract, and its fulfillment depends on how well the reciprocity works. To the extent that the individual and the organization are able to satisfy each other's needs, the individual will tend to identify himself with the organization and to consider himself and his role as symbolic of that for which the organization stands.

Levinson identified the central terms of the contract, particularly for the individual, as the needs, which each person has in different measure, that must be satisfied if the person's relationship with the organization is to be productive—needs for ministration, maturation, and mastery.

Ministration needs are, for a teacher, needs "for closeness, for gratification, and for support, protection, and guidance" (Levinson, 1968, p. 147). They are idiosyncratic in that each of us requires their satisfaction at different levels. One teacher may need a great deal of support in his work, another may demand very little, but each has to have what he needs. The extent to which the ministration needs of an individual are satisfied by his organizational relationships symbolizes for him the degree to which the organization "cares."

The notion of maturation needs implies that given appropriate conditions, each person will develop his potential to whatever extent he can. Maturation needs tend to be unrecognized by a person except, perhaps, in retrospect.

If they are met, the person unfolds; if they are not, he vegetates. Occasionally someone may ask, for example, why an obviously intelligent man is in a lowly position. Apart from that kind of observation, it may never be apparent to the man himself or to others that he might have been able to do better, that he has not grown as he might have, or even that he is stunted. Maturation needs could even be viewed as anti-stunting needs (*ibid.*, p. 174).

The development of potential requires a climate that provides opportunities for creative activity and adequate reality testing—checks and balances. Human growth tends not to occur in freedom and creativity unbounded by the real world or lacking in feedback on the results of one's efforts. A teacher can pursue an unlimited number of creative classroom endeavors and, in the process, sense a great deal of personal growth and development. Unless, however, he submits his efforts to some test of reality—Did they produce the results he intended and how does he know?—the sense of growth is not substantiated.

Need for mastery refers, in general, to drives for the competence and skill that enable us to have some control over our environment; the need to feel that we are not at the mercy of conflicting environmental forces, that we can respond to and even redirect those forces to serve our own goals. For the teacher, important competences and skills may well embrace more than those germane to the classroom, including, for example, the ability to deal adequately with colleagues on the faculty, the central office bureaucracy, or the principal of the school. Need for mastery deals with having a sense of control over those aspects of one's environment that make a difference in one's day-to-day functioning. Some of my colleagues, for example, become quite upset and frustrated because they find themselves unable to influence the central administration, so they spend a great deal of time in meetings trying to establish a basis for control. My own concern with trying to influence central administration (which is clearly part of my environment) is minimal. I am neither better nor worse than my colleagues—just different and perhaps a little less frustrated.

If relationships between supervisor and teacher constitute a microsocial system, with the supervisor an agent of the macroorganization, the concepts of the psychological contract and the

reciprocation process as it is adapted to the interaction of supervisors and teachers may be summarized as in Figure 15.1. Both
supervisor and teacher bring expectations to their relationship.
These expectations form the psychological contract whose terms
deal with needs for ministration, maturation, and mastery. If the
reciprocation process works, the teacher's needs are satisfied, and
he will be mentally healthy, that is, he will have a wide variety of
sources of gratification, will treat others as individuals and not as
role holders, will be flexible, instead of stereotypically rigid under
stress, will accept his own limitations and assets, and will perform
his job actively and productively.

The scheme, though it seems theoretically sound, is deceptively
simple; the processes are exceedingly complex and their implementation requires a great deal of supervisory skill. For example,
with regard to the ministration needs of the teacher, the supervisor
has to be a skillful interpersonal diagnostician. A teacher is not apt
to tell his supervisor how much interpersonal closeness he needs in
order to function well, nor his requirements for protection and
support, even if he were aware of them. The supervisor must sense
these needs in the teacher's behavior and, in being aware of how
well he can fulfill these needs, be prepared to offer the teacher
other sources of gratification if he is incapable of doing the job
himself. With regard to the teacher's maturation needs, particularly
because they are unrecognized or unmentioned, the supervisor must
create the atmosphere that will enable the teacher to experiment
and grow as a person and must learn to work with a teacher so that
the teacher will test the reality of his developmental activities
appropriately. With reference to the teacher's needs for mastery,
the supervisor probably has to be a counselor from time to time. It
would be through this kind of interaction, unless the supervisor
picks up cues in other situations, that the teacher's feelings of lack
of potency and control over his environment might surface.

At this point a supervisor might well say—and with justification—
"Oh, come now, you're suggesting that I be all things to all people
in an almost God-like fashion. Come down to earth." It is true, of
course, that no one supervisor can be expected to have the knowledge and skill that would enable him to deal with every teacher he
encounters productively, to fulfill the contract. Life just does not
work out that way. People at work tend to develop a mode of

FIGURE 15.1   The Psychological Contract and Reciprocation

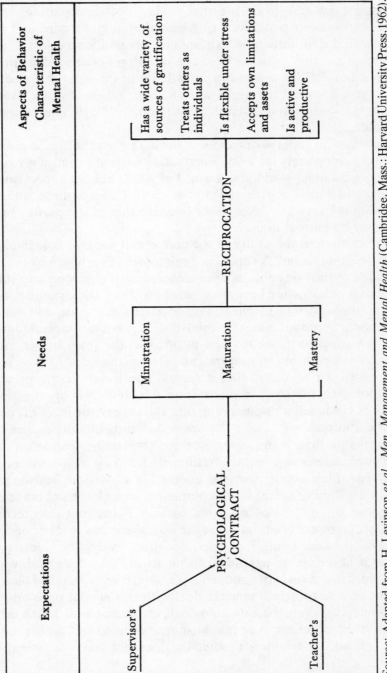

Expectations	Needs	Aspects of Behavior Characteristic of Mental Health

Supervisor's
Teacher's
PSYCHOLOGICAL CONTRACT

Ministration
Maturation
Mastery

RECIPROCATION

Has a wide variety of sources of gratification

Treats others as individuals

Is flexible under stress

Accepts own limitations and assets

Is active and productive

Source: Adapted from H. Levinson *et al.*, *Men, Management and Mental Health* (Cambridge, Mass.: Harvard University Press, 1962).

interpersonal and group life that makes do, representing a compromise between conditions to which they might aspire and those they would find untenable. An implicit bargain is struck, the terms of which are that each party to the situation acknowledges that he cannot have all he wishes but he will settle for what it appears he can have. Some of his needs are satisfied; others are not. But the balance is "satisficing" (March and Simon, 1958). People, somehow, get along.

So it is with supervisors and teachers. The psychological contract is rarely completely fulfilled. Some satisfying compromise is reached between an ideal world and a world in which neither supervisor nor teacher can exist together. Without such a compromise, the relationship is likely to cease, either because one of the parties breaks it off or by mutual consent.

What, then, is the utility of the concept of the psychological contract in supervision? A supervisor might be well advised to consider the idea of the contract, its dimensions, and the process of reciprocation as a device for becoming more aware of the dynamics of his relationship with a teacher. The teacher's behavior will tell the supervisor about his needs for ministration, maturation, and mastery. But the supervisor needs to be attuned to the level on which the teacher is operating so that he can pick up the cues.

There is, it seems to me, a second use for the concept of the psychological contract in supervision. Much as it is appropriate to think of the teacher's demanding that the supervisor meet his needs, so the students may make the same demands of the teacher. It is conceivable that, if the supervisor and the teacher can learn about the implications of contract fulfillment for their relationship, they can also think about it in the context of classroom learning. My teenage daughter's most bitter complaints about her teachers seemed to occur when "he doesn't listen to us." Translated into terms of the psychological contract, what she was saying was that her ministration needs were being frustrated because, really, "he doesn't care enough about us as people to listen to us." A supervisor who is conceptually aware of, and able to interpret, behavior like this might be able to help a teacher deal with this sort of problem.

Contracts, even the psychological, are reciprocal. Much as the supervisor represents a potential source of need fulfillment for the teacher, so the teacher, though he does not have organizational control of the relationship, can potentially satisfy the supervisor's needs, particularly for ministration and mastery, but less so for maturation. The supervisor needs from the teacher what the teacher needs from him: a certain measure of warmth, closeness, and caring, as well as a relationship that promotes his need for mastery of his environment, not in any autocratic sense but in the sense of a developing awareness of competence. The teacher, by way of the style of his interaction with the supervisor, exerts a great deal of control over the extent to which the supervisor's needs can be met.

How does all this happen? How does the relationship become mutually enhancing for both teacher and supervisor? Again we must focus on the supervisor. His behavior and his sensitivity and awareness of the teacher will determine how well the reciprocity will work. If his needs are being frustrated in his interaction with the teacher, he had best look to himself for the initial diagnosis. If the problems of supervisory relationships are not first solved by or through the supervisor, the relationship will probably degenerate or be severed altogether.

THE INTEGRATING AGENT

One role that a supervisor plays, but which is almost universally overlooked, is that of providing the means by which teachers (mostly new teachers) are made a part of the system. It is to this role that we now turn our attention, keeping in mind the idea of reciprocity of relationships that is the focus of this chapter. The point of departure is another conceptual transfer from general organization theory to what has been referred to as the microsocial system between the teacher and the supervisor.

Barrett (1970) postulates three integration models or mechanisms that may link the goals that an individual has with the supraordinate needs of the organization. These models are of exchange, socialization, and accommodation. They may not—in fact, in most cases, probably do not—develop out of planned strategies, but are more likely to be part of the informal structure of the organization. Barrett points out that "organization members spontaneously commit themselves to the pursuit of individual *goals*. They do not necessarily commit themselves spontaneously to the pursuit of organizational objectives" (p. 3). Thus, when a teacher goes to work in a school, his initial concerns are automatically egocentric. If the school desires a teacher to commit himself to objectives beyond his own goals, it should expend some thought on how the commitment is to be made. If the supervisor wishes to broaden the teacher's perspectives of school life and of their relationship, he will have to give some thought to the manner in which it is to be done and not rely on chance.

The *exchange model* is similar to the classic bargaining situation: "We want your services to do a job. In return for your commitment of time, energy, and skill to things we consider important, we are prepared to reward you accordingly." Sometimes the rewards are explicit, for example, the salary; sometimes they are more informal, for example, a supervisor will show interest in a particular project or praise a job he judges to have been well done. Whatever the medium of exchange, formal or informal, the transaction is made by bargaining. An unintended consequence is that the organization trains its members not to go beyond the limits of the original bargain unless further rewards are forthcoming. In addition, there comes a time, different for each of us, when the offer of additional rewards has no effect. We are satiated.

The *socialization model* depends on social influence. Through the use of persuasion or modeling behavior, either by the leader or the worker's peers, attempts are made to get the individual to value the organization's objectives and expend energy to attain them. As the process is successful, it is not unusual for the individual to give up some of his egocentric needs, particularly if they happen to conflict with what the organization considers important. In any event, it appears that, as a socialization strategy is used, the individual's goals and the organization's objectives will find more in common with one another.

The *accommodation model* runs counter to the socialization model. In the latter, the organization tells the individual that, if he opens himself up to influence and observes the behavioral models that are presented to him, he will see their worth and will follow them. The accommodation model takes the individual's goals, needs, and motivations as they are and tries to adapt the organization's structure and operations to them. The organization's objectives are not necessarily changed, but relationships are such that "the pursuit of organizational objectives will be intrinsically rewarding and will provide for the simultaneous pursuit of the individual's existing goals" (Barrett, 1970, p. 11). The primary mechanisms of accommodation are concerned with role or job design and participation. Job descriptions are developed and changed from time to time so that they permit the individual to move toward his own goals while accomplishing the organization's objectives. Or the individual participates in such organizational activities as objective setting, problem solving, and decision making, which enable him to influence the setting and alter it if he can. In the accommodation, as in the socialization model, it is assumed that there will be a broader overlap of the individual's goals and the organization's objectives than there is in the exchange model.

Only rarely is any one of these models likely to emerge in its pure form in an organization. They tend to exist alongside one another, with one of them providing the predominant organizational theme. Assembly-line work is mostly a matter of exchange. Schools seem to emphasize socialization. Some organizations, tending toward participative management, might symbolize accommodation.

Barrett's notion of social mechanisms that integrate the goals of individuals with the objectives of the organization can, I think, be transfered to the relationship between supervisor and teacher. "Behavior begets behavior." As has been suggested a number of times, if the supervisor questions the efficacy of his work with a teacher, he should first check his own behavior.

By way of moving the integrating mechanism notion out of the organizational context and into that of supervisors and teachers, then, we can create an image of three interacting climates, each related to a particular mechanism. The behavior by which the teacher reciprocates will reflect the supervisor's mechanism.

The Exchange Model

What is communicated from supervisor to teacher in the exchange model is that teaching is a job like any other job: you put in your time, perform adequately, refrain from irritating your supervisors, and are rewarded accordingly. The relationships between supervisor and teacher reflect this image. So long as the teacher comports himself correctly (from the supervisor's point of view), he will receive the expected rewards. The commitment of excessive energy, either to the job or to the relationship with the **supervisor** is discouraged, particularly if the commitment would make the teacher's efforts more visible than the job requires. The teacher reciprocates. He picks up his cues from the supervisor and starts to behave and evince the attitudes that will indicate his commitment to the job strictly within the limits of his contract. He is careful, for example, not to arrive in school too early in the morning and not to stay there very long after the school day is finished. He becomes quickly aware of what kinds of behavior the supervisor approves of. He gives and he gets, and both parties establish a way of working together.

The Socialization Model

The cues that the supervisor sends out in a climate of socialization are much more diffuse than they are in a climate of exchange. The supervisor indicates to the teacher that, "the best way for you to relate yourself to the school and what it is doing is to watch what I do and how I feel. In addition, watch the other teachers so that you can find out how people operate together here. If you do this, it won't be long before you find your needs being satisfied, and you will also be making a contribution to the total effort." Socialization is symbolized by paternalism and benevolent modeling relationships. It leaves room for the satisfaction of the teacher's idiosyncratic needs, but usually only within the models that are built. This point holds for what transpires between supervisor and teacher and between the teacher and his colleagues.

The teacher responds in kind. Particularly because the supervisor constitutes an important source of the teacher's rewards (actually, a matter of exchange), the teacher lets himself be socialized into a benign submissiveness. He gives the supervisor his allegiance and, in turn, receives guidance and support.

In order for the socialization process to work, the models (the supervisor and other teachers) that are presented to the teacher must be appropriate for him. People tend to be selective about those with whom they want to identify. It is difficult to mandate models without a concomitant rigid structure of rewards and punishments, which few schools have. This may be part of the reason that some teachers are misfits in one system but not in another; their models may simply not have been ones with which they were able to identify.

The Accommodation Model

The supervisor employing a socialization model says to the teacher, "come towards me and you will learn the things I think are important. Your needs will be integrated into mine (the system's)." In the accommodation model the supervisor moves toward the teacher. He first examines the teacher's skills, needs, and aspirations and then, within broad limits, seeks ways in which the system can adjust itself to the teacher's goals while maintaining its own requirements and objectives. The supervisor becomes a collaborative helper, an agent of the larger system who is interested in the teacher's problems and has both the skill and material resources to help solve them. He is not, however, the pawn of the teacher, to bend at the teacher's every whim. He maintains the overall organizational view and provides reality-testing procedures for the teacher's ideas. Reciprocally, the teacher collaborates with the supervisor. As the process develops, and particularly as a result of the reality-testing role played by the supervisor, the teacher starts to sense the breadth of the organization's boundaries and the ways in which he can alter or expand them so that his own goals and the school's objectives have a considerable degree of congruency. The relationship itself between supervisor and teacher becomes focused on problem solving in a more or less egalitarian manner. Little emphasis is placed on rewards and punishments or on socialization pressures from the supervisor or colleagues.

These brief and hypothetical images of the supervisor in each of the integrating models have been purposefully hyperbolic, to make the images clear. The social situations, too, have been overdrawn. It would be unrealistic to expect that any effort by a supervisor to integrate a teacher's goals with the organization's objectives would be limited to behavior characteristic of exchange, socialization, or accommodation. What becomes important in the way that the supervisor deals with the teacher is the dominant relational mode of their interaction. Behavior begets behavior. Exchange models produce social climates in which exchange is the premium; teachers will tend to reciprocate socialization efforts in relatively predictable ways; they will alter their behavior under conditions of accommodation.

These notions should help a supervisor to monitor himself with a teacher *if* he is aware of his style and the interactional dynamics that emanate from it. I pursue this general idea further in the next chapter, which is concerned with the supervisor as an interpersonal interventionist.

16   Supervision as
Interpersonal Intervention

The focus of my argument concerning the problematic nature and effectiveness of supervisor-teacher interaction has been on the interpersonal dimension of the relationship. This position represents much more than a philosophical point of view. That is, there seems clearly to be a body of knowledge, albeit incomplete, that carries with it the strong suggestion that the character of the interpersonal transactions that occur between supervisor and teacher is related, in large measure, to the extent that the two will be able to work productively together. The issue, of course, is not that the two need "love" each other. Rather, the point is that teaching and supervision are both, primarily, intense and complex human interactive functions. Matters of technique, methodology, and curriculum tend to be dealt with effectively in supervision to the degree that the interpersonal ground of the relationship between supervisor and teacher can be described as communicatively open, maximally trusting, and minimally defensive.

These points lead me to suggest the need to reconceptualize the function of supervision and the role of supervisors in a way I think fits the needs of teachers, supervisors, and schools—even if these needs are presently unrecognized. What I have in mind is to conceive of the function of supervision as *interpersonal intervention* and the role of the supervisor as that of *interpersonal interventionist*,

Adapted and reprinted by permission from A. Blumberg, "Supervision as Interpersonal Intervention," *Journal of Classroom Interaction*, 13 (no. 1, December 1977): 24-31.

that is, a person whose job requires that he intrude in particular ways into a teacher's personal and technical system to achieve certain ends or products. The product most typically associated with supervision in the schools is an improved quality of instruction in classrooms. I add two additional products to be sought: the personal and professional growth of teachers and the personal and professional growth of supervisors. Few people in education or the community at large, I suspect, would argue with the first, improving the quality of instruction, as the essence of supervision. By the same token, I have a hunch that many would disagree with my position on the other two products, the mutual growth of supervisor and teacher, as critical to the effective rendering of help to the teacher. Nonetheless, it seems clear to me that, if the function of supervision as it is presently conceived in the schools is to grow beyond what appears to be a relatively devalued function by great numbers of teachers to one that is held in high esteem, it must ultimately include a concern with the potential mutual growth aspect of the relationship.

I am well aware that the normative structure of schools and teachers does not support in any strong way the position I take, though there is some evidence of concern by individual teachers. For example, Gwynn (1969, p. 76) reports a continuing study of the ways in which both preservice and in-service teachers thought supervisors could be of help to them. Of the twenty-four "ways in which a supervisor can help," one of them was categorized "with my problems—professional, community, social." It was ranked fifth and received, curiously, more support from experienced teachers than from preservice or first-year teachers. Though Gwynn's results may be somewhat out of date, it is possible that teachers sense and need something of which the system is unaware. For example, I frequently ask my students, "When was the last time your supervisor (or principal) engaged you in a discussion of their personal or career goals with the object of being helpful to you?" It is only the rare case where, in a class of thirty-five or so, more than one or two hands are raised affirmatively. I presume it would be the height of folly to ask supervisors the companion question: "When was the last time you sought help from teachers concerning problems you might have with your own personal and professional development?"

As I interpret the current concerns with competency-based

supervision (Harris and King, 1974) and clinical supervision, neither of them approaches the problem of supervision in the schools from the perspective that I am suggesting. By and large, both of these approaches appear to give most emphasis to the curricular, methodological, or technological aspects of teaching. There appears, in both of them, to be little concern with the nature and quality of the human relationship that exists between supervisor and teacher. For example, the Harris and King project referred to above proposes three major competency "domains" that are central to supervision: problem solving, human relations, and job-task. Within these domains, eleven basic competencies have been specified, and, of the eleven, only one may be properly categorized as focusing on the interpersonal system of the supervisor and teacher. Further, there are seventy-five separate functions connected with the domains, out of which three appear to bear on supervisor-teacher interaction and relationships.

I have no comparable data to report relative to clinical supervision. I do, however, have anecdotal reports from students of mine who are involved in student teaching supervision with a "clinical" model. The gist of these anecdotes is that the supervisors, at least, feel constrained by the structure of the model and feel it is a mechanical, rather ritualistic, "going through the paces" experience. As one student supervisor reported, "I am made to feel that I am dealing with things and techniques, not people." There is no question, of course, that the learning and testing of different teaching methodologies and techniques are important. The question at root, in my judgment, concerns the nature of the relationships and subsequent transactions that occur between supervisor and teacher as the methodologies and techniques are learned. Put into research design terms, the issue involves the character of the process variables that mediate supervisor-teacher interaction.

In addition, but not at all an afterthought, the question also involves the substance of the supervisory transaction that goes beyond issues of methodology or classroom control, for example. To pursue this point further, it is instructive to learn about positions taken in another helping profession toward the nature and substance of the supervisory relationship. In *Coping with Conflict* (Mueller and Kell, 1972), a book about the supervision of psychotherapists and counselors, one finds some ideas that are germane at this point, if only to hold up an image of what might be relevant to supervision in the schools. The following quotations, all from Mueller and Kell, convey the flavor of the argument.*

[Students] have a way of squirming out of casebooks. As they come alive, . . . [students] may shed their inhibitions . . . causing . . . [the teacher] anxious moments [p. 3].

Learning *what* is [good teaching] is an insufficient goal of supervision unless both parties recognize that a major part of what is [good teaching] is the way in which the [teacher] sees himself [p. 5].

So long as the supervisor and [teacher] focus their attention solely on the [students'] behavior and assume that managing that source of anxiety (i.e., the [teachers']) is a sufficient goal of supervision, the process of supervision will remain didactic at best [p. 6].

If the supervisory relationship is to develop along the lines we propose, . . . then that relationship must be founded in trust, openness, warmth, and honest collaboration. The essence of supervisory relationships is no different from that of any significant human relationship and unless that common essence (i.e., trust, openness, warmth, and honest collaboration) exists, the supervisory relationship will not be actuated [pp. 7-8].

These statements imply a concept of supervision and supervisor-teacher relationships which, if transferred into the context of public education, goes far beyond what is currently the experience and training of most supervisors. The suggestions implicit in them for a more fulfilling and productive function of supervision in the schools may be restated in the following way:

1. An appropriate focus of at least some part of the supervisor-teacher transaction should be on those elements of the classroom situation that tend to induce anxiety in the teacher and the ways in which the teacher deals with that anxiety. This is not to suggest that all teachers are anxious. It is, however, to make the point that there are conditions in every classroom that produce teachers' anxiety, that sometimes it is overwhelming, thus immobilizing, and that an extremely important function of supervision is to help the teacher understand its source and work with it . . . Much as the classroom may produce anxiety in the teacher, so may the supervisory situation produce it for the supervisor. If this statement

---

* I have taken the liberty of substituting, in brackets, more educationally relevent terms than the ones used originally by Mueller and Kell. The original reads "clients" instead of [students], "therapist" instead of [teacher], and "therapeutic" instead of [good teaching].

seems out of context, let me suggest that the reader, in retrospect, examine his own emotionality during the last time he tried to deal with the anxiety of another person.

2. So long as the thrust of supervision is on curricular and methodological matters to the neglect of behavioral matters—those of the teachers in the classroom and of the teachers and supervisors in their interaction with each other—the outcome of supervision will fall short of its potential. Metaphorically, knowing the words is not a sufficient condition for singing a song. One must also know and be able to sing the music *and* want to sing!

3. To the extent that the focus of supervision remains solely on the behavior of students as the source of the teacher's problems, the supervisor's role will be that of a didactic teacher. The suggestion is that, as long as problems of teaching exclude the teacher as a person, the better are the chances that supervision will be a prescriptive process with slight chance for growth of either the teacher or the supervisor.

4. In order for supervisor-teacher relationships to be growth producing, they need to be seen as *significant* human relationships, not matter-of-fact, ritualistic ones, as appears so often to be the case. Indeed, as was discussed in Chapter 6, the more the supervisory relationship was characterized, behaviorally, by the components of a supportive interpersonal climate, the more productive and important it was from the point of view of the teacher.

5. At some time in the supervisor-teacher relationship, attention needs to be given to the personal and professional growth problems of the teacher, if only to test whether the teacher is experiencing any such problems. What is *not* at issue here is whether the supervisor should be a psychotherapist or try to play psychotherapist. What *is* at issue is the need, as I see it, for the supervisor to convey an authentic "reaching-out" to the teacher as a person.

THE SUPERVISOR AS AN INTERPERSONAL INTERVENTIONIST

If educational supervision is to move in the directions that have been proposed above, it seems obvious that the concept of the role of the supervisor needs to change. The change is from a role that may be described primarily as that of experienced curricular and methodological technician who comes bearing gifts or knows best how things should be done to one where the prerequisite skills and understandings are most closely associated with being able to help another with personal, interpersonal, and group problems. In addition, this role requires the supervisor to be a competent pedagogical technician. Further, and underlying this concept, is the notion that the process of learning in supervision, for both teacher and supervisor, is an experiential, not a didactic one.

The rationale for conceiving of supervision in this light has been implicit in the comments that have been made to this point. Explicitly, the rationale is as follows:

1. At its roots, teaching involves the creation of learning opportunities in an environment whose essential human dynamics are interpersonal and group in nature.

2. Problems that teachers confront and that interfere with the creation of learning opportunities have their roots, again, in the human dynamics of the classroom setting, though they may be conceptualized by the teacher and a supervisor in other terms—curricular or methodological competencies of the teacher. It does suggest, however, that they are the figure and not the ground of the teaching-learning process. Thus, whatever the technological or pedagogical skills of a teacher may be, they become actuated in an environment which is either subtly or openly characterized by issues of power, motivation, communications, peer-group relations, norms, and both intragroup and intergroup conflict.

3. The primary task of the supervisor is to intervene and help the teacher deal with these categories of human problems in the classroom so that teachers' competencies may be most adequately used.

The concepts of intervention and intervenor have received their most thorough consideration from Argyris (1970). "To intervene is to enter an ongoing system of relationships, to come between or among persons, groups . . . for the purpose of helping them . . . the system exists independently of the intervenor" (p. 15). The intervenor, thus, is separate, but related to the client system.

This view values the client system [i.e., the teacher, for our purposes] as an ongoing, self-responsible unity that has the obligation to be in control over its own destiny. An intervenor, in this view, assists a system to become more effective in problem solving, decision making, and decision implementation in such a way that the system can continue to be increasingly effective in these activities and have a decreasing need for the intervenor [p. 16].

Flowing from this concept of the intervenor role are three primary tasks or processes. The first is the generation of valid information associated with the problem. The second is to maintain the client's system's discreteness and autonomy, thus the necessity for free, informed choice. The third is concerned with the development of the client's internal committment to the choices made, the issue being that, if commitment is low, the changes of lasting learning and change resulting from the intervention are minimal.

We must move down the ladder of Argyris' abstraction to the role of a supervisor as an interpersonal intervenor. It seems to me that a fundamental premise is involved. It is that this concept of supervision as interpersonal intervention implies a sort of world view on the part of a supervisor that I believe not to be widely held. It holds that adults, when confronted with appropriate data about themselves and the situation in which they are working where their adultness is acknowledged and accepted, will make decisions for themselves that are appropriate for them. This is a widely accepted democratic ethic. But let us move from the fluffiness of it to some obvious behavioral and emotional questions. Can a supervisor "let" a teacher make what seem to be wrong decisions and respect and support the teacher for making them? If these decisions turn out to be wrong, can the supervisor refrain from taking an "I told you so" stance? Can a supervisor "let" a teacher fail? Can a supervisor "let" himself fail? In the face of rejection of the supervisor's help by the teacher, can the supervisor still convey regard for the teacher as a person? How does the supervisor handle his feelings of being rejected: With anger? With acceptance? With empathic understanding of the teacher?

One can go on and on. Ultimately, however, the answers to these and similar questions need to be provided, not by a paper-and-pencil test, but by the supervisor through behavior. From what I have observed of the behavior of supervisors, most of them would have a great deal of difficulty answering them, behaviorally, in a growth-producing way. They would find difficulty "letting" a teacher make the "wrong" decision, "letting" a teacher or themselves fail, not reacting to rejection with anger and concurrent desires to punish, for example. And they would have these difficulties not because they are bad or stupid people; rather, the difficulties would arise because most of us have been trained, unwittingly, I suspect, to deal differently with the people for whom we are responsible. That is, our training leads us to understand and accept the premise that organizations are built around the idea that "father (or mother) knows best." And the institutions in which we work tend to support what might be called this "benevolent partner-guilty child" stance. If the difficulties are to be overcome, it means that we must deal with the problem of both individual and organizational change.

THE GENERATION OF VALID INFORMATION

The nature of the information that the supervisor-intervenor gathers in the course of working with a teacher is a matter of deep significance, much more so than meets the casual eye. At issue is the postulate (Tichy, 1975) that the information that an intervenor focuses on in his work is reflective of the assumption he makes about his role and the diagnostic position he takes about the nature of system problems. What information the supervisor focuses on, then, is projective of how that supervisor sees his role and function. Further, the manner in which the data is collected, collaboratively with the teacher or noncollaboratively, is reflective of the manner in which the supervisor conceives of role relations with the teacher. Thus, if the data collected by the supervisor are concerned only with curricular methodology and are collected without any suggestions from the teacher, one might infer that the supervisor sees problems of teaching almost exclusively in terms of method, and the supervisor sees his role, vis-à-vis the teacher, *as a teacher*, or, perhaps, as a benevolent-paternalistic problem solver.

The information-gathering stance of the supervisor as interpersonal intervenor is, first of all, collaborative with the teacher. This stance conveys an egalitarian view of the supervisor-teacher relationship—one of two professionals analyzing and working on problems together. The nature of the data to be collected ranges over a wide variety of possibilities, some of which are teaching method, the behavioral style of the teacher, the behavior of the students related to the teacher's behavior style, the ways in which the teacher deals with conflict in the classroom, the ways in which the teacher deals with his own anger or warmth, the nature of the relationship between the supervisor and the teacher, the ways in which supervisors and teachers deal with their anger, warmth, and dependency toward each other.

The focus of the data-collecting efforts of the supervisor as interpersonal intervenor, then, is on the wholeness of the supervisor-teacher microsystem and not merely on some disconnected parts of it.

FREE AND INFORMED CHOICE

The underlying principle at work relative to the supervisor-intervenor's efforts to create a situation of free and informed choice on the part of the teacher is to maintain the separateness and autonomy of the teacher as a client-system. Because a condition of free choice implies that the client makes those decisions that are relevant to him, "Free choice makes it possible for the clients to remain responsible for their destiny" (Argyris, 1970, p. 16). There is another consequence of free choice that has already been alluded to. It is that, as the supervisor works to create this condition with a teacher, the implicit suggestion is that the teacher is an adult, not a child. This is not merely a platitude. The consequences of an adult-adult relationship are much different from those that may be characterized as parent-child, as even people familiar with the popularized versions of Transactional Analysis (Berne, 1964) know. Most importantly, for our purposes, the chances of *mutual* growth for supervisor and teacher are greatly enhanced in the former and only dimly possible in the latter.

INTERNAL COMMITMENT

The task of developing the internal commitment of the teacher to a course of action in the process of supervision is simple on its face, highly complex in action. Again, Argyris (1970, p. 20) spells it out succinctly. When one becomes internally committed to a course of action, thus owning it and feeling responsible for it, "the individual has reached the point where he is acting on the choice because it fulfills his own needs and sense of responsibility, as well as those of the system."

There are both practical and philosophical consequences to the supervisor-intervenor's concern with working on the development of internal commitment on the part of the teacher. Practically, without such commitment, both the interaction between supervisor and teacher and any "problem-solving" that comes of it takes on a gamelike quality. The game is not necessarily of the win-lose variety, but it may be one that is implicitly designed to end in a tie with neither side having made any permanent encroachment on the territory of the other. For the supervisor, this may mean creating the illusion (perhaps self-deceiving) of being interested in the teacher's problems and of his own involvement in the supervisory process. For the teacher, also engaged in creating illusions, it may mean trying to convey to the supervisor that their work together has been helpful and contains potential for long-term growth. The results of this game, if successfully played by both parties, is that each maintains what he sees to be his integrity, and no one loses except, possibly, the youngsters in the classroom.

Under conditions of internal commitment—the teacher to problem solutions and the supervisor-intervenor to the process of helping—it no longer becomes necessary to play the game. Things are simply more honest, or they have the potential to be that way.

Philosophically, the development of a condition of internal commitment reinforces the adultness of the relationship with its consequent potential for mutual growth. Included in this idea is the "all-rightness" of either the teacher or the supervisor to be openly *noncommitted* to the extent that each can admit feelings on nonproductiveness about the situation. This might lead to an open decision either to sever the relationship or seek other avenues by which to pursue it.

In my mind, and by way of summary, the role concept of the supervisor as interpersonal intervenor is a model for adult learning. It focuses not only on the problems of classroom teaching and learning, but also on the ingredients of the supervisor-teacher relationship that contribute to or detract from the mutual and personal learning of each party in that relationship. It is collaborative, and it is also based on the notion (Steele, 1975) that the "facts are friendly." This means not only facts related to the classroom and what goes on it, but also those facts related to the supervisor-teacher microsystem and what goes on in it. Relative to the latter, I take it to be important for the supervisor and teacher to learn to engage in reciprocal feedback and self-disclosure. The teacher needs to be able to disclose feelings of insecurity, for example, as well as tell the supervisor what it is about his behavior that is helpful or unhelpful. And the same holds for the supervisor. Further, the supervisor as interpersonal intervenor implies, critically, voluntarism. Intervenors need to be free to choose their clients and clients need to be free to choose their helpers. It makes no more sense to think that any supervisor can help every teacher than it does to think that any teacher can help every student. (This point of view only makes sense if good teaching is seen as a matter of learning to use appropriate methods, and the supervisor has knowledge of these methods while the teacher does not.)

Is there a place within this role concept of supervision that I have proposed for the evaluation function that many supervisors now enact? The answer, I think, is "No" at least as far as the manner in which this function is presently conceived. It seems rather hypocritical and dishonest for a supervisor to engage a teacher in collaborative work and interpersonal effort and then to "fail" that teacher if these efforts do not pan out productively. After all, it could be that the supervisor failed and not the teacher. What is required is some sort of evaluative arrangement between supervisor and teacher whereby each knows what both success and failure mean—and what are the consequences of each, collaboratively agreed to. The implication of this is that the function of hierarchical, unilateral evaluation of teacher by supervisor will cease to be. If this state of affairs ever came to be, my hunch is that there would be no more incompetent teachers in the schools than there are now when evaluation of teachers is done by supervisors who "know a good teacher when they see one."

17   Teachers Supervising Teachers

All of the preceding chapters have been written on the assumption that the present structure of supervision in the schools—an emphasis on one-to-one relationships—is not likely to change in the near or, perhaps, even the distant future. Given that assumption, the research that has been presented and the concepts that have been discussed seem to fit well into that structure and the processes that derive from it.

But is that the sum total of it all? Is there not a vision of the schools as social systems and of the process of supervision within those systems that might be different and more productive for all concerned? If we had no such vision or if we felt we had reached the limits of our ability to think about what schools might be, then this book would have ended at the close of the last chapter. That we have reached the limits of our ability to think about what schools might be is a position I find hard to accept. Indeed, there are examples of the nature of schools having been rethought, mostly in nonpublic settings. What goes on as a result is different from our typical experience. I am not referring to the frequently abortive situations that may be characterized as laissez-faire playpens. Rather, I refer to those situations in which conscious and deliberate efforts are made to alter the relationships among the people who work and learn in schools. These efforts are directed away from the notion that schools are places where the primary function of teachers is to impart knowledge and that of supervisors is to help teachers do it better. They are directed toward making schools places where, though youngsters do indeed learn, the overarching focus is one of people consciously, collaboratively, and humbly concerned about the problems of teaching and learning. Schools are, indeed, uncertain settings, and most appropriately so given how much we do not know about the elegant complexities of the entire teaching and learning enterprise.

These last three chapters, then, raise the issue of supervision in the context of what might be. The presenting question is: Can teachers supervise teachers?

Teachers, of course, have long given help to their colleagues in an informal manner. In point of fact, a small but growing body of data is slowly becoming available that indicates that the primary source of assistance that teachers use in their efforts to solve the problems they face on a daily basis is other teachers. Millikan (1979), for example, in a study of a sample of secondary-school teachers in Edmonton, Alberta, as to the source and character of help they sought and received, found that the number of instances in which teachers assisted each other far outweighed the number of times that they called on their formal supervisors or consultants. A pilot study of the nature of adult-adult interaction in the schools (DeSanctis and Blumberg, 1978) yielded similar information. In this project a sample of teachers was asked to record the instances and purposes of their conversation with other adults during the course of a school day. Of the numbers of times they spent talking about matters related to instruction or classroom management, 64 percent was with other teachers, 23 percent with professional staff personnel, 7 percent with their principal, and, interestingly, 6 percent with nonprofessional personnel, custodians, cafeteria workers, and so forth.

One might take the position that the situation could scarcely be otherwise, and I would certainly agree. Teachers are much more readily available to each other than to central office personnel, for example. They see each other before and after school, in the halls, and at lunch much more frequently than they might see their principal or an instructional specialist with multischool responsibilities. What is of more than passing interest, though, is the rather small number of times that teachers seem to raise questions of instruction or curriculum with their principals. For whatever reason, principals appear not to be the people to whom teachers turn, as a rule, when they need assistance with problems related to teaching.

There is some evidence to suggest that teachers develop and use an informal system through which they appear to try and deal with the majority of the problems they encounter in their work. They do this, more than likely, because they see their colleagues grappling with similar problems. And, if the data that has been discussed earlier in this book has any validity at all, they do it because colleagues are less threatening and easier to approach than professional staff personnel or their principal.

Teachers apparently do use each other as peer supervisors if supervision is interpreted broadly to mean the offering of any kind of mutual assistance on the job. Why not let the matter rest there, content with things as they are? It is a good question, particularly if one takes to heart Sarason's (1971) proposition, as he wrote about problems of change in the schools, that "the more things change the more they remain the same." His perspective of the massive attempts that have been made to change the schools in the past two decades or so is that, despite these efforts, schools remain essentially the same kind of organizations they were—and perhaps always have been. In general, it is probably true today (though there have to be some glaring exceptions) that teachers relate to each other, to their principals and other supervisors, and to youngsters in ways that vary little from those of prior years. And what teachers do in the classroom (or what the principal does in the course of a day) is, likewise, probably not substantially different from what has occurred in schools for many years. I know, for example, that when I visit schools, particularly secondary schools, my sense of what is occurring in them suggests almost a nostalgic return to my years in high school forty years ago. But, although schools do appear to be relatively static social systems, changes do occur, if slowly. And among them is what appears to be a growing emphasis on teachers serving as supervisory-helping agents for one another in a somewhat systematic fashion. Central to the concept of team teaching, for instance, is the notion that teams of teachers will work together, plan together, help each other, and perhaps, in some cases, even serve as critics for each other. That the idea of teaming has not produced the desired effects, in many cases, is not the point. The point is that the concept has made its way into the system and has, in some situations, had productive results. In some schools that are not structured around the team concept, there have, in addition, been apparently successful efforts to develop peer-oriented supervisory structures as an integral part of the formal system (Amidon, Keyes, and Palisi, 1966; Abramson, 1972).

It is obvious that the practice of peer or group supervision is not sweeping the country although the idea appears to have great potential. The point here is not to criticize the schools for not having taken advantage of their own internal resources, much as that seems to be the case. Such a criticism may be warranted, but that is a position I am not ready to take. Rather, the question is: Are there ways of building on the already existing informal system through which teachers help each other so that the help becomes less chancy and potentially more effective? And, further, given that such ways do exist or might be invented, should they be used in all cases? Might it not be better simply not to tamper with the system on the notion that it is behaving in a "satificing" manner (March and Simon, 1958) now and that the results of efforts to change it will hardly be commensurate with the energy required. Might it not be better to let things happen if they will and not try to introduce a new program that may well be ignored as many other innovations have been after proponents suggested that they were the answer to all problems associated with the schools?

These are two types of questions: one involves feasibility; the other, desirability. The answer to the former is clearly in the affirmative. There are ways to develop structures and processes that would enable schools to capitalize on the informal supervisory-helping systems that seem to be part of their generic makeup. Most of this chapter, indeed, is a discussion of alternative ways this might take place.

As for the desirability of developing such structures and processes, the answer is not so clear cut. This may sound a little ridiculous to the reader who may ask, "If we can do it, if we can develop ways of making what we do in the schools potentially more productive, why don't we just go ahead and do precisely that?" The reason for my hesitancy is related to the history of the process of inducing change into the schools rather than to the particular technological substance of the change. Given, for example, Sarason's penetrating analysis of change in the schools and his conclusion that "the more things change the more they remain the same," I find myself reluctant to offer yet another prescription for change while I have knowledge that so many previous prescriptions seem not to have affected the system in any startling ways.

The issue is not, of course, that teachers, principals, or other helping agents do not want to do a better job. In point of fact, Lortie's (1975) analysis of the work of teachers, with its emphasis on the psychic rewards that teachers derive and seek from their jobs, would suggest just the opposite, that they would continually be seeking ways to become better so that more of these rewards would be forthcoming. The issue, in my mind, is typically not one of motivation. Rather, it is apt to be more a question of how proposed changes are developed and implemented—a matter of process—than anything else.

An example will make the point clearer. On occasion a school district or a school requests that I consult on problems of supervision. The request is often to help them develop a better instrument for use by supervisors as they observe teachers and then talk with them about their observations. My usual response is that I would prefer to discuss the problem before making a decision about whether or not to go ahead with the project. Just such a situation occurred recently. On talking with the person in the central office responsible for the project, I suggested that it might be a good idea if discussions about it were held with representatives of the people who would be involved (teachers, department heads, principals, and supervisory staff from the central office). He agreed, and a full day of meetings was held.

The result of these meetings convinced me that the critical problem the district faced was one of communication and trust, not the development of "a better mousetrap." Further, I was convinced and informed the person responsible that, if the district went ahead with the project without first working on and trying to improve staff relationships, it would not matter what kind of an instrument was created. Things would remain the same. The district chose to ignore the process issue, developed a new instrument (without my help), and, as I understand the results, things have, indeed, remained the same.

Back, then, to the question of the desirability of trying to develop a structured means of making what informally takes place among teachers relative to their helping each other into a more formal and systematic process through which a wider range of expertise can be brought to bear. It would certainly seem a desirable thing to do *if* the process of developing the structure is a collaborative one that takes into consideration not only the needs of the teachers but the objectives of the school. If the strategy adopted by the central office or principal is simply to propose and implement a program of peer or group supervision, my hunch is that it will develop in form and not substance and eventually pass into welcome oblivion, as have many previous good ideas, and scarcely be mourned.

The question of what form a particular system of peer supervision should take is best answered by the response, "There are no 'shoulds.'" Schools are different, as are teachers, principals and other supervisors. A system that fits well in one school may be ineffectual in another. But if there are no "shoulds" there are certainly a number of alternatives. A discussion of a few of them will be the focus of most of the remainder of this chapter.

First, it is necessary to speak about some of the organizational and role factors that need to be considered if a school seeks to move in the direction of some type of peer supervisory structure. Some of these have been discussed previously, but they are discussed again in the specific context of this chapter. And they relate, of course, to the question of the desirability of this specific change and how to bring it about.

The rule of thumb that assumes primacy here is, "People ought to know what they're getting into." To gloss over some of the problems that will almost certainly develop as teachers attempt to help each other in a manner that reflects some goal-oriented structure is folly if not downright dishonesty. In point of fact, not to talk with teachers about what is involved simply communicates to them in an indirect but powerful way that they are not adult enough to make appropriate decisions about themselves and their work. Hence, the following:

The effective implementation of a type of system that is the focus here requires, first of all, a normative change of attitudes among school people concerning what a school is all about and the role and behavioral responsibilities that derive from this "aboutness." What schools seem to be about, for the most part, is that they serve as dispensaries (Schaefer, 1967). That is, they dispense information and skills. Schools also speak to the task of inculcating (dispensing) democratic ideals and so forth, but that notion would seem to be more for public consumption. It bears little resemblance to what happens in most schools on a daily basis. These points should not be taken as criticism of what schools or teachers do. Rather, they are observations of a particular state of affairs. The point is, however, that this state of affairs speaks directly to role behavior. If a school is essentially a dispensary, then teachers are in the business of dispensing things as efficiently and effectively as they can. And the role of supervisory personnel is to help make teachers better dispensers (and also, if I may be permitted the slight pun, to try and dispense with those who are not doing a good job of dispensing).

If a school is to be a place where the adults in it become actively engaged in helping each other, they will need to develop a different concept of the school and also, as I have indicated, of their role. Such a shift in concept does not exclude the notion of dispensing, but it adds to it the idea that schools can be, and perhaps ought to be, places where teachers learn ever more about the processes of teaching and learning and where supervisors continue to learn how to assist in those processes. The phrase Schaefer (1967) uses to think about this kind of a school is that it might be "a center of inquiry about teaching and learning" and, thus, not a dispensary. Merely announcing that a school is now such a "center" will not, of course, make it one. Certain factors of school life need to be considered and dealt with, and some of them are considered below.

FACTORS OF SCHOOL LIFE AND SUPERVISION

Structure of the Work of a Teacher

Despite the creation of "open" schools, team teaching, and so forth, teachers are, by and large, lone operators. They plan their work by themselves and carry out their plans in isolation. Even though they talk with their colleagues about what they do in a classroom, they are alone when they do it, at least as far as other adults are concerned.

This aloneness has several effects on teachers and on teaching. First, it implicitly creates and sustains the idea that teachers are *supposed* to be alone. If they were not, why would we have created schools as they are? In short, the concept of schools as dispensaries has had the unintended consequence of making schools into organizations where being isolated from one's peers while one is working is a way of life. Further, this way of life has come to be valued. The specific value that is attached to it is called privacy, which may be a pseudonym for "let me make my mistakes by myself."

But there is another side to the aloneness facet of a teacher's work life. Goldstein and Knobloch characterize it well in their book, *The Lonely Teacher* (1971). That is, much as teachers value their classroom privacy and may discourage attempts to make it less private, they also seem to sense their isolation, some of them strongly so, and wish somehow that things were different. My own observations, at a minimum, suggest this is precisely the case. That is, if teachers (and sometimes their supervisors) are provided with, or provide themselves with, the opportunity to talk about and try to solve problems that they think are important and if they perceive themselves not to be engaging in an academic exercise, they find it exhilarating. And this is so for what appear to be two reasons. First, they seem to find intelligent and deliberate efforts to work on and learn about problems of teaching and learning a satisfying activity. Second, being with colleagues—other adults—is pleasing by itself. They are not lonely.

The structure of the work of teachers, then, would seem to foster an approach-avoidance conflict for teachers relative to their attitudes toward the development of the idea of peer supervision— or toward the school as a place where teachers learn from each other. On the one hand, the structure puts a premium on privacy, on the idea that what a teacher does in a classroom is that teacher's business. On the other hand, the structure creates forces that work in the opposite direction, toward being with and working with one's peers.

Vagueness of the Technology of Teaching

The supervision of teachers, whether that function is performed by a person whose organizational role is that of supervisor or by colleagues, would be a much simpler affair if there was *a* way of teaching. There is not. No two teachers deal with problems they confront in precisely the same manner, and what happens in teaching, like other so-called "people" professions, is much a function of individual predispositions. This is, at one and the same time, the beauty of teaching and the thorn in its side. That is, much as there is no set way of doing things, thus enabling the teaching-learning process to be an open and potentially creative one, so this very fact makes it difficult to help teachers in ways that are customarily thought to be helpful. The classroom management problems typically encountered by a teacher, for example, are not the same as those encountered by an apprentice carpenter who is trying to learn how to cut a square edge on a beam. In the latter case, the master carpenter can be very precise in showing the apprentice what to do. It is a matter of technique, with a limited number of alternatives, and pieces of wood rarely talk back. Teaching, however, is quite imprecise. There are many ways to deal productively with the same problem. Modeling behavior may be only marginally helpful (Gibb, 1954) because the person doing the modeling is, after all, acting on his own idiosyncratic predispositions, which may be incompatible with those of the teacher who needs help.

It would seem that any program of peer supervision needs, as a prior condition, to focus on helping teachers learn better how to help each other. What this means, in turn, is that the peer supervision strategy has to be a collaborative problem-solving one. Hardly anyone would argue with this point of view. The problem is that, for the most part, teachers have not learned, either as part of their college training or their day-to-day work, how to collaborate with one's peers in a problem-solving way. This conclusion is not intended to put down teachers. Rather, it states what appears to be a fairly general fact of school life that could scarcely be otherwise. The focus of teacher education is appropriately on teaching as teaching, not on working with other teachers. And the focus of in-service education, which is by no means a universally acclaimed activity, is typically on methodological or curricular issues. Practically nowhere in a teacher's preservice or in-service training is there a pointed concern with the problems of relating to or working with other teachers. This would make it seem foolhardy to develop plans for peer or group supervision without helping teachers learn productive ways of helping each other.

Tenured Teachers—and More of Them

Chapter 13 gave attention to the problems of supervising tenured teachers. The existence of a tenure system, and the additional fact that the percentage of tenured teachers in schools has increased greatly as the school-age population has declined, also bears on matters of group supervision. Just as the structure of a teacher's work creates both driving and restraining forces concerning supervising one's peers, so does the fact of tenure cut both ways.

What seems to come to mind most readily as people talk about tenured teachers is their freedom. And, curiously, it is their freedom to reject things they do not like and their freedom to refuse involvement in affairs outside their classroom that receive most attention. If they so choose, they can be fairly immovable, psychologically if not physically.

There is, however, another side to the picture that has to do with the fact, mentioned earlier, that the percentage of tenured faculty in schools is increasing rapidly. The potentially positive outcome of this situation, as opposed to the negative mood of the previous paragraph, is that schools are becoming more stable organizations. Thus, schools and teachers are in a position to contemplate their collective future in ways that would have been impossible in the past. Simply put, more teachers are likely to be together in a school for a longer period of time than would have been the case but a few years ago. What this means is that there is more opportunity to think through long-range plans than has been possible heretofore since more of the same people will be around to act on those plans. Thus, though the prerogatives of tenured teachers may hamper efforts at peer supervision, the large numbers of tenured teachers on school faculties may, under appropriate conditions, work in the other direction. All of which brings us to the role of the principal.

Role of the Principal

One thing we know about school principals: no two of them are any more alike in what they think and how they conduct themselves than are any two teachers. That there are "many roads to Rome" for the principal has been documented in a book (Blumberg and Greenfield, 1980) that considers the work perspectives of a number of extraordinary ones. What, then, can be said in general about the role of the principal in the development and maintenance of a system of group supervision? I do not wish to be prescriptive here, and so I offer my ideas in propositional form. The bases of the ideas are not new; nor are the ideas themselves necessarily startling. But they bear discussion in the context of supervision.

—The more a principal exhibits active concern with what teachers are doing and how they relate to each other, the more teachers will exhibit similar concern.

—The more the principal actively conceives of a school as "a center of inquiry about teaching and learning," the more teachers will do the same.

—The higher the value the principal places on, and behaves in, an openly communicative and collaborative style, the more teachers will be inclined to risk being open and collaborative.

—The more a principal structures into school operations an open feedback system concerning his behavior, the more teachers will be inclined to test similar mechanisms about their own behavior.

—The more a principal communicates by behavior that running a school is an exercise in continual testing, not certainty, the more teachers will conceive of their efforts in a like manner.

—The more a principal is willing to be open with the teachers about his failures on the job, the better the chances that teachers will be open with each other about their failures—and their successes, too, I might add.

—The more a principal communicates by his behavior that seeking help is an "all right" thing to do, the more teachers will be apt to seek help from each other.

This list of propositions could undoubtedly be expanded. As it stands, however, it contains some ideas that are critical to the development of peer supervision. Perhaps as important, the propositions focus on the centrality of the principal's behavior in moving a school in the direction of a more open, help-seeking, and help-giving environment. And principals are, indeed, central to the organizational zeitgeist of a school, a fact that has been documented any number of times. The principal's behavior cannot help being an organizational model, whether or not he recognizes this.

I must make note of a "sleeper" in the list: the proposition concerning the desirability of developing a feedback system that focuses on the principal's behavior and functioning. If the development of a program of group supervision in a school involves opening the activities of teachers to observation and discussion, it seems reasonable that the principal might buy into that idea, too, relative to his activities. This is not a matter of "what's good for the goose is good for the gander." Rather, the objective is to create a system that uses its resources in the most open way possible. And teachers can be powerful resources for principals.

I do not pretend to think that I have dealt with all the factors in school organizational life that might affect a program of peer supervision-helping. There are, for example, problems of time, questions possibly relating to the teachers' union and the union contract, the role of curriculum specialists, and the attitudes of teachers in other schools. It seems to me, however, that the issues that have been discussed are the most focal and problematic ones. If they could be dealt with, others might assume secondary importance.

Finally, let me say that I *do not* know of any schools that actively and deliberately conceptualize themselves as "centers of inquiry about teaching and learning." It is even possible that such an articulation to self may not be important, though I think it might be helpful as a guide to thinking. I *do*, however, know of schools that have instituted programs that have tended to move the faculty in that direction without any self-conscious attempt to articulate it. For example, I have known of schools where:

—The principal and numbers of teachers met together regularly on weekends to work on curriculum and materials.
—The principal, a Gestalt therapist, held quasi-therapy group meetings with his faculty so that they could examine themselves and their teaching in light of Gestalt theory.
—The principal invited those teachers who wished to meet with her after school one day a week to talk about problems of teaching in that school. This is a rather simple thing to do, but it is apparently bearing fruit; teachers are talking with each other in a school where they rarely did before.
—The faculty, under the leadership of its department heads (I mentioned this case earlier), is becoming involved in a total school effort to examine itself and share its resources.
—Individual teachers agreed to tape-record a segment of their classroom behavior and then present it to a group of colleagues for descriptive—not evaluative—analysis and feedback.

None of these situations represents an earthshaking event. What they do represent, though, is slight (in some cases, more) movement away from the unitary concept of schools as dispensaries toward something that may hold greater promise for all concerned. I do not know of any colleges or universities where this is happening—not even in colleges of education.

18　Socialization and Supervision

It was suggested in Chapter 17 that teachers should engage in a great deal of informal interaction directed at helping one another on matters related to improving their instructional effectiveness. The discussion that follows builds on this possibility, draws upon socialization theory in exploring issues related to the phenomenon of instructional supervision, and, more particularly, identifies factors that may impede or facilitate socialization for interpersonal competence and the work of instructional supervisors, be they teachers or some other member of the school or central office staff.

An extensive literature about the socialization of adults in organizational settings provides the basis for the ensuing discussion. Brim and Wheeler (1966), upon whose thinking much of the first section of this chapter is based, suggest that socialization may be broadly thought of as a process by which an individual acquires the knowledge, values, and behaviors needed to function in society. In the context of instructional supervision, socialization may be thought of as the process by which one acquires the knowledge, values, and behaviors needed to be an effective supervisor, that is, one who is able to influence teachers, help them grow professionally, and improve their effectiveness as teachers.

This chapter was written especially for this book by Professor William Greenfield of Syracuse University.

ADULT SOCIALIZATION

Much of adult socialization involves creating new arrangements of what has been learned previously. Learning a new role is thus largely dependent on what has been learned in prior circumstances. In the case of the instructional supervisor, who more likely than not has spent some portion of his career functioning as a teacher, for example, learning and performing the role of instructional supervisor is likely to be influenced to a large extent by the character of the supervision he experienced in his earlier role as teacher. This may in some instances have been an excellent growth-producing exchange between supervisor and teacher that did in fact enable the individual to improve his performance as a teacher. On the other hand, and I fear this may be the more general case, the quality of supervision experienced by the teacher during those earlier years may more often have been poor, and the teacher may unwittingly have acquired some behavioral expectations and attitudinal sets about "supervisors" that are in fact dysfunctional to effective supervision.

Three factors are related to the process of learning a new role. These include the individual's motivation to learn and perform the new role; his knowledge of the norms, attitudes, and behaviors associated with the role; and his ability actually to enact a satisfactory role performance. In reference to the earlier discussion of the relation of experiences as a teacher to performance as an instructional supervisor, knowledge, ability, and motivation may be thought of as outcomes of earlier socialization experiences that intervene in the process of learning a new role. Thus, one of the objectives of socialization during the adult years, in addition to the acquisition of new material, is the recombination and synthesis of old material.

The relationship between previous experience and new learning has significance not only for the supervisor, as in the previous example, but for the teacher who is now, in turn, to be supervised. If the supervisory effort to help teachers grow professionally and improve their performance as a teacher is to be effective, the supervisor must understand what he is asking the teacher to do in learning a new skill, acquiring new knowledge, or changing his attitudes. If the teacher is to act upon the supervisor's suggestion, doing so may, in fact, necessitate a recombination and synthesis of old material (what one can already do or what one already knows) in order to accept or implement the new material, and, in some instances, the teacher may actually have to *unlearn* previously acquired material in order to learn the new material. Even when these possibilities are recognized by the teacher and supervisor, and I suspect that this is not often the case, the learning task for the teacher may present quite a challenge, even to the most capable and motivated teacher.

A related aspect of adult socialization involves learning how to mediate conflicting role demands. As a person learns more complex roles and as he is required to perform a range of different roles, the possibility for role conflict increases. We see this in the case of the teacher who may be required to befriend a child in order to facilitate learning and, at another point in time, may be required to discipline that same child for misconduct in the lunchroom. Or we can see it in the case of the school principal charged with the responsibility to evaluate teachers and, at the same time, to serve as a resource and friendly counsel available to help resolve instructional problems.

The numerous ways of dealing with this problem of role conflict include compromise among competing demands; avoidance of the situation; arranging conflicting demands in a time sequence that the individual can manage; and becoming consumed, frustrated, and perhaps incapacitated by the conflict. Individuals often mediate conflict through the use of "metaprescriptions," or guides used by an individual in the process of compromising among competing role demands. The nature of the metaprescriptions developed by teachers and supervisors for improved effectiveness or for seeking and providing help on instructional matters present interesting but virtually unexplored questions. As teachers enter the occupation, what attitudes and expectations do they acquire about their relationship to supervisors and other teachers concerning matters related to seeking advice on their performance or effectiveness as teachers? Do teachers, as suggested in the previous chapter, develop a metaprescription that guides them to other teachers rather than to their supervisor when they need help on instructional matters? Do they have the feeling that admitting some shortcoming or exposing an instructional problem or inadequacy to their supervisor will result in a poor evaluation or some other sort of negative sanction? Do supervisors shy away from intervening in a class or otherwise offering to help a teacher improve their ability because they think it will be perceived by the teacher as intrusion into the teacher's territory (perhaps an attitude carried over from their own experience as a teacher)? We might learn a great deal about factors and forces bearing on the phenomenon of instructional supervision if we were to merely ask teachers and supervisors to catalogue their meta-prescriptions vis-à-vis their interaction with one another, that is, to develop a taxonomy of the "guidelines" teachers and supervisors use in deciding the who, what, why, when, and where of their interaction with each other.

Socialization Setting

Another aspect of adult socialization is that it frequently occurs within the context of a complex organization. The model in Figure 18.1 depicts six dimensions related to adult socialization in organizational settings. Three are located at the organizational level, and three represent the individual being socialized. Theoretically, socialization will be most effective when the setting is characterized by clear norms, abundant practice opportunities, and selective reward structures, and when the individual is both motivated and able to learn and perform the role.

FIGURE 18.1   Framework for Analysis of Socialization in
                     Organizations

		Intervening Mechanisms		
		Organizational	Individual	
Independent → Variables	Norms	Capacity to present clear norms	Capacity to learn the norms	Socialization Outcomes
	Performances	Capacity to provide performance opportunities	Capacity to perform	
	Rewards, Sanctions, Motives	Capacity to selectively reward performance	Motivation to perform	

Source: O. Brim, Jr., and S. Wheeler. *Socialization after Childhood: Two Essays* (New York: John Wiley and Sons, 1966). Reprinted by permission.

While the model in the figure was developed especially to describe processes that occur in organizations that have a special mandate to change or resocialize people (schools, universities, prisons, and mental hospitals, for example), these same dimensions seem relevant to role learning by adults in any organizational setting. A major issue, given this conceptualization, is that differently organized settings probably have varying effects on the people involved. In addition, individuals who differ in their prior role-learning experiences will likely vary in their motivation and ability to learn and perform new roles. Socialization processes and outcomes, thus, are highly dependent upon variations in both the structural properties of the settings and the personal characteristics of the individuals involved. This emphasis upon the contribution of organizational structure to socialization outcomes differs from the more traditional or common focus upon the responses of individuals to socialization pressures.

The model suggests a number of implications for supervisors and teachers regarding, generally, an increase in the instructional effectiveness and, more specifically, the professional growth of teachers. It calls attention to many factors bearing upon the individual role-learning situation of both the teacher and the instructional supervisor. The following series of questions concerns factors salient in the socialization of either a teacher or an instructional supervisor:

—Are the particular attitudes, knowledge, and behaviors needed to perform the role effectively presented clearly to the supervisor or the teacher?
—What opportunities are available for individuals to gain some practice in using this knowledge or skill?
—When appropriate performances are executed, are there rewards for compliance or effective behavior?
—How capable is the individual of learning what is required to perform the role effectively?
—Can the individual put these ideas into practice appropriately? How motivated is the individual to learn these new behaviors, attitudes, or knowledge, and is he sufficiently motivated to put them into practice?

This general scheme might be used as a guide in designing or evaluating the work of supervisors or in planning strategies intended to improve the performance of teachers or supervisors. Workshops or conferences aimed at improving teacher performance in the classroom might be more effective if they were to take these questions into account. Supervisors might be more helpful if they were able to perceive and articulate what it is a teacher needs to do to be more effective, and to work with that teacher in terms of his capacity to learn and perform and his motivation to perform. How many supervisory conferences have fallen on deaf ears for lack of motivation on the part of the teacher? How many times have teachers been told to manage their classroom discipline problems more effectively, yet they received no clear information on what to do, or had no opportunities to practice using the required knowledge and behaviors in a simulated or natural setting?

In a similar vein, and taking a cue from some of the data discussed in the preceding chapter, what social (structural) arrangements might occur in schools to facilitate informal teacher interaction regarding matters of instructional effectiveness or, more generally, matters related to improving a teacher's performance in the classroom? Is it possible, by redesigning the structural conditions of the setting in which teachers work, to make it easier and more likely that teachers will develop and relate to one another based on a norm of professional collegiality—to pursue their work and their relations with each other guided by a sense of their school as a "center for inquiry and learning"? There are, for example, schools with open spaces and teaming arrangements. These have usually been adopted and modified in the name of increasing instructional effectiveness, but little has been done in terms of exploring the potential of these and other arrangements for changing the quality and content of teacher interaction, thereby perhaps inducing professional growth.

Such changes in the school environment might influence the supervisor's understanding of the instructional situation and the character of his work with individual teachers. Opportunities to observe two or more teachers working simultaneously would seem, on the surface at least, to provide a broader view of similarities and differences among teachers and of strengths and weaknesses in their teaching methods. In such an environment, a supervisor might more easily encourage one teacher to observe another teacher at work (ostensibly modeling preferred behaviors or attitudes or actively and successfully solving an instructional problem with which the observing teacher is having difficulty).

Much has been left unsaid here regarding adult socialization and the potential of such a framework for informing the work of supervisors and our more general understanding of the phenonomenon of instructional supervision. Many factors come into play, on both an individual and structural level, in influencing the instructional effectiveness of teachers. The reader desiring more detail on these issues is encouraged to examine David Goslin's *Handbook on Socialization Theory and Research* (1969). This book, accompanied by Brim and Wheeler's book entitled *Socialization after Childhood: Two Essays* (1966), provides a much more complete discussion of these ideas.

PROFESSIONAL SOCIALIZATION

While the preceding comments have rather generally focused on a variety of issues associated with adult socialization, the remainder of this chapter deals more specifically with dilemmas attending the professional and organizational socialization of supervisors, and the relation between interpersonal competence and effective instructional supervision.

A profession has been variously defined. A professional occupation is distinguished from other occupations by the degree to which professions are characterized by systematic theory, authority based upon expertise, broad community sanction, a code of ethics, and a professional culture (Greenwood, 1966). Occupations may be classified along a continuum from less professional to more professional, depending on the degree to which the membership is characterized by these five attributes. Professional socialization refers to the process by which persons learn and perform according to the norms, values, and behaviors held to be necessary for performing a particular professional role (doctor, lawyer, priest, teacher, or nurse, for example).

Educators, as a group, claim to be a profession. While one can dispute the degree to which educators reflect the various attributes of a profession described above, it seems clear that, as an occupational group, educators are engaged in a process of professionalization. That is, their activity as a group is increasingly oriented toward the more professional end of the occupational continuum referred to above. As a consequence, teachers and instructional supervisors frequently experience the dilemmas associated with being a professionally oriented member of a bureaucratically oriented organization.

One of the distinguishing characteristics of professionals is their claim to authority on the basis of expertise. The organizational work roles of educators are differentiated according to task specialization; teachers with specialized knowledge in mathematics are not usually employed to teach history or literature. This is reflected in certification practices, which in turn have had a considerable effect upon the nature of undergraduate and graduate training programs in education, and, specifically, upon the orientations of, and problems experienced by, instructional supervisors.

These training programs tend to reflect the effects of the process of occupational professionalization in their increasing emphasis upon the acquisition of "specialized knowledge" as a central focus of teacher preparation. In a parallel fashion, programs of graduate study engaged in by teachers aspiring to assume roles as instructional supervisors (principalship, staff specialist, curriculum coordinator, and so forth) are increasingly characterized by a heavy emphasis upon the acquisition of special, "expert" knowledge. Programs preparing educational administrators reflect a professional orientation in this respect. Yet an assumption basic to the bureaucratic organization of most public schools is that the supervisor, at whatever level, operates to a large extent on the basis of authority relating to office or position in the organizational hierarchy, not on the basis of professional expertise.

There is, thus, a dilemma for the supervisor influenced by a professionally oriented preparation program. Such training teaches one that professional acts are legitimated by the degree to which they are in accord with the professional's special knowledge. A heavy emphasis on the acquisition of special, expert knowledge is expected to serve the autonomous professional well in the performance of his task. From an organizational superior's viewpoint, however, the justification for the behavior of a subordinate is the extent to which it reflects and complies with the organization's rules and regulations. The implication is that the act requires the approval of some other person in a superior position. This is quite different from the way decisions are made by truly autonomous professionals. The instructional supervisor adopting the professional norm of expertise is, therefore, likely to experience much personal frustration when survival in an assigned position in the school hierarchy depends upon conformity to organizational rules and regulations— rules that may conflict with his base of expertise. This dilemma is perhaps most evident in the common expectation that school principals will both evaluate teacher performance and help teachers grow professionally. Extensive research and the frequent testimonials of both supervisors and teachers suggest that the two expectations are largely incompatible.

The major point of the preceding discussion is that professionally oriented training intended to prepare more competent and effective instructional supervisors may not be having the desired effect. Indeed, if professional socialization in formal preparation programs is complete, graduates are very likely to have acquired knowledge, values, and behavior dispositions that are quite incompatible with some of the organizational role expectations held for supervisors. The factors operating to influence compliance with organizational norms are discussed next.

ORGANIZATIONAL SOCIALIZATION

The process by which one learns the knowledge, values, and behaviors requisite to performing an occupational role within the context of a particular organization, or organizational subunit, is referred to as organizational socialization (Schein, 1968). While the training content and acquired professional role orientations may be similar for individuals, actual role behavior will likely differ because organizational demands differ. An example is the instructionally oriented principal who, because of organizational control and coordination needs, is required to spend most of his time in administrative activities. This reduces the amount of time available for working closely with teachers and becoming integrally involved in instructionally significant matters.

Organizational socialization is a process that recurs throughout a person's career, each time one changes positions in an organization or when a person leaves one organization to enter another. The phenomenon is found both in the schools that train professionals and in the work organizations where such individuals are employed. It is distinguished from professional socialization in its focus on the particular structure of the organizational setting in which the process occurs. At times it may be a conscious socialization effort by agents of the organization, but it frequently occurs without the awareness of either the organization's members or the individual affected. It is an elusive and ubiquitous process that happens so frequently during a person's total career that it is often overlooked, and yet it is an extremely important process that can make or break a career and can enhance or limit the effectiveness of the work of teachers and instructional supervisors.

While many different forces determine how and to what extent professionals learn the requirements and acquire the skills needed to perform their roles, the structure of most occupations is such that the majority of role learning occurs in an organizational context of one kind or another. The case of instructional supervisors is illustrative, and in some respects it may be unique. The prospective supervisor is, from the time he first begins school as a student until he enters teaching or becomes a supervisor, influenced by the group he eventually joins and serves, that is, teachers. All of this occurs in an organizational context not much different from that in which he might eventually function as a supervisor. The long-term character of the organizational socialization of educators makes it a potent process, even though its effect on professional growth and development is neither obvious nor well understood.

The nature of the supervisor's career, in education as in other occupations, is such that one begins in a low position in the organizational power hierarchy and, if one performs to the satisfaction of superiors, the person is promoted to successively higher and more influential positions. During the time it takes to prove one's loyalty to the organization and to demonstrate one's performance effectiveness, it is often necessary to hold in limbo much of what has been learned during professional training for the role. The result is that a lot of what was learned is often forgotten by the time the person is in a position to apply general principles learned during the professional preparation period. And, even if it has not been forgotten, much professionally relevant knowledge, many attitudes, and certain skills may have been "put aside" in response to pressures of organizational socialization that required the adoption, even if only temporarily, of certain metaprescriptions needed at the early stages of the person's teaching career. Indeed, if the professional training was at all visionary, the teacher who aspired to be an instructional supervisor may have had to "unlearn" many things in order to survive in a school organization that puts a high premium on order, stability, and conformity. The frustration induced by the necessity to unlearn (or put aside) some of the content of professional training programs may be reflected in the frequently voiced metaprescription that, "What I learned in graduate school is just theory and has no practical value on the firing line."

To summarize, organizational socialization is a process by which an individual learns and complies with the organizational norms and values required for satisfactory role performance. In the case of instructional supervisors, this process may begin as early as one's first involvement in schools as a student. There is clearer evidence that it occurs during the teaching years, during involvement in a professional preparation program, and again upon entering a supervisory position. The potency of what is learned during professional socialization may be diminished by organizational socialization attendant upon the supervisor's role in schools.

The next portion of this chapter builds on the preceding discussion of professional and organizational socialization by examining the relation of interpersonal competence to the process of instructional supervision and exploring how conditions in the school environment might impede or facilitate the acquisition and use of such skills by the instructional supervisor.

Interpersonal Skills and Instructional Supervision

Every conception of the role of instructional supervisor, or model of the process of instructional supervision, has implicit within it the requirement that the supervisor must rely heavily upon interpersonal and verbal skills in the course of helping teachers grow professionally and, more specifically, of improving the quality of teaching and instruction. For example, a basic reader on general supervision by Heald, Romano, and Georgiady (1970) includes forty-eight articles on supervisory behavior and factors related to instructional supervision, and the large majority of these are directly concerned with the character of the interpersonal relations of supervisors and teachers. Implicit in all, and explicit in most, of these discussions is the fundamental necessity of the supervisor to communicate *verbally* with teachers, usually on a face-to-face basis. This may seem so obvious, so commonplace, as to be unworthy of note. But the centrality of this interpersonal exchange to the work of supervisors is a phenomenon that has not been explicitly addressed to any great extent in the training of supervisors, in their recruitment and selection, or in the research literature about instructional supervision. The point is, some individuals have more well-developed verbal and interpersonal skills than others, and these skills are crucial to enacting most, if not all, conceptions of the role of instructional supervisor—as well as the process of instructional supervision. Supervisors who have difficulty or are otherwise uncomfortable in verbal, face-to-face interpersonal interaction with teachers, are unlikely either to enjoy or to be very proficient at their job.

An implicit major assumption underlying phenomena of adult socialization is that, like supervisory phenomena, the socialization process itself depends in large part upon some manner of interpersonal exchange between individuals. In both cases, the repertoire of interpersonal skills possessed by the individuals involved in the process greatly influences both the nature of the process itself and the character of the outcomes.

Thus, instructional supervision, like teaching, is essentially an interpersonal activity. Students of instructional supervision have historically argued the importance of interpersonal competence vis-à-vis the effectiveness of instructional supervisors; few, however, have actually examined the impact of interpersonal phenomena on the process and outcomes of instructional supervision. And I have found no examples in the literature on instructional supervision of either what is meant by interpersonal competence or what factors might promote the acquisition and development of interpersonal competence among instructional supervisors.

In the literature concerned with instructional supervision, the works of Blumberg and Amidon (1968), Blumberg and Cusick (1970), and Blumberg (1973) stand out as the best examples of efforts to understand the influence of interpersonal phenomena upon the process and consequences of the work of instructional supervisors. In an effort to place the influence of the interpersonal behavior of instructional supervisors in proper perspective, Blumberg developed a conception of supervision that attaches primarily to the interpersonal aspects of supervisor-teacher interaction. He argued for a reconceptualization of the supervisor's role—from methodological and curriculum specialist to "interpersonal intervenor." Although Blumberg presented a clear and well-developed case for such a reconceptualization, he neither explained what interpersonal competence on the part of a supervisor might mean nor indicated what factors might be related to the development and enactment of such competencies.

Socialization for Interpersonal Competence

What do we mean by interpersonal competence? Interpersonal competence is that skill or set of abilities that enables an individual to shape the responses he gets from others (Foote and Cottrell, 1955). In the case of instructional supervision, the supervisor may be thought of as interpersonally competent to the extent that he is able to influence a teacher in the direction desired. In public schools this generally means some improvement in the quality of teacher instruction in classrooms. From the perspective of Blumberg's concept of the role of the supervisor as that of "interpersonal interventionist," this means that the supervisor must "intrude in particular ways into a teacher's personal and technical system to achieve certain ends or products."

As Weinstein (1969) observes, interpersonal competence is "the ability to accomplish interpersonal tasks . . . the ability to manipulate others' responses" (p. 755). While it is believed by many that "manipulating" another person toward some particular end is somehow professionally undesirable and connotes the idea of inauthenticity, the conception is, by itself, value-free and relative to the actor's aims. The real issue, in terms of interpersonal competence, is not manipulation of another's responses per se, but, rather, the purpose underlying the manipulation.

An instructional supervisor may be self-serving in his manipulation of a teacher, as in the case of the supervisor who gets a teacher to do or change something in a classroom merely to make the supervisor "look good" to his superior. On the other hand, the supervisor may manipulate a teacher (obtain a desired response on the part of the teacher) in order to improve the quality of classroom instruction, as in the case of influencing the teacher to try out an instructional strategy that is known to be more instructionally appropriate and effective for a particular category of learner than the one the teacher currently happens to be using. In both instances, the supervisor is interpersonally *manipulating* the teacher; in the latter case the manipulation is professionally appropriate and desirable, but in the former case it clearly is not.

Weinstein (1969), building on the work of Foote and Cottrell (1955), Thibaut and Kelley (1959), Goffman (1959 and 1961), Homans (1961), Blau (1964), and Garfinkle (1964), offers a conceptual framework explicating elements related to interpersonal competence and focusing specifically on the character and process of interpersonal interaction. His analysis is based on the relationships among ten interconnected concepts:

Interpersonal task—The response one actor is attempting to elicit from another.

Interpersonal competence—Being able to achieve interpersonal tasks.

Lines of action—What one actor actually does to elicit a desired task response from another.

Encounter—Any contact between people that involves an interpersonal task by at least one party to the exchange.

Situation—All the potentially meaningful stimuli present in an encounter.

Defining the situation—The process by which participants in an encounter select and organize situational stimuli into a coherent understanding of what is actually occurring during an encounter.

Projected definition of the situation—These are lines of action by one actor intended to influence another actor's definition of the situation.

Working consensus—This is the definition of the situation to which participants in the encounter jointly subscribe.

Situational identity—All relevant situational characteristics determining who the actors are and what they represent to one another.

Identity bargaining—The process by which actors influence their own or each other's situational identity.

The last concept, that of identity bargaining, is, as Weinstein says, "pivotal in being interpersonally competent" (p. 757). The character of the situational identity we project and maintain for ourselves and others results from the process of identity bargaining and significantly affects one's capacity to influence another, that is, to get a desired response. The supervisor who enters a supervisory encounter with a teacher and fails to anticipate the strong likelihood that he and the teacher may very well hold different understandings or definitions of the situation (help versus evaluation) is not likely to anticipate the need to engage in a process of identity bargaining. Because of this, the supervisor probably may not be able to develop the kind of working consensus required to elicit effectively a desired response from the teacher.

Following Weinstein's conception, the skills needed by the supervisor to establish and maintain an identity that facilitates being able to influence the teacher depend upon the supervisor's being able to take the role of the teacher and predict accurately what effect certain lines of action taken by the supervisor will have upon the teacher, upon the supervisor having in his possession an extensive set of possible lines of action to enact, and upon the supervisor's possession of the interpersonal ability to use those lines of actions that are effective and appropriate to the situation.

Previous Experience and Role Socialization

Now, what are the conditions that might influence the development of interpersonal competence by the supervisor? While one's interpersonal competence is developed in large measure as a result of the countless interpersonal exchanges encountered during the period extending from infancy through adulthood, it is posited here that the interpersonal competence of the instructional supervisor is largely influenced by the nature of his experience as a teacher. For example, during the teaching years one has a varying number of opportunities to become interpersonally involved with other teachers in the work setting, and the content of these interpersonal encounters may vary from nonwork-related matters (who won the ball game last night), to professional concerns about each other's or a third party's teaching strategies or abilities. In other words, there may be many or only a few opportunities for one teacher to engage another in discussing or exchanging views on instructional or other matters.

In addition to the differences in opportunities teachers have for such interpersonal encounters, those which do take place usually occur in a context shaped by peer-group and organizational norms regarding such matters as teaching styles, the value or appropriateness of different modes of instruction, criteria for evaluating teacher effectiveness, the efficacy of certain supervisory behavior, the character of the relations between supervisors and teachers, and the like. In other words, those encounters that do take place do not occur in a normative vacuum; instead, they are shaped and influenced by many situational factors.

So, in addition to variances in the opportunities a supervisor might have to engage in interpersonal encounters with teachers during the supervisor's teaching years, there also are differences in what one learns about teachers, teaching, supervisors, and supervising during that period. The learning that results may actually occur in an unconscious and certainly in an informal manner, but it is proposed here that the nature of the supervisor's experience during the teaching years significantly affects his subsequent performance as a supervisor.

Supervisors who have had extensive opportunities to acquire and practice the sort of content-specific interpersonal skills alluded to above will, in all likelihood, develop more interpersonal competence and a greater repertoire of appropriate lines of action than supervisors who have not had such experiences. Given the nature of the teaching occupation and the structure of the setting in which teachers work, it does not seem unreasonable to suggest that supervisors who have had an extended opportunity to benefit from this sort of "anticipatory" role socialization process (Merton, 1968) are the exception rather than the rule.

As mentioned in a previous chapter, teachers tend to work in isolation from one another, and they do not engage in extensive interpersonal interaction as a part of their normal daily routine. Instead, most teachers spend most of their time in direct contact with groups of children. That is, most of their daily work experience is with children, not adults. While one might argue that such encounters offer prospective supervisors many opportunities to learn and practice interpersonal skills, it seems unlikely that the particular lines of action employed or the tactics used to influence children will be appropriate to the requirements of the supervisor-teacher encounter. Indeed, one might speculate that an extensive history of this sort of interpersonal experience might account, at least in part, for the "parent-child" character of many supervisor-teacher relationships.

Most supervisors have just not had a very extensive history of adult-adult relationships as an integral part of their prior work experience, and much of their most recent socialization for interpersonal competence was focused on relations with children, not adults. Indeed, upon entering the world of teaching, many individuals have been forced to learn new metaprescriptions, new lines of action more appropriate to adult-child relationships—skills that are essentially inappropriate to influencing adults. Adult-child relationships do not benefit those teachers who hope to become supervisors. Prospective supervisors need to expand their adult-adult relationships.

If this is a possibility, and I believe it is, then it may be necessary to resocialize teachers so they might indeed acquire and develop the interpersonal competence necessary for effective instructional supervision. A possible avenue for such learning is to structure the work situation in schools so that teachers have more opportunities for adult-adult work relationships, particularly where teacher performance and instructional effectiveness are a primary focus of attention. Doing so may permit teachers in general, and prospective instructional supervisors in particular, to learn and practice lines of action appropriate and effective in influencing adults in the context of a school organization. We know from some limited research (Millikan, 1979, DeSanctis and Blumberg, 1979) that the number of times teachers call upon one another for help or assistance far outweighs the number of times they call upon their formal supervisors or consultants.

This situation seems to offer potential as a sort of natural socialization opportunity. Teachers who interact with their peers learn and practice many of the interpersonal skills and develop the repertoire of tactics they are likely to require for effective supervision. This informal learning situation can present them with the opportunity to engage in the process of identity bargaining, so necessary to developing a working consensus conducive to helping another teacher solve instructional problems; to develop a capacity for empathy (projecting themselves into the situation as it is experienced by the other); to acquire a sensitivity to knowing which lines of action are most appropriate for a given interpersonal situation; and to become more skilled at employing the interpersonal skills needed to develop a mutual definition of the situation that facilitates one teacher's ability to influence another.

19   Supervision: An Organizational Category in Search of Itself

Curiously, thinking about what to say here and deciding how to organize it have been difficult tasks for me. This is curious because, though my interests in matters concerning the schools are not confined to supervision, without much doubt that field of educational practice has consumed a substantial portion of my research, teaching, and writing time over the past fifteen years or so. One would suspect that having devoted so much time and energy to a topic and having perhaps made some modest contribution to thinking in the field would surely have enabled me to organize and write with my customary ease. That I have not been able to do this (indeed, even as I write I am still experiencing some uneasiness) sends an unmistakable message to me, and that message is reflected in the title of this chapter.* Much as I think that the field of supervision in the schools is at loose ends with itself, so, in a way, am I wondering a bit whether the work I have engaged in has really had substantial impact in ways other than to have enlarged my vita. I like, of course, to think that it has, but the questions are still there.

To address one's colleagues by disclosing self-doubt about the importance of one's work and, thus, by inference, about

---

* I take the liberty and hope the reader will not view it as egocentric that I present this final chapter practically verbatim from a paper I presented at the National Invitational Conference on Instructional Supervision at Kent State University in December 1978. The conference was sponsored by the Council of Professors of Instructional Supervision. In point of fact, I had this chapter in mind when I wrote the paper. The ideas and concerns I expressed then make sense at this writing, much as they did at the time the address was given. The title of the paper was the same as the title of this chapter.

the importance of theirs may seem a bit odd, but it is meant as a prelude to the main thrust of my remarks. First, I suggest that the traditional one-to-one focus of supervision in the schools, with which most of us have been concerned, has no future. Though it may well be that people charged with helping teachers teach better have experienced some isolated successes, it seems clear to me that the work of supervisors, by whatever name they go, has had little effect in raising the quality of instruction in systems as a whole. If there is evidence of this having happened, I am unaware of it. The second aim of this chapter, in light of the initial position, is to suggest a need to rethink the problem of improving instruction so that it is not associated primarily with teachers as individuals but with schools as normative, organic systems. So long as we conceive of the problem as involving *a* person dealing with another—or, perhaps, a small group—we will have been successful at keeping busy, but ultimately will have had little effect on the quality of education.

Finally, in these introductory remarks, I must state two major biases that I hold about the work that we, as professors and supervisors, do. First, I hold a bias against labels. Thus, with all due respect for the thinking and work of many, I reject such labels as clinical supervision, competency-based supervision, creative supervision, and synergistic supervision for two major reasons. For one thing, the labels are simply not descriptive of anything that may happen, and they are not at all discrete. May not, for example, "clinical supervision" be "creative" or "synergistic"? Or could it not be the other way around? And are not all supervisory strategies based on competencies? Let me cite an example of some of the problems that we run into as we put labels on our ideas. In an article anticipating educational developments in the twenty-first century and their relationship to "clinical supervision," Shane and Weaver (1976) make the following statement: "When properly construed, then, clinical supervision involves assisting teachers to develop through direct, guided experience those skills needed for diagnosing and meeting the needs of a wide array of children or youth" (p. 55). Now, I must ask, "Are these activities and goals restricted to those who are practicing 'clinical supervision'?" What do we call the activity that does what the authors suggested, but does not follow the particular structure that Cogan (1973) has elaborated? I hope you see my point.

Another reason for my dislike (perhaps, more appropriately, disdain) for labels and labeling is more profound. Quoting my colleague, Jerry Harvey (1976), my attitude is also based on ". . . Bion's (1974) assertion that the way one can render a powerful idea impotent is to institutionalize it in the form of a word which restricts its meaning . . ." (p. 5). We in education seem to have been particularly prone to do that, for whatever reasons I am not sure. Examples abound, and I need not repeat the litany of good ideas that have been given names, become institutionalized, and have passed by the wayside or been bastardized.

I cannot resist telling you of one situation with which I am currently familiar. In a community not far from where I live, a new elementary school was completed a year or so ago. It was designed to be an "open" school—a label that has both physical and sociopsychological meaning. Well, within a fairly short time the teachers built barricades between the various learning areas, some of them quite decorative, I might add. So, in effect, we have an "open" school that is not open.

My second bias is somewhat different in kind from the first. It is that, relative to the schools and supervision, I am much inclined to de-emphasize program structure and to emphasize process. This is a figure and ground sort of thing that has its roots much more in data than in ideology, as was true of my concern about labeling. The point is, of course, that all social systems require a structure or they would not exist. But the structure, as I see it, provides the skeleton within which and around which various human relationships are enacted and work technologies are employed. And, though structural arrangements influence who talks to whom and about what, it is, in my opinion, the character of the relationships that are developed in the process of work that makes the difference in classrooms and in supervision. It would be possible to cite research results from a number of different fields that support this position, but it is too familiar a one to require that. And I suspect that many, if not most, of you hold a similar bias—an emphasis on process and not structure. The point is that, holding this position, I find myself with little concern for developing models to do something. I have more concern for helping supervisors or those who would be supervisors understand the impact that their behavior has on others, as well as the nature of the relationship that might result from their behavior.

Let me do what may appear to be a turnabout. It may at this point sound contradictory for me to say that I do not believe we can adequately think about theory and research in supervision without being concerned with the organizational structure of the schools, but I do not think it is contradictory. I think it is incredibly important for us to develop as keen an understanding of school organizational structure as possible since, as I have noted, the structure is the context within which action occurs. In various ways it affects how things happen, the processes and relationships that occur every day in a school. Without some relatively systematic sense of the structure of schools, much of what happens in schools— the work of teachers and the work of supervisors, for example—can become an unintelligible aggregate of random interactions.

How best, then, can one conceptualize the structure of schools as organizations? For too long schools have been lumped in a global conceptual pot as relatively standard bureaucracies that contained some elements that made them different. My position is that, though schools do indeed have ideal-type bureaucratic elements—division of labor, hierarchical authority structure, and so forth—they are quite different from other organizational types at the same time they exhibit some similarities. This difference has been nicely conceived and elaborated by Weick in an article entitled "Educational Organizations as Loosely Coupled Systems" (1976). The notion of being "loosely coupled" helps a lot of what happens in schools make sense. It suggests, for example, that the activities and intentions of one actor in the system are only loosely related to the activities and intentions of another actor. Some examples: What teacher A does in a classroom typically has no relationship to what teacher B does. What a teacher does in a classroom may or may not be related to what a youngster learns. And, for our purposes, what a supervisor does with a teacher is only loosely coupled with what the teacher does in the classroom. I suspect, incidentally, that this loose coupling in the supervisor-teacher relationship is cause for no small amount of frustration on the part of the supervisor.

But loose coupling is not completely adequate in explaining schools, for, in some parts of their organization and function, schools are very tightly organized or woven. Stemming from their· argument that the purpose of an educational system is to exchange standard types or categories of socialized people with society, Meyer and Rowan (1975) make the point that, "In such matters as controlling who belongs in which category, educational organizations are very tightly, not loosely, organized" (p. 1). Thus, tight control is exercised over who is a student, teacher, principal, guidance counselor, or supervisor. And there is a tight relationship between, for example, gaining membership in the category "second-grader" and having been a "first-grader." You cannot be the former without having been the latter. The issue is, though, that, even as the organization exercises tight control over its categories and the rituals through which one is admitted to a category, the activities that occur within the categories are very loosely coupled with the category itself. Thus, as in the examples above, given two second grades in the same school with the same curriculum, what transpires within each is loosely coupled internally in that the connections between teacher intentions and student behavior are vague, and loosely coupled with the other in that there is no necessary connection between what occurs in one and what occurs in the other.

More directly, let us move to the case of supervision and supervisors in the schools. "Supervisor" is an organizational category. In most states, the process of becoming a member of that category (to be certified as a supervisor) is rather tightly woven in that it requires the successful completion of certain ritual activities that, in themselves, are loosely coupled with the functions that supervisors are supposed to perform and the results they are expected to produce. In New York State, for example, in order to obtain supervisory certification one must have been a teacher for three years, have taken thirty semester hours beyond the baccalaureate degree, eighteen of which must be in educational administration, and have taken a university (or college) approved and supervised internship. That is all! But even that is probably more than is demanded in some other states.

But what of the activities and functions performed by a person once he has been admitted to the category of supervisor or whatever title (helping teacher, resource teacher, instructional specialist) a particular system gives to that position? What purposes do they serve? The questions can be approached on two levels: organizational and day-to-day work. Organizationally, my argument stems from another provocative paper by Meyer and Rowan (1977). Their suggestion, first, is that organizations, primarily those that do not have to meet the demands of technical production and exchange (the schools, for example), "are driven to incorporate the practices and procedures defined by prevailing rationalized concepts of organizational work and institutionalized in society. Organizations that do so increase their legitimacy and their survival prospects, independent of the immediate efficacy of the acquired practices and procedures" (p. 340). This fits part of my notion of what the organizational structure of schools is all about. That is, schools are not structured by the demands of technical production and exchange except, as was noted earlier, they are geared to develop categories of people that are exchanged with society. Society reciprocates by allowing schools to exist. The schools develop categorical roles (like supervisor) to maintain themselves and, in the process, increase their legitimacy and their survival prospects.

What purpose, then, is served by the activities of people who occupy such categorical roles in organizations such as the schools? Meyer and Rowan suggest that, in these cases: "Activity . . . has ritual significance; it maintains appearances and validates an organization" (p. 355). The implication is very strong that in the present case—our concern here with supervisors and supervision, an organizational category in which there is no accepted or standard technology and which is scarcely ever evaluated as to both its effectiveness and efficiency—the primary *organizational* function that is served by the activity of supervisors of whatever stripe is to maintain appearances and validate the organization. Nothing negative should be attributed to this position. In point of fact, it is probably very important for the maintenance of schools as organizations that such activities be performed.

On the level of the day-to-day, here-and-now function of supervision, the issue of what purpose supervisory activities serve takes on a different light. That is, as we turn our attention to the interpersonal transactions that characterize supervision on a daily basis, the organizational functions tend to fade, to become part of the ground, as it were. Precious few data are available to help us understand the situation. We do know that there is a wide variance of opinion among teachers concerning the utility of the supervision they receive. As might be expected, the gamut runs from the opinion that supervision is a "waste of time" to the opinion that it is "quite helpful." A key to accounting for these responses is, perhaps, found in the behavioral style of the supervisor. But inquiry into the evaluation of supervisory functioning misses the point somewhat in this discussion. That is, while it may tell us a bit about how teachers appraise what goes on, it does not tell us what does go on or what purpose it does, or perhaps should, serve.

Let me then report to you the results of two studies in which I have been engaged. The first was rather casual and informal, but I hope it serves as a prelude to more systematic inquiry. What I was interested in was, on the surface, simple. I wanted to know the kinds of problems teachers talked about with supervisors, the content of their discussions, and whether teachers were helped by their supervisor or whether they saw their supervisor as primarily a source of task or emotional support. The sample was small (forty teachers) but it came from two different groups. The results obtained from these groups reinforced each other, thus leading me to think that I was not dealing with a deviant segment of the population, at least in the geographic area in which the data were collected.

The results, briefly, were that the most commonly discussed problem was concerned with teaching methodology and materials, followed by discipline, school organizational issues, and teachers' classroom behavior. The respondents were fairly evenly split concerning whether they were helped by the supervisor. Slightly more said that they were than that they were not, and most help was received, as might be expected, on problems that dealt with classroom methodology and teaching materials. Finally, for our purposes and perhaps most importantly, the respondents were almost evenly split between seeing their supervisor primarily as a source of skill in teaching or of emotional support. Thus, and in an interesting way, though nothing that got talked about between these teachers and their supervisor had to do, on the face of it, with teacher needs for emotional support, almost half of them said that they saw this as a primary function of supervisory activity. If these results are reinforced in further study, they would have something important to say to supervisors and to the focus of their training. If, for example, a fair amount of task-oriented supervisor activity is indeed ineffective, if teachers have unarticulated role expectations for supervisors relative to needs for emotional support, and if being a teacher also means being lonely (Goldstein and Knoblock, 1971), it is at least possible to conceive of a shift in our concern about what supervisors do and for what they should be trained, even if we choose not to alter our ideas about the way supervision is presently conceived. The shift might be from a heavy focus on the task of improving instruction, at which supervisors may be only moderately effective, to one where the notions of task and social-emotional support are linked. I doubt that we would lose much in the process.

Findings from the second study, much more rigorous in design than the one just mentioned, show the problem of supervisory activity from a different angle. Stemming from our interest in the organizational character of schools and from the fact that little is known systematically about how teachers spend their out-of-classroom time during the course of a school day, this study focused on the transactions that teachers had with other adults while school was in session. I concentrate on only that small part of the results that seems to relate to our concerns.

As might be expected, a content analysis of the nature of the adult transactions in which teachers engage during a school day revealed three major areas of concern: task problems associated with instruction and student behavior, organizational matters, and socializing. Most transactions focused on organizational matters (40 percent), and those that were concerned with task and socializing were almost even in frequency (31 percent and 20 percent, respectively). A chi-square test applied to this data yielded a significance level of .05. From our data, problems of organizational maintenance, as opposed to problems of teaching, are discussed by teachers with other adults more frequently than would be expected by chance.

The analysis was taken a step further. We were interested in knowing who it was that teachers talked to relative to their major concerns. The specific piece of information that bears on our concerns at this conference deals with task transactions. Of the times that teachers talked with other adults about task matters, 61 percent involved other teachers; 24 percent, professional staff; 8 percent, administrative staff; and, interestingly, 7 percent, nonprofessional staff. An immediate inference is that teachers in our sample did not see their administrators as potential sources of help on classroom problems. It is somewhat amusing that they talk with them about these issues only about as much as they discuss them with nonprofessional staff. What is more important, however, is the idea that they interact with other teachers concerning task problems about two and a half times more frequently than they do with professional staff personnel (supervisors, helping teachers, guidance counselors, and so forth).

One's response to this finding might be, "But of course. Teachers are more readily available during the course of a day than are their organizationally specified 'helpers.'" This is so, and it is precisely this set of circumstances that, combined with other things we know about schools, teachers, and teaching (see Lortie, 1975, for example), leads me to offer a proposal intended to make the activity of supervisors more task productive than organizationally ritualistic and self-justifying.

I must say, at this point, that I am not optimistic about the chances of my proposal being adopted in the schools, or even in *a* school, in either the near or relatively distant future. Nevertheless, I take it as the responsibility of those of us who are supposed to spend most of our time thinking, researching, and writing about education and the schools to offer proposals that might move the field beyond where it is, even though such proposals may, on the face of it, seem improbable of attainment. Thus, though I have no doubt that what I am about to suggest will be distinctly different from what is, I offer it for the fun of thinking about what might be and the possibility that we, both you and I, might be stimulated to consider, experiment, and implement the proposal should it gain credibility.

My proposal for improving instruction and, by inference, changing the organizational function of supervision, is not new, though in the past it seems to have received rather short shrift at the hands of both academics and practitioners. It has been stated in the obverse by Schaefer (1967, p. 1) and quoted by Dreeben (1970, p. 1), who "deplores the fact that 'society has not expected the school to be systematically reflective about its work—to serve as a center of inquiry into teaching . . . ,' that schools have been regarded as dispensaries." What is being called for, then, is a reconceptualization of the essential function of the school from one in which certain things are dispensed—formally, information and skills; informally, attitudes—to one in which, put succinctly, everyone—

pupils, teachers, supervisors, guidance counselors, and principals—
has the responsibility to learn.

There are several reasons for my suggestion that, in order to
improve instruction and enable supervisors to serve (in Meyer and
Rowan's terms) more than an organizationally ritualistic and self-
justifying role, it is necessary to reconceptualize the role and function of schools. Some of them have already been stated implicitly.
But let me not shadowbox. Let me be, instead, forthright.

1. There is little evidence that supervision as it is currently conceived has had any appreciable effect on the nature of the overall
processes of teaching and learning in the schools. It is probably
true that individual teachers have been helped from time to time,
but, given the loosely coupled organizational character of a school,
one would suspect that little if any sort of contagion effect has
taken place in any sort of systematic way.

2. The present system whereby one person works with another—
or, perhaps, a small group—is doomed to failure, if it has not failed
already, if our interests go beyond the individual teacher to include
the nature of the system. There simply are not enough skilled
teaching and learning helpers to go around. And, even if there were,
we can be quite sure that school districts would not pay for them.
As we all know, the trend is more toward reduction in personnel.

3. I think that all of us at this conference are, like supervisors,
engaged in what are essentially organizationally ritualistic activities. This is not to say that we, like some supervisors and teachers,
do not have some productive effect on individuals. Undoubtedly
we do. But it does seem to me that our books, our research, and our
teaching helps, more than anything else, to justify us, our positions,
and our universities. That point may be hard for us to take, but I
believe it to be true, at least as far as the *organizational* function
of our activities is concerned.

In summary, then, my reason for suggesting the necessity of
reconceptualizing the nature of the school depends upon *whether
we are interested in the systemic improvement of instruction and
in making schools centers of inquiry into teaching.* If we are not
interested in these things, it might be better if we were to acknowledge that fact to ourselves, at least, and go about the business of
doing the things we know how to do best, which means more of
the same. I simply do not believe that our present structure and
mode of operation is working—certainly not on any grand scale.

If we are to reconceptualize schools, we also need to rethink the role of the people who inhabit them on a daily basis—a large order. I confine myself to the role of the supervisor, or, more broadly, to whoever might have some overall responsibility for the improvement-inquiry effort. I do this by resorting to the fantasies of teachers that appeared in Chapter 4. For your convenience, two of the fantasies, one of the supervisor's house today and one of the supervisor's house in the future, are repeated here.

Fantasy of a Supervisor's House Today

One approaches the house via a long, winding driveway. You cannot see the house from the road. The lawn surrounding the house is very green because it is made of astroturf. The house itself is square and has a flat roof. There is nothing romantic about it. There are no windows in the house. A number of things strike you as you enter. Everything is in its place. The furniture is very austere, and it is nailed to the floor. There is a picture on the wall that is a flowchart, in color, of administrative positions. Diplomas hang next to the flowchart. There are floral arrangements composed of artificial flowers. The lighting system is stark and very bright. The house is very clean. It has a central cleaning system with vacuums in the walls. In the house are janitorial supplies and textbooks. There are also disconnected bodies sitting in straight rows.

Fantasy of a Supervisor's House in the Future

The house is a round one. There are lots of two-way windows. It is located in sort of a parklike atmosphere. The house seems friendly and can be expanded. It is all on one floor and has a large revolving entrance door making it easy to enter or leave. The fact that it is round and on the floor conveys an egalitarian, not bureaucratic, atmosphere where all resources have equal input. In the inside, around the wall, there are lots of partitioned enclosures, each with a revolving door. The partitions separate the enclosures from a "commons" area, but do not totally enclose them. The "commons" is used for discussions between the occupant of the house and visitors.

I think it unnecessary to go into a detailed interpretation of these fantasies again. I suspect you will enjoy doing it on your own more. But a few comments are necessary. Relative to the "house today" one clearly gets an image of sterility, order, and, for me, at least, an odd feeling of fragmentation, mostly from the last sentence. Supervisors, of course, are not dull or unfeeling people. But in all likelihood they do work and convey attitude sets in ways that, for the most part, reinforce the expectations the system has of itself. Otherwise, they would have difficulty surviving. In the "house in the future" things are clearly different. I get a sense of wholeness. In a way, this fits my image of a collaborative house of inquiry. The psychology of it is clear. The supervisory role, if schools were to be reconceptualized in ways I have suggested, would change to become more congruent with the school. If this were to happen, it is just possible that supervision would not be a "category in search of itself."

It is clear, then, that my developing orientation toward supervision focuses on the supervisor in a school that itself has developed from a system that dispenses to a system that inquires while it is in the process of helping its members to learn. And supervisors should, perhaps, manage the inquiry process while they are also learning. Although I espouse this orientation, I must also confess that I myself continue to behave much the way I always have. I reinforce by my teaching, research, and writing that which I have said is systemically relatively ineffectual because it is quite comfortable.

This final chapter has become, in a way I had not consciously intended, a rather personal document. Indeed, I had developed a number of research questions that I had anticipated would find their way into this book before it ended. They seem rather inappropriate at this point. I did not understand this personalized thrust until I reread and reflected on the comments I made when I began the chapter. You may recall that I expressed some uneasiness at the task of writing it, and I suspect that the uneasiness is by now obvious to the reader. It may be a cue that I, too, am a "category in search of self." In a way, I hope so.

Epilogue

When one puts the last period to the last sentence of a book, it is with a sense of relief, exhilaration and, perhaps, exhaustion. It is finished, complete. Yet the final sentence in the last chapter makes it clear, I think, that, while the manuscript is finished, the problem with which the book has dealt—the nature of the human and work relationships of supervisors and teachers—remains. It is of great day-to-day importance for the practitioner. It is somewhat less pressing for those of us who teach about and inquire into the character of supervision. As I have suggested at various points in this book, the task that confronts people (myself included) in the latter group is far less taxing than that which confronts those who engage in the day-to-day business of running the schools. It seems appropriate to direct a final few words specifically to the practitioner, not with the idea that these words will "complete" things for them, an obviously impossible task, but to acknowledge the wide gap between the work worlds of those who "talk about" and those who "do" something. It seems clear to me that the responsibility for closing that gap rests much more with the talkers than the doers. These last few comments constitute a small effort to reach out, gently and with humility.

Earlier in the book I took note of Seymour Sarason's contention that "the more things change the more they remain the same." In many ways that contention is a solid one, but it also seems to me that changes are taking place that do and will continue to change the work of supervisors and teachers. To mention a few prominent examples, the suprastructure of schools on the local, state, and federal level seems to be becoming increasingly more bureaucratized. There appears to be a growing emphasis on managerial, noneducational functions in school organizations, which is accompanied by heightened adversarial relations between teachers' unions and school boards. The interacting phenomena of declining enrollments and school closings have added a new dimension to the life of supervisors and teachers not previously experienced. And the overall turbulence of what has come to be called our postindustrial society has certainly found its way into the daily world of schoolpeople.

Precisely what effect these circumstances will have on the schools and the people who work in them is a question that is hard to answer or even, perhaps, to begin to answer. My suspicion, though, is that they will increase the level of tension in the system and that it may be at this point that the focus of this book will have relevance for the practitioner in a way that has not previously been discussed. That is, implicit throughout the book is an approach to the work relationships of people in the schools that runs counter to the tension-inducing forces that seem to be developing. This approach is not one of "soft" human relations aimed at making people happy. Rather, its concern is with a straightforward acknowledgement that interpersonal, group, and organizational conflicts do exist; that hiding from them or conceiving of and then dealing with them as win-lose situations only serves to increase the tensions that seem endemic in schools; and that there exists a body of knowledge and a growing body of skills that can enable people to deal better with the tensions and conflicts that arise.

I find myself wishing I could provide an easy answer to supervisors or would-be supervisors who might say, "OK, your argument seems reasonable, tell us where to start." There is no easy answer; nor is there ever any one answer to fit every situation. Nonetheless, it does seem to me that it is possible for a school, with minimal financial outlay, to start thinking and acting along the lines implied above so that the school moves in the direction of becoming a more interpersonally competent organization. The following thoughts might help.

First, a caveat: so long as a school is conceived of as simply a series of compartments in which adults deal with youngsters several hours each day, the concept of developing an interpersonally competent organization is meaningless. Organization means, among other things, relatedness. Compartmentalization conveys separateness. The school principal is the key. The extent that the principal behaves (not just talks) in ways that foster the notion of relatedness will be reflected in the willingness of teachers and other supervisors to devote time and energy to each other. The issue, first of all, then, is one of conceptual and attitudinal set—and behavior that is congruent with that set.

Given that set, or movement in that direction, some things that could happen in a school are:

—Supervisors and teachers could engage in a series of role-negotiating sessions in which both parties become explicit about what they want from each other and what they are prepared to give each other. This might have the effect both of making expectations more realistic and developing a more open communications climate in a school.

—Supervisors and teachers could agree to tape-record supervisory conferences and then listen to them with the idea of learning together about their interpersonal behavior. They could use the behavior category system discussed in Chapters 10 and 11, but that is not necessary.

—Supervisors and teachers could develop microteaching practice sessions (perhaps to replace faculty meetings) after which the supervisor and teacher would hold a conference, tape-record it, and criticize it based on the supervisor's behavior in the conference.

—Supervisors and teachers could jointly establish criteria for assessing the quality of teaching in a school.

—Supervisors and teachers could jointly establish criteria for assessing the quality of supervision in a school.

—Supervisors and teachers (with some outside help) could use their in-service days to develop interpersonal skill instead of the usual fare (teaching methods, discipline, and so forth), which tends to receive less than enthusiastic endorsement from teachers in any event.

It would be foolhardy to suggest that any one of these ideas or any combination of them would guarantee a "New Jerusalem" for supervisor-teacher relationships. They are small steps in need of continual reinforcement. There might, however, be an added bonus:

Engaging in them might encourage supervisors and teachers to think and talk openly about a couple of subjects that rarely seem to be discussed—themselves and their school as a place to work.

Bibliography

Abramson, P. "When Teachers Evaluate Each Other." *Scholastic Magazine* (September 1972): 26-28.

Amidon, E., K. Kies, and A. Palisi. "Group Supervision." *National Elementary Principal*, 45 (no. 5, April 1966): 54-48.

Argyris, C. *Intervention Theory and Method*. Reading, Mass.: Addison-Wesley, 1970.

Armstrong, H. *A Teacher's Guide to Teaching Performance Evaluation*. Worthington, Ohio: School Management Institute, 1972.

Bakke, E. *The Fusion Process*. New Haven, Conn.: Yale University, Labor and Management Center, 1953.

Bales, R. *Interaction Process Analysis*. Reading Mass.: Addison-Wesley, 1951.

Barrett, J. *Individual Goals and Organizational Objectives*. Ann Arbor, Mich.: University of Michigan, Institute for Social Research, 1970.

Barrett-Lennard, G. *Dimensions of Therapist Response as Causal Factors in Therapeutic Change*. Psychological Monograph 562. Washington, D.C.: American Psychological Association, 1962.

Benne, K., and P. Sheats. "Functional Roles of Group Members." *Journal of Social Issues*, 4 (no. 2, Spring 1948): 42-47.

Berne, E. *Games People Play*. New York: Grove Press, Inc., 1964.

Bidwell, C. E. "The School as a Formal Organization." In *Handbook of Organizations*, edited by J. March. Chicago: Rand McNally, 1965. Pp. 872-1022.

Bion, W. "Experiences in Groups: III." *Human Relations*, 2 (no. 1, 1949): 13-22.

———. *Attention and Interpretation*. New York: Basic Books, 1974.

Blake, R., and J. Mouton. *The Managerial Grid*. Houston: Gulf Publishing, 1964.

Blansfield, M., R. Blake, and J. Mouton. "The Merger Laboratory: A New Strategy for Bringing One Corporation into Another." *Training Directors Journal*, 8 (no. 5, 1964): 2-10.

Blau, P. *Exchange and Power in Social Life*. New York: John Wiley and Sons, 1964.

Blumberg, A. "Supervisory Behavior and Interpersonal Relations" *Educational Administration Quarterly*, 4 (no. 2, Spring 1968): 34-45.
————. "A System for Analyzing Supervisor-Teacher Interaction." In *Mirrors for Behavior*, VIII, edited by A. Simon and G. Boyer. Philadelphia: Research for Better Schools, Inc., 1970. Pp. 34-1.1 to 34-1.15.
————. "Supervision: What Is and What Might Be." *Theory into Practice*, 15 (no. 4, 1976): 284-292.
————. "Supervision as Interpersonal Intervention." *Journal of Classroom Interaction*, 13 (no. 1, December 1977): 24-31.
————, and E. Amidon. "Teacher Perceptions of Supervisor-Teacher Interaction." *Administrator's Notebook*, 14 (no. 1, September 1965): 1-4.
————, E. Amidon, and W. Weber. "Supervisor-Teacher Interaction as Seen by Supervisors." Unpub. MS, Temple University, Philadelphia, 1967.
————, and P. Cusick. "Supervisor-Teacher Interaction: An Analysis of Verbal Behavior." *Education*, 91 (November 1970): 126-134.
————, and W. Greenfield. *The Effective Principal: Perspectives on School Leadership*. Boston: Allyn and Bacon, 1980.
————, M. Loehr, and P. Goldstein. "Content and Process in Supervisor-Teacher Interaction." Unpub. MS, Syracuse University, Syracuse, New York, 1978.
————, and W. Weber. "Teacher Morale as a Function of Perceived Supervisor Behavior Style." *Journal of Educational Research*, 62 (no. 3, 1968): 109-113.
Brewster, K. "On Tenure." *AAUP Bulletin*, 58 (no. 4, 1972): 381-383.
Brim, O., Jr., and S. Wheeler. *Socialization after Childhood: Two Essays*. New York: John Wiley and Sons, 1966.
Cogan, M. *Clinical Supervision*. Boston: Houghton Mifflin, 1973.
————. "Rationale for Clinical Supervision." *Journal of Research and Development in Education*, 9 (no. 2, Winter 1976): 3-19.
DeSanctis, M., and A. Blumberg. "An Exploratory Study into the Nature of Teacher Interactions with Other Adults in the Schools." Unpub. MS, Syracuse University, Syracuse, New York, 1979.
Dreeben, R. *The Nature of Teaching*. Glenview, Ill.: Scott, Foresman and Co., 1970.
Festinger, L. *Theory of Cognitive Dissonance*. New York: Harper and Row, 1957.
Flanders, N. *Teacher Influence-Pupil Attitudes and Achievement*. Cooperative Research Project 397, Final Report. Washington, D.C.: U.S. Government Printing Office for the U.S. Office of Education, 1960.
————. "Interaction Analysis and Clinical Supervision." *Journal of Research and Development in Education*, 9 (no. 2, Winter 1976): 47-57.
Fleishman, E., and E. Harris. "Patterns of Leader Behavior Related to Employee Grievances and Turnover." *Personnel Psychology*, 15 (1962): 43-53.
Foote, M., and L. Cottrell, Jr. *Identity and Interpersonal Competence*. Chicago: University of Chicago Press, 1955.
French, J. R. P., and B. Raven. "The Bases of Social Power." In *Studies in Social Power*, edited by D. Cartwright. Ann Arbor, Mich.: University of Michigan, Institute for Social Research, 1959. Pp. 150-167.

Garfinkle, H. "The Routine Grounds of Everyday Activities." *Social Problems*, 11 (1964): 225-250.

Gibb, J. "Is Help Helpful?" *Association Forum* (February 1954): 25-27.

———. "Defensive Communication." *Journal of Communication*, 11 (no. 3, 1969): 141-148.

Goffman, E. *The Presentation of Self in Everyday life.* Garden City, N.Y.: Anchor Books, 1959.

———. *Encounters.* Indianapolis, Ind.: Bobbs-Merrill Book Co., 1961.

Goldhammer, R. *Clinical Supervision.* New York: Holt, Rinehart, and Winston, 1969.

Goldstein, A., and P. Knoblock. *The Lonely Teacher.* Boston: Allyn and Bacon, 1971.

Golembiewski, R. *Men, Management and Morality.* New York: McGraw-Hill, 1965.

———, and A. Blumberg. "Confrontation as a Training Design in Complex Organizations: Attitudinal Changes in a Diversified Population of Managers." *Journal of Applied Behavioral Science*, 3 (no. 4, 1967): 525-547.

Goslin, A. (ed.). *Handbook of Socialization Theory and Research.* Chicago: Rand McNally, 1969.

Greenwood, E. "Attributes of a Profession." In *Professionalization*, edited by H. Vollmer and D. Mills. Englewood Cliffs, N.J.: Prentice-Hall, 1966.

Guetzkow, H., and J. Gyr. "An Analysis of Conflict in Decision-Making Groups." *Human Relations*, 7 (no. 3, 1954): 367-382.

Gwynn, J. M. *Theory and Practice of Supervision.* New York: Dodd, Mead, and Company, 1969.

Harris, B. M., and J. D. King. *Professional Supervisory Competencies.* Report of the Special Education Training Project. Austin: University of Texas, 1974.

Harris, T. *I'm OK—You're OK: A Practical Guide to Transactional Analysis.* New York: Harper and Row, 1962.

Harvey, J. "Eight Myths OD Consultants Believe In . . . and Die By." *OD Practitioner*, 7 (no. 1, 1976): 5.

Heald, J., L. Romano, and M. Georgiady (eds.). *Selected Readings on General Supervision.* New York: Macmillan Co., 1970.

Heishberger, R., and J. Young. "Teacher Perceptions of Supervision and Evaluation." *Phi Delta Kappan*, 57 (November 1975): 210.

Herzberg, F., B. Mausner, and B. Snyderman. *Motivation to Work.* New York: John Wiley and Sons, 1959.

Homans, G. *Social Behavior: Its Elementary Forms.* New York: Harcourt, Brace and World, 1961.

Horney, K. *Our Inner Conflicts.* New York: W. W. Norton, 1945.

Kahn, R., D. Wolfe, R. Quinn, J. Snoek, and R. Rosenthal. *Organizational Stress.* New York: John Wiley and Sons, 1964.

Katz, D., and R. Kahn. *The Social Psychology of Organizations.* New York: John Wiley and Sons, 1966.

Laing, R., H. Phillipson, and A. Lee. *Interpersonal Perception.* New York: Springer, 1966.

Leavitt, H. J. "Applied Organizational Change in Industry." In *Handbook of Organizations*, edited by J. G. March. Chicago: Rand McNally, 1965. Pp. 1144-1170.

Levinson, H. *The Exceptional Executive*. Cambridge, Mass.: Harvard University Press, 1968.

———, C. Price, K. Munden, H. Mandl, and C. Solley. *Men, Management and Mental Health*. Cambridge, Mass.: Harvard University Press, 1962.

Lieberman, S. "The Effect of Changes in Roles on the Attitudes of Role Occupants." *Human Relations*, 9 (no. 4, 1956): 385-402.

Likert, R. *New Patterns of Management*. New York: McGraw-Hill, 1961.

Lortie, D. *Schoolteacher*. Chicago: University of Chicago Press, 1975.

March, J. G., and H. A. Simon. *Organizations*. New York: John Wiley and Sons, 1958.

Maslow, A. *Motivation and Personality*. New York: Harper and Row, 1954.

———. *Eupsychian Management*. Homewood, Ill.: Richard D. Irwin, 1965.

McGregor, D. *The Human Side of Enterprise*. New York: McGraw-Hill, 1960.

"Methods of Evaluating Teachers." *NEA Research Bulletin*, 43 (1965): 12-18.

Merton, R. K. *Social Theory and Social Structure*. New York: Free Press, 1968.

Meyer, J. W., and B. Rowan. "Notes on the Structure of Educational Organizations: Revised Version." Paper presented at the meeting of the American Sociological Convention, 1975.

———, and B. Rowan. "Institutionalized Organizations: Formal Structure as Myth and Ceremony." *American Journal of Sociology*, 83 (no. 2, 1976): 340-363.

Millikan, R. "Consultative Needs and Practices in Selected Senior High Schools in Alberta." Unpub. diss., University of Alberta, 1979.

Mosher, R., and D. Purpel. *Supervision: The Reluctant Profession*. Boston: Houghton Mifflin, 1972.

Mueller, W. J., and B. L. Kell. *Coping with Conflict*. New York: Appleton-Century-Crofts, 1972.

National Education Association. *The Elementary School Principalship in 1968*. Washington, D.C.: NEA, Department of Elementary School Principals, 1968.

Pelz, D. "Influence: A Key to Effective Leadership in the First Line Supervisor." *Personnel*, 29 (no. 3, 1952): 209-217.

Rogers, C., R. Rablen, and A. Walker. "Development of a Scale to Measure Process Change in Psychotherapy." Unpub. MS, University of Wisconsin, Madison, 1958.

Sarason, S. *The Culture of the School and the Problem of Change*. Boston: Allyn and Bacon, 1971.

Schaefer, R. J. *The School as a Center of Inquiry*. New York: Harper and Row, 1967.

Schein, E. "Organizational Socialization and the Profession of Management." *Industrial Management Review*, 9 (no. 2, Winter 1968): 1-16.

Schutz, W. *FIRO*. New York: Holt, Rinehart, and Winston, 1958.

Shane, H. G., and R. A. Weaver. "Educational Developments Anticipating the 21st Century and the Future of Clinical Supervision." *Journal of Research and Development in Education*, 9 (no. 2, 1976): 10-18.

Siegel, E., and S. Siegel. "Reference Groups, Membership Groups, and Attitude Change." *Journal of Abnormal and Social Psychology*, 55 (1957): 360-364.

Simon, A., and G. Boyer (eds.). *Mirrors for Behavior*. Philadelphia: Research for Better Schools, Inc., 1970.

Steele, F. *The Open Organization*. Reading, Mass.: Addison-Wesley, 1975.

Stone, I. *Lust for Life*. New York: Doubleday and Co., 1954.

Suehr, J. "A Study of Morale in Educational Settings Utilizing Incomplete Sentences." *Journal of Educational Research*, 56 (no. 2, 1962): 75-81.

Thibaut, J., and H. Kelley. *The Social Psychology of Groups*. New York: John Wiley and Sons, 1959.

Tichy, N. "How Different Types of Change Agents Diagnose Organizations." *Human Relations*, 28 (no. 9, 1975): 771-799.

Tuckman, B., and W. Oliver. "Effectiveness of Feedback to Teachers as a Function of Source." *Journal of Educational Psychology*, 59 (no. 4, 1968): 297-301.

Tukey, G. "Comparing Individual Means in the Analysis of Variance." *Biometrics*, 5 (1949): 99-114.

Weick, K. "Educational Organizations as Loosely Coupled Systems." *Administrative Science Quarterly*, 12 (no. 1, 1976): 1-19.

Weinstein, E. "The Development of Interpersonal Competence." In *The Handbook of Socialization Theory and Research*, edited by D. Joslin. Chicago: Rand McNally, 1969.

Weller, R. *Verbal Communication in Instructional Supervision*. New York: Teachers College Press, 1971.

Wiles, K. *Supervision for Better Schools*. New York: Prentice-Hall, 1953.

Woodward, J. *Management and Technology*. London: Her Majesty's Stationery Office, 1958.